1800

1803 The first convict settlers brought to Port Phillip Bay, the future city of Melbourne

1804 Hobart founded

1812 War between the United States and England

1813 Wentworth, Lawson and Blaxland cross the Blue Mountains

1824 Jedediah Smith finds the great South Pass over the Continental Divide

1824 *The Australian*, the colony's first independent newspaper, begins publication

1829 Captain Charles Fremantle takes possession of the whole of New Holland westward of N.S.W.

1830 Peter Cooper drives his steam powered Tom Thumb Locomotive to Baltimore

1837 The city of Melbourne founded

J. H. Williams arrives as the first American Consul in Australia

1839 The United States Surveying and Exploring Expedition berths in Port Jackson

1842 Sydney created a city

1844 Samuel Morse introduces the electric telegraph into the United States

1845 The first clipper ships are built in New York and Boston

1845 Charles Sturt reaches the middle of the continent from South Australia

1848 Gold discovered at Sutter's Mill by James Marshall

1848 Gregory and von Mueller explore the north and interior of Australia

1850

1850 An Australian Constitution Act separates Victoria from New South Wales and grants representative government to South Australia and Tasmania

1851 The America's Cup syndicate formed

1851 Edward Hargraves discovers gold at Summer Hill Creek in New South Wales

1852 Transportation ceases with the last group of convicts despatched to Tasmania

1853 Commodore Perry opens Japan to free and easy access by the United States

1853 Samuel McGowan establishes the first telegraph line in Australia, linking Melbourne with Williamstown

1854 The Eureka Stockade Rebellion occurs

1856 The secret ballot introduced in Australia

Tasmania given self-government

1859 Oil struck in the first petroleum well by Edwin L. Drake of Oil Creek, Pennsylvania

1859 Queensland separated from New South Wales

1860 Burke and Wills cross the continent to the Gulf of Carpentaria

1861 The Confederate States of America formed. Confederate forces fire on Fort Sumter and begin the Civil War

Australia and America 1776-1976

The United States of America and the Commonwealth of Australia can both be held to have arisen out of the American Revolution. For the Revolution robbed the British Crown of its greatest possession outside India, and gave the immediate impetus to the foundation of English settlement in Australia. To a great extent it is true that the establishment of both nations arose out of the efforts and sufferings of the outcasts of England.

The close parallelism of historical development in both countries has received little serious study so far. In commissioning this book as a way of commemorating the bi-centenary of the American Revolution on July 4, 1776, the Australian Government has enabled the author to identify and broadly characterise a new zone of study for historians of both countries. In doing so, he has opened up an area of fascinating general interest at a time when the relations between the two countries are, in fact, of growing significance.

This book does not attempt to make a complete chronological comparison of events, but it traces themes of development which place in context the historical similarities in the two countries. In anecdotal style the author, an accomplished journalist and historian, offers revealing glimpses of individuals and happenings connecting the peoples, problems and progress of the two countries. *Australia and America 1776-1976* is an inviting stimulus to the recognition and study of the historical background to the relationship between the two countries.

1776~1976
AUSTRALIA AND AMERICA THROUGH 200 YEARS

1776~1976
AUSTRALIA
AND AMERICA
THROUGH
200 YEARS

NORMAN BARTLETT

FOREWORD BY MALCOLM FRASER
PRIME MINISTER OF AUSTRALIA

INTRODUCTION BY MANNING CLARK
EMERITUS PROFESSOR OF AUSTRALIAN HISTORY
AUSTRALIAN NATIONAL UNIVERSITY

Published by Sam Ure Smith at
THE FINE ARTS PRESS, SYDNEY
1976

This first edition published 1976
by the Fine Arts Press Pty Limited
34 Glenview Street, Gordon 2072
in collaboration with
The Australian Exhibit Organization
Department of Administrative Services
Canberra, A.C.T.
Published with the assistance of
The Literature Board of the Australia Council
© Copyright The Australian Exhibit Organization 1976

National Library of Australia Cataloguing-in-Publication data:

Bartlett, Norman, 1908-
    Australia and America Through 200 Years, 1776-1976.
    Bibliography
        0 86917 000 7
    1. Australia—Relations (general) with United States
    2. United States—Relations (general) with Australia
        I. Title
    301. 299407

Set in Linotype Times Roman 10/ 12 Point
by Terrey Hills Typesetters, Sydney
Editorial and design by Charter Books, Sydney
Printed and bound by the Griffin Press,
Adelaide

FOREWORD

Australians and Americans share a dedication to preserve and foster the ideas of democracy and freedom which are under threat in many parts of the world today. There is little doubt that our common pursuit of conditions where every citizen can achieve self respect is a strong basis for the warm friendship we have developed.

This great ideal was fervently expressed two hundred years ago in the form of the American Revolution, where men and women fought to be free. Today—because of that revolution—men and women fighting for freedom around the world still look to the United States for inspiration.

During World War I in the trenches of France and some twenty years later in the Pacific we were proud to fight side by side with Americans for that freedom.

America has used these two hundred years to build the most prosperous country in the world. It has used this prosperity to undertake aid programmes unrivalled by any country at any time and has become a symbol and a force for decency and humanity. Australia is proud to share with America the close economic, social and cultural links which have developed ever since the *Philadelphia* sailed into Port Jackson in 1792.

Some of the great names of Australian history are Americans. We owe a lasting debt to such men as George Chaffey, the pioneer of irrigation in Australia; J. C. Williamson, a giant in Australian theater, and Walter Burley Griffin, designer of our national Capital.

Some of the great democratic institutions in Australia were inspired in America. The founding fathers of the Australian Federation looked to America for help in drawing up the Australian Constiution, and from America we borrowed the idea of Federalism itself.

Australia today stands alongside America in its efforts to maintain international security and stability. We see in our alliance not only an instrument to make Australia more secure, but one which can contribute significantly to the solution of global problems.

This book by Norman Bartlett in this bi-centennial year for America is timely in its examination of 200 years of developing rapport between our nations.

Malcolm Fraser

AUTHOR'S NOTE

This book could not have been written without the assistance of people, organizations and authoritative works of reference on the history of both countries.

I am especially indebted to Professor Manning Clark, of the Australian National University, who suggested the theme and gave generously of his time to encourage the work itself. Officers of the Australian Exhibit Organization, especially Susan Warren, a graduate of the Louisiana State University, provided a great deal of assistance in the collation of data and illustrative material. Special thanks are due in the latter context also to Mr. Rex Harris, Director of the Australian Information Service, New York, and to the officers of the National Library, Canberra.

The final preparation of the manuscript was made possible by the assiduous assistance of my wife with the final editing, correcting and typing of the work.

Of the numerous works consulted, those of greatest general interest include Emeritus Professor C. M. H. Clark's monumental work in progress, *A History of Australia*, and the recent *A New History of Australia*, edited by Professor Frank Crowley. R. A. Swain's Roebuck Society Publication No. 8, *To Botany Bay* (Canberra, 1973), was extremely useful in compiling early chapters. Colin Simpson's *The New Australia* (London, 1972) is the best recent account of contemporary technological and mining developments. Colin Cross's *The Fall of the British Empire* (London, 1968) contributed to the later chapters.

On the American side, I owe a good deal to Vernon L. Parrington's classic *Main Currents in American Thought*, Bernard de Voto's *Westward the Course of Empire*, the BBC's *Alistair Cooke's America*, Barbara W. Tuchman's *The Proud Tower*, Robert A. Hart's *The Great White Fleet* (Boston, 1965), J. W.

Oliver's *History of American Technology* (New York, 1956), William R. Brock's *Conflict and Transformation* and the two volumes of Daniel J. Boorstin's *The Americans*. J. C. Furnas's *The Americans: A Social History of the United States 1587-1914* was of particular value throughout.

Norman Bartlett

CONTENTS

THE ILLUSTRATIONS

INTRODUCTION

Although the beginning of European civilization in Australia was a child of the American Revolution, no writer has previously attempted to trace the contribution of the United States of America to the history of this country. There have been useful discussions of that influence during the early years of our history by writers such as Gordon Greenwood and Lloyd Churchward, and brilliant generalizations on Australia by American authors such as Mark Twain and Jack London. But no writer has so far attempted to survey the whole field. So the committee appointed by the Australian Government to report on the most appropriate ways in which Australia could mark the bi-centenary of the American Revolution on 4 July 1776 proposed that such a book should be written.

It was fortunate that it was possible to commission Norman Bartlett to write the book. For he not only had the energy and the gift to do the work in the time available, but he also had the wisdom and experience demanded for the task. He was born in England and educated at State schools in Western Australia and the University in that State. After some years as a journalist in Perth he served with the Royal Australian Air Force in New Guinea, the United Kingdom, France and Germany. After the war he worked as a press attache and information counsellor in Bangkok, New Delhi, Tokyo and London till he retired in 1973.

During those years he found time to write books such as the novel *Island Victory*, and the prose works *Land of the Lotus Eaters* and *The Gold Seekers*, which gave him a place in the literary history of this country.

The year after he retired he began to work on a thesis for the degree of Doctor of Philosophy in History at the Australian National University. The quality of the work he produced while writing his thesis on the early intellectual history of Australia demonstrated his fitness to write on the contributions made by Australia and America to each other's history.

The reader may judge and enjoy Norman Bartlett's achievement. At the risk of anticipating that pleasure it seems to me that he has done quite magnificently what all first works attempt to do. He has shown the way: he has ploughed the first furrow so well that others will now find it much easier to till the field. For too long Australian intellectuals, writers, publicists, and all those who are curious to find out why we are as we are have looked to the British Isles almost exclusively to find out how that civilization of Europe came to this ancient uncouth continent. Now, thanks to works such as this one, we know we must also look to the United States. So this book is one way of saying thanks, and one quite important way of helping all of us to take the blinkers off our eyes, and see the world as it is.

Manning Clark

1

Prelude to Botany Bay

Terra Australis Incognita, the last-but-one continent discovered by Western man, lay high above the white scallop shell of Antarctica, cradled in the reef-littered waters of the Southwest Pacific—a huge, flat palm of blazing red earth and tawny grassland, bare to the sun, a shaggy pelt of eucalyptus and cedar edging its eastern coast above the pounding surf, wooded humps rising at the southeastern and southwestern corners, a great stretch of arid stony plain between. Since unrecorded time water flowing over wrinkled sandstone and shale spread broad, alluvial sands across wide southeastern valleys that glittered with gold. In the far northwest, flat-topped hills, almost solid lumps of iron, rose starkly from the earth.

In the shallow, emerald green seas lapping northern shores on east and west, sea-serpents, manatees, giant turtles and sharks shared sun, air and warm water with sea slugs and pearl oysters. Where the continent faced the chill Southern Ocean seals possessed the broken ledges of ancient rookeries, and yearly the great fin-backed whales passed on their mating pilgrimage to warmer seas.

To the north lay New Guinea and stretching away to the northwest the scattered mountain backbones of what are now Indonesia and Malaysia. In a time when dry land bridged the islands, groups of nomads wandered through the centuries from some genesis of *homo sapiens*, probably in Asia, until at last thirty or forty thousand years ago, they could go no further and spread out in thin trickles over the empty continent. The endless search for food took them into the thin savannah forest of the warmer inland and along more hospitable coasts where short, swift, rain and snow-fed rivers ran tumbling to the sea.

The climate was too arid and the savannah soil too thin for the development of primitive agriculture. Native animals—hopping marsupials and nocturnal tree-climbers for the most part—were unsuitable for domestication. Only the dingo or warrigal lay down with man beside his lonely camp fires under the vast night sky where Atnatu with his wives, the stars, watched benignly over the fate of his people.* As the glaciers of the ice age melted and the seas flowed in across the land-bridge from Asia these Paleolithic men and women were left alone with kangaroos, koalas, wombats and that strange web-footed, duck-billed, earth-burrowing mammal, the platypus, to share an inhospitable environment without the basic requirements of civilization—agriculture and animal husbandry.

Millennium followed millennium and man elsewhere passed from the Old Stone Age to the New Stone Age moving slowly up the ladder of civilization, discovering the arts of sowing and reaping, forging iron and casting bronze, building houses of wood and stone, raising temples and palaces, exchanging goods and tracing trade routes. Some fifteen thousand years ago, ancestors of the American Indians began to range throughout the Americas, developing a rich diversity of cultures and societies. Meanwhile, the rice-rich deltas of Asia provided a fecund people with sufficient surplus for temples and palaces, cities and markets, craftsmen and poets, as well as courtesans and dancing girls. In the Great Southland, cut off from these fertilizing streams, men still chipped flints for tools and hunted with wooden spears and curved boomerangs.

Hardy sea-going peoples from the islands to the north sometimes ventured into the shallow seas of the continental shelf to gather aphrodisiac bêche-de-mer for languid mandarins and rajahs in the lacquered palaces of Asia. For these intruders the sea offered riches enough. The harsh barren breast the ancient continent bared towards the Indies offered no flowing milk and honey to tempt invaders. In time, other men with lighter skins and more rapacious instincts, came from distant lands to rape the earth of its treasures of iron and gold, and to begin that fructifying cycle of seedtime and harvest that lies at the root of all civilized beginnings.

European man, searching for treasure to plunder, first crossed the Atlantic early in the eleventh century, when Vikings came upon self-sown wheatfields and wild grapes in Vinland, probably Nova Scotia. But the Vikings were only visitors; nearly five hundred years passed before Columbus opened the way to European domination of the Americas. Within fifty years of Columbus reaching the West Indies Spanish conquistadors had plundered the whole of Central America and Peru, exterminating the ancient civilizations that had grown there. In 1513, Balboa first saw the Pacific from "a peak in Darien" and in 1565 Magellan rounded South America through the strait that bears his name. Magellan met his death in the Philippines and his crew returned home north of New Guinea, completing the first voyage around the world.

From Mexico the Spaniards marched north through what are now Arizona, New Mexico and Kansas in search of fabled cities where gold was said to hang on trees. All they found was desert and alkaline marshes and hostile Indians

*Different groups of Aboriginals had various beliefs in a Supreme Being; Atnatu was the god of the Kaitish people of the northern central area.

sheltering in seemingly impregnable pueblos cut into towering rock. Meanwhile, Breton fishermen, laughing off the Pope's gift of the Americas to Spain, worked the cod banks off Nova Scotia while hardy French hunters and trappers penetrated the forests and tundra of Canada-to-be in search of fur and beaver pelts to clothe the aristocracy of Paris.

Six years after Columbus discovered the West Indies the intrepid Portuguese mariner, Vasco da Gama, rounded the Cape of Good Hope and opened the gateway to India and the East Indies. By 1511, the Portuguese had established themselves on the west coast of the Malay Peninsula at Malacca, which had trading links with China. A few years later the newcomers had reached Canton (1516) and after protracted negotiations received permission to open a trading factory at Macao (1557), at the mouth of the river approach to Canton. The Chinese thereafter confined all foreigners to this area and all foreign trade had to be conducted through Canton. In the wake of the Portuguese came the English (Drake circumnavigated the globe in 1577-80), the Dutch and the French, operating through the English East India Company (1600), the Dutch East India Company (1602) and the French East India Company (1604).

In 1565, Spanish seamen took advantage of favorable winds to open a trade route through the northern Pacific to the Philippines. From then on a fleet of galleons—the famous Manila galleons—traveled annually between Panama and Manila. Earlier, Spanish seamen had traveled up the west coast of North America and named California, taking the name from a romance published in 1510, which claimed that "on the right hand of the Indies is an island called California, very close to the Terrestrial Paradise. . . ." California, according to this account, was peopled by black Amazons and had no other metal but gold.

Over forty years later, Drake sailed along the same coast and further north, searching for a quick route home through the illusory northwest Passage. He named part of the coast New Albion and captured one of the Manila galleons before completing his circumnavigation of the world. Meanwhile, the Spaniards, still searching for the legendary Great Southland to convert and plunder, discovered the Solomon Islands but failed to establish a plantation colony there. On one of these voyages, Pedro Fernandez Quiros, a godly Portuguese subject of the King of Spain, cast anchor on 3 May 1606, in a great bay of "a land more delightful, healthy and fertile" than he had yet seen. This, he told himself, was surely the fabled Southland, rich in gold and pearls, where he was destined to found the New Jerusalem. Offering thanks to God for safe passage across perilous seas he ordered an altar built on a white beach lapped by gentle waves.

With friars chanting and soldiers wearing the blue cross of a newly created Order of the Knights of the Holy Ghost, Quiros named the waters where his ships lay the Bay of St. Philip and St. James, and claimed the land for Pope and King, plus "all the lands which I sighted and am about to sight, and all

*William Dampier, buccaneer, master navigator
and forerunner of Captain James Cook*

Left: *Christopher Columbus, first modern navigator to visit the Americas*

this region south as far as the Pole, which from this time shall be called *Australia del Espiritu Santo,* with all its dependencies and belongings; and this for ever, and as long as right exists. . . ."

Eighteen months later Quiros was back in Madrid and two small coins, which he gave to a beggar, were his sole reward for discovering what he believed would be the New Jerusalem. His discovery, as time would show, was not *Terra Australis* but Santa Cruz in the New Hebrides. Luis Vaez de Torres, his pilot and companion in adversity, sailed home by another route, giving his name to the strait that lies between Australia and New Guinea.

In 1619 the Dutch East India Company established its island headquarters at Batavia in Java. Dutch seamen had already learned to use the Roaring Forties eastward from the Cape, turning northward in the longitude of their East Indies possessions. The merchantmen sometimes overcarried and made landfalls along the western coast of an inhospitable land they called New Holland, but saw little there that would interest company ledger-keepers at Batavia or the Hague. In 1642, Governor-General Anthony van Diemen at Batavia commissioned Abel Tasman to sail south and east in search of new lands with trading resources (that is, settled and civilized) and a navigable route to Spanish South America. Tasman touched on an area he named Van Diemen's Land (later renamed Tasmania) and discovered the coast of New Zealand, where Maoris killed and ate some of his seamen.

In 1688, the English buccaneer William Dampier spent three months on the northwest coast of New Holland and like his Dutch predecessors found it a barren wilderness inhabited by "the miserablest People in the World!" A subsequent voyage in 1699, this time as captain of a naval ship, did nothing to change his mind. By then, with British settlements in Virginia, Maryland and New England, the Lords of the Admiralty were not particularly disappointed at the negative results of Dampier's voyage, though they court-martialed him and declared him unfit to command any of his Majesty's ships.

During the seventeenth and early eighteenth centuries, the countries of Europe were mostly ruled by aristocratic cabals immersed in dynastic struggles. Only in Holland and England did governments give full weight to commercial considerations although merchants were increasingly important in France. England and Holland were commercial and colonial rivals but England had the edge as the English governed a manufacturing as well as a trading economy. The dynastic wars that convulsed Europe during the eighteenth century involved France, Spain and England and spread to India and America.

England emerged from these wars as the paramount sea power in the Pacific and Indian Oceans as well as in the Atlantic, although Manila was restored to Spain under the terms of the Peace of Paris (1763). Admiral

George Anson's Pacific exploits against Spain stimulated English interest in the Pacific, where France now became England's greatest rival. Three British naval expeditions under Byron, Wallis and Cateret crossed the Pacific between 1764 and 1767 and in the latter year Captain Samuel Wallis in H.M.S. *Dolphin* discovered Tahiti. This, together with renewed French interest in the area, encouraged fresh study of the voyages of Quiros and Torres and of the possible location of a Great Southland somewhere in the South Pacific.

Among papers captured during Britain's brief occupation of Manila in 1762 were accounts of early Spanish explorations in the Pacific. Alexander Dalrymple, a young writer with the East India Company in Madras, learned Spanish in order to be able to translate these documents. The result was *An Account of the Discoveries made in The South Pacifick Ocean previous to 1764* (London, 1767). Among other things Dalrymple, a skilled navigator and hydrographer, posited the existence of *Terra Australis Incognita*, although he placed it too far south and east and peopled it with settled and possibly civilized inhabitants.

In 1768, with war again raging in Europe and the Chevalier de Bougainville already in the Pacific in the name of England's hereditary enemy, France, the Lords of the Admiralty read Dalrymple's book with attention and took down the leather-bound volume containing Quiros's *Memorials*. They had lost Manila to the politicians and needed a base for a Pacific Squadron. The Royal Society of London gave their Lordships the opportunity they sought. In February 1768, the Society wrote to its Patron, King George III, praising his love of science and suggesting an expedition to newly discovered Tahiti to observe the transit of Venus on 3 June 1769, for "the like appearance will not happen for more than a hundred years."

The Royal Society recommended Dalrymple as leader of the expedition. The Admiralty and Mr. Joseph Banks, a rich young botanist among those promoting the project, opposed his appointment: the Admiralty because they were loath to permit a non-naval officer to command a King's ship contrary to regulations; Mr. Banks because he had a protégé, Yorkshire-born Master's Mate James Cook, who had been his modest and highly efficient companion in scientific work off Newfoundland. The Admiralty promoted forty-year-old Cook First Lieutenant and gave him command of a converted Whitby coal "cat", *Endeavour Bark*, 368 tons, rotund and copper-bottomed, perfectly suited for the task she had to do.

James Cook had learned his business in the coal trade out of Whitby along the bleak Yorkshire coast facing the North Sea. He served an apprenticeship with John Walker, a Quaker coal-shipper in the Baltic trade, but had refused command of a coal cat to join the Royal Navy. Within a month he was Master's Mate but he spent thirteen years in the same noncommissioned rank though highly regarded for his astronomical knowledge, hydrographical skill, fine seamanship and exemplary record. He now found himself promoted from the naval survey of the coast of Newfoundland to captain of a king's ship, at a wage of five shillings a day plus £120-a-year for victualing.

H.M.S. *Endeavour Bark* sailed from Plymouth on 26 August 1768, with ninety-four men aboard including Mr. Banks, his friend, Swedish botanist Dr. Solander, two artists to record scientific and geographical discoveries, two liveried footmen and two negro servants. As they sailed down the Channel crowds were parading London streets shouting "Wilkes and Liberty", while coffee-house gossips deploring the "licentious and republican" spirit abroad in the American colonies, where the repeal of the Stamp Act had failed to appease "factious and designing" men intent, it seemed, on nothing less than running their own affairs in their own way for their own benefit.

When she sailed there were two Americans aboard the *Endeavour*: Virginia-born Second Lieutenant John Gore, a fine seaman and keen sportsman, and Midshipman Mario Matra, or Magra as it appeared in the muster roll, a bespectacled, serious-minded Tory from New York. As loyal officers in His Britannic Majesty's Royal Navy, Gore and Matra wanted no truck with seditious republicanism. Before a month was out they had a shipmate, a fellow-American of more Republican spirit.

On 10 September, according to Mr. Banks's journal, the voyagers "dined in Africa, and took leave of Europe for Heaven knows how long, perhaps for ever." They spent five delightful days at Madeira where the Governor accorded them the "unsought honour of an official visit." At Funchal, chief port of the Madeiras, a young American sailor named John Thurmond was granted the unsought honor of joining the British Navy and taking part in what turned out to be one of the world's historic exploring expeditions. To make good a crew shortage Captain Cook had resorted to the fine old British custom of sending out a press gang. Thurmond, crew member of a New York sloop, was brought aboard *Endeavour* struggling, fighting and yelling that King George of England was nothing more than the son-of-a-bitch.

Unlike Gore and Matra John Thurmond never again saw Europe or America, except for the east coast of Tierra del Fuego, where it was so cold that Mr. Banks's two negroes, dead drunk on an excess of rum, froze to death. Gore, Matra and young Thurmond were the first Americans to set foot on Australian soil. Thurmond died and was buried at sea before the voyage was over. Gore lived to sail again with Cook, and Matra later dreamed that Australia might one day become a new America.

Captain Cook and his party duly observed the transit of Venus—obscured, Cook reported, by "an atmosphere of dusky shade round the body of the planet"—and ten days later sailed on the second leg of their historic journey. Cook was now carrying out Admiralty sealed orders which suggested he chart the undiscovered eastern coast of New Holland from Tasman's Van Diemen's

Land to Quiros's New Jerusalem. First, he established the separate existence of the north and south islands of New Zealand. Then, at daylight on 20 April 1770, eight days after the British Chancellor, Lord North, decided to retain the most obnoxious of all British duties on American commodities, the tax on tea, Cook's first lieutenant, Zachary Hicks, sighted "sloping hills covered in part with trees and bushes, but interspersed with large tracts of sand." It was the eastern coast of New Holland. By the end of the year the continent was still a great unknown but Cook had made it a recognizable shape on the charts of the world.

Mr. Banks had mixed feelings about the new land. His first good view, through a break in the clouds with water spouts wavering along the horizon, was like a corner of Arcady: "The country this morn rose in gentle sloping hills which had the appearance of the highest fertility, every hill seemed clothed with trees of no mean size; at noon a smoke was seen a little way inland, and in the evening several more." A week later, leaning on the port rail, he compared the country with "the back of a lean cow, covered in general with long hairs, but, nevertheless, where her scraggy hip bones have stuck out further than they ought, accidental rubs and knocks have entirely bared them of their share of covering."

At daylight on 29 April Cook recorded, ". . . we discovered a bay which appeared to be tolerably well sheltered from all winds, into which I resolved to go with the ship." Ten "Indians" gathered on a small hill to watch the ship sail into the bay. Cook sent the master in the pinnace to sound the approach. Some of the "Indians", lithe, naked, dark brown men with straight hair and full beards, came down to the cove a little within the harbor and "invited our people to land by many signs and words."

At 2:00 P.M. the *Endeavour* anchored under the south shore but by then the "Indians" seemed to have lost all interest in the proceedings. Several fishermen landed from frail canoes and scarcely lifted their eyes. A naked woman with three children came out of the bush to meet them carrying wood. She glanced at the ship but showed neither surprise nor concern. They "began to dress their dinner," Mr. Banks observed, "to all appearances totally unmoved by us. . . ."

Later in the afternoon, when a shore party approached the rocks to land, two of the fishermen came down "each armed with a lance about ten feet long, and a short stick, which he seemed to handle as if it was a machine to throw the lance . . . resolved to dispute our landing . . . though they were but two, and we thirty or forty." The "Indians" refused to parley and a harmless exchange of spears and shots occurred before the defenders ran away. During the next week men from the *Endeavour* landed to gather wood and locate fresh water, Banks and his scientists botanized and collected specimens, and Cook walked this way and that noting the quality of soil and herbage.

Sir Joseph Banks, scientist and patron of Australian development

Benjamin Franklin, like Banks, a modern scientific spirit in a new world

Groups of "Indians" watched these proceedings with interest from afar, throwing a spear or two in protest. They rebuffed all attempts to parley and refused to accept proffered presents. "All they seemed to want," Cook wrote, "was for us to be gone." On 7 May they had their wish. The *Endeavour* nosed out of Botany Bay—a name of ill-omen in the years to come—having inadvertently fixed the site for the first British colony in the Pacific.

The eighteen years between Captain Cook's discovery of eastern Australia and the arrival of the First Fleet, under Captain Arthur Phillip, R.N., at Botany Bay on 18 January 1788, were momentous years in the history of the world. The British lost America, gained India and continued to compete for domination of Pacific trade routes. Louis XVI and Marie Antoinette inherited an increasingly insecure throne in near bankrupt France. A melancholy young Corsican named Napoleon Bonaparte passed out of the Ecole Militaire in Paris and was posted as second lieutenant to garrison duties at Valence in southern France. He read Rousseau and Goethe's *Sorrows of Werther* and made notes on a wide range of miscellaneous subjects, such as "Boston is more than ten degrees colder than London" and "After three years of war America was recognized (as an independent nation) by France in 1777." It took the English Government six years longer to recognize the independence of the American colonies.

On 4 July 1776, Congress carried the American Declaration of Independence, drafted by Thomas Jefferson with revisions by Benjamin Franklin and Samuel Adams. More than seven years later, on 3 September 1783, after a succession of humiliating defeats inflicted by Washington's "Ragged Army" and in face of sustained hostility at sea from France and Spain, the English Parliament acknowledged the document's validity. British recognition of the United States of America ended the American Revolution but it did not establish American suzerainty over the whole of North America south of Canada and the Great Lakes. The French and the Spaniards saw to that. They wanted to confine the United States east of the Appalachians but Americans saw the Mississippi, discovered by the Spaniard De Soto and explored by the Frenchman La Salle, as their natural western boundary.

Beyond the Mississippi lay Louisiana, not the compact southern state now known by that name but a huge tract of wilderness comprising the present-day states of Louisiana, Arkansas, Missouri, Oklahoma, the Dakotas, Nebraska, Iowa, Minnesota, Kansas, Colorado, Wyoming and Montana. Nobody really ruled the handful of trading posts and garrisons scattered through this great watershed, but Spain claimed suzerainty. In 1801, Spain yielded it to Napoleon under secret treaty but retained possession of Mexico and Upper California, already colonized by Franciscan missionaries. Spanish-Americans soon lost any competitive impetus they might have had and lazed on their southwestern ranchos. Meanwhile, Russia and Britain showed a sustained interest in the increasingly important fur trade associated with the northwest Pacific coast.

Throughout the revolutionary war, the Lords of the Admiralty did not abandon their interest in the Pacific. They spared time and money to send Captain Cook on two more voyages. Between 1769 and 1780 Cook, now a post-captain and Fellow of the Royal Society, ended two Admiralty pre-occupations: the whereabouts of *Terra Australis Incognita* and the search for the Northwest Passage. *Terra Australis* existed but was no longer *Incognita* so far as the charts of the Pacific were concerned. The Great Southland was not where Dalrymple and others said it should be. Nor did it have developed resources open for trade or plunder. Dampier's New Holland and Cook's New South Wales comprised the west and east coasts with Torres' Strait above and the Southern Ocean below. The rest was a comparatively simple matter of charting and the far greater task of discovering, in due course, what lay between Mr. Banks's scraggy bovine backbone and Dampier's arid mangrove-edged coastline.

Cook's third voyage (1776-79) ended the equally persistent hope that an open passage north of the Americas led from the Atlantic to Cathay and the Indies. From a base in New Zealand Cook crossed and recrossed the Pacific from Antarctic to Arctic. There was nothing east of New Zealand but scatters of islands and the long coastline of North America, with the Spaniards edging up from the south, the Russians moving down from the north and Drake's New Albion between. The Admiralty was still interested in finding a safe, commodious harbor which might one day serve as a base for a Pacific Squadron but by sheer bad luck Cook missed one of the world's best harbors, Port Jackson. Though he had named it on his first voyage, he had failed to penetrate to the magnificent spread of water and scores of comfortable coves hidden behind the almost overlapping headlands.

Three Americans accompanied Cook on his last and greatest voyage: John Gore, who had been second lieutenant on the *Endeavour*, now first lieutenant aboard the *Resolution*, Cook's own ship; John Ledyard, a Connecticut Yankee, corporal of marines on the *Resolution*; and Simeon Woodruff, gunner's mate on *Discovery*, commanded by Charles Clarke. The two ships were again converted Whitby coal cats, stout craft ideally suited to Cook's purpose. Among officers and crew, besides those already mentioned, were men destined to become voyagers and explorers in their own right, including William Bligh, sailing master aboard the *Resolution*, notorious in later years for the mutiny on the *Bounty* and the Rum Rebellion in New South Wales; and Midshipman George Vancouver, who followed Cook on America's northwest coast and gave his name to Canada's best-known Pacific port.

John Ledyard, an American-born adventurer impressed into the Royal Marines, declared himself a traveler and a friend of mankind. Certainly he crowded enough colorful incident into thirty-six years to make him an American folk hero, a sort of sea-going Daniel Boone. Born in 1751 at Groton on the Connecticut coast, the son of a sea captain who died when the boy was eleven, young Ledyard declined to be a missionary to fulfil his mother's ambition or a lawyer to please his uncle. Instead, he ran away to sea from Dartmouth College in the spring of 1773, "like an Indian, in a dugout canoe."

Ledyard first went to sea as a sailor on a trading vessel bound for the Barbary coast. In 1774 he deserted ship at Falmouth, in Devon. The Watch picked him up at Bristol and offered him the alternative of shipment to the Guinea plantations or enlistment in the British Army. Not unnaturally, he chose the latter and, because of his education, soon became a corporal of marines. Pleading reluctance to fight against his fellow-countrymen in the revolutionary war he managed to talk himself into third-ranking place in the complement of eleven marines and a drummer-boy aboard Cook's *Resolution*.

In the Aleutian Islands and at Nootka Sound on the northwestern coast of North America, Ledyard made his first acquaintance with the fur trade. To learn more he volunteered to locate a Russian fur-trading post and, with the help of two Indian guides, succeeded in bringing several Russians back to the *Resolution*. Russian fur-traders had been active in the Aleutians and along the Alaskan coast since 1741 following the remarkable and tragic exploration of the area by Vitus Bering and Alexei Chirikof. Russian activity prompted the Spaniards to move northwards from Mexico and establish settlements at San Diego, Monterey and San Francisco. After Cook's voyage the Spaniards sent further exploring parties which reached latitude sixty-one degrees, somewhere near the present boundary between Yukon Territory and Alaska, before giving up and returning south.

Meanwhile, Lieutenant Gore and Corporal Ledyard had seen enough fur-trade possibilities to excite their interest. Captain Clarke took command of the expedition after Cook's death but died himself in ice-bound seas a few months later. John Gore then crossed with the ships to Canton where the few sea-otter furs acquired at Nootka Sound brought £2,000 worth of silk, tea, porcelain and similar China goods. Cook's account of the fur trade and Gore's successful salesmanship in Canton stimulated British interest in the economic development of the northwest coast. The first British trading ship went to Nootka Sound in 1785. Others followed from Bengal, Bombay and England, sent by the East India Company or with its blessing.

Ledyard, who in 1782 deserted the King's service at Huntington, Long Island, had similar plans for American shipowners. The times were propitious but American merchants were not ready to take advantage of them. Ledyard tried to enlist interest in an American commercial expedition to the northwest

The Boston Massacre. The beginning of independence

coast but not until six years after he arrived back in America did American ships begin to exploit northwestern waters.

If American shippers were slow to catch fire from Ledyard's stoking they lost little time in entering the tea trade from Canton. The tax on "English tea" from China had been one of the "tyrannous iniquities" Samuel Adams and the patriots had raged against when Charles Townsend, as Chancellor of the British Exchequer, had tried to make Americans pay for what he considered American wars against the Indians and the French. Following the Boston Massacre on 5 March 1770, when a small body of redcoats fired on an aggressive, jeering mob, killing and wounding several patriots, the British attempted to appease colonial sentiment by removing the duties on lead, paint, paper and glass. However, Lord North, Townsend's successor, retained the tax on tea—to maintain the principle as George III put it—and thereby virtually made the American Revolution inevitable. The war over, Americans lost no time in going directly to Canton to obtain tea and other China goods, hitherto supplied to them via Britain by the monopolistic East India Company.

As early as February 1784, Robert Morris, a Philadelphia merchant, sent the *Empress of China* from New York to Canton. Morris's ship is generally regarded as the first American ship to reach China with a cargo for trade although the re-rigged eighty-ton Hudson River sloop *Experiment*, which had no business attempting such a hazardous journey, made the trip about the same time. Another early ship to show the Stars and Stripes in the China Sea was the *Canton*, under the command of Thomas Truxtun, from Philadelphia. Captain Cook was the unofficial and unacknowledged patron of all these voyages and many that followed, for American seamen made ready use of his exact and detailed journals and the published works of those who sailed with him. These included John Ledyard's *Journal of Captain Cook's Last Voyage to the Pacific Ocean and in Quest of the North-West Passage, between Asia and America* (Hartford, Connecticut, 1783), which depended for its charts and nautical detail on an unofficial record published in London in 1781 and almost immediately pirated in Philadelphia. The official record begun by Cook was completed after his death in the Friendly Islands on 14 February 1779 by his second lieutenant, King, and appeared three years later.

By 1786, America's China trade had grown to such an extent that Congress sent Samuel Shaw to be American Consul in Canton, still the only port in the Chinese Empire open to foreigners. The narrow earth lanes and alleys of the old city, with its blue-gray brick buildings and scarlet lacquered temples and bridges, was much as it had always been. Along the riverfront, where factories served as combined warehouses, offices and dwellings for a growing number of European and American businessmen, things were different. Ships from many nations crowded the estuary, and the Portuguese-designed *lorchas* which plied from the crumbling and picturesque Portuguese colony of Macao carried the news of the world, albeit a little late, from anchored ships to anchored factories, for the Chinese authorities would not allow foreign ships up-river within cannon shot of the city proper.

Shaw, an ex-major in the Revolutionary Army, had not been in his new post long before he heard rumors that the British planned to establish a colony along the coast of Cook's New South Wales. Some said it would be a settlement of American Loyalists, driven from their homes by victorious patriots. Others said it would be a dumping ground for convicts huddled in hulks along the Thames, since the Americans had refused to take them as plantation labor from contractors who had hitherto shifted the burden from official shoulders. Shaw reported the rumors to Washington although by now there was an American Minister in London fully aware of the problems the new Prime Minister of Great Britain, the Right Honorable William Pitt, faced in the aftermath of the American war.

The whole mercantile system of trade, so derided by Scottish Adam Smith in *The Wealth of Nations* (1776), had crumbled with the loss of the American colonies. An entirely new system was necessary, but in a Britain where the East India Company still commanded considerable power and prestige, reconstruction of the British Empire on the free trade and utilitarian lines demanded by Adam Smith and Jeremy Bentham promised to be a long-term affair. Two immediate problems could not wait on the development of new economic theory or the deliberations of humanitarians and philosophers. First was the need for accommodation and compensation for 100,000 Americans who had remained loyal to King George and the British connection. Second, a means of disposal had to be found for convicts liable to transportation who, before the war, had been shipped off to the American plantations at the rate of a thousand a year.

Solution to the first problem was reasonably prompt and efficient although not everyone agreed that the right people had been sent to the right places. Solution to the second problem, hotly debated before and since, unwittingly laid the foundations of a New Britannia in another world—in the minds of some a nascent United States of Australasia, destined to emulate in the southern hemisphere the growth and influence of the United States of America in the northern hemisphere.

2 New Worlds for Old

Australia's First Fleet, with pioneers far different from the godly Puritans who had founded New England 158 years before, arrived at Botany Bay on between 18 and 20 January 1788. The Governor, Captain Arthur Phillip, R.N., London-born son of a German teacher, was fifty and had been at sea since he was fifteen. He had charge of a company of about fifteen hundred people, more than half of whom were convicts, transported in eleven ships whose combined tonnage was less than that of a modern transatlantic liner.

"The wind was fair, the sky serene, though a little hazy, and the temperature . . . delightfully pleasant," wrote Captain Watkin Tench, of His Majesty's Marines, in his *Narrative of the Expedition*; "joy sparkled in every countenance, and congratulations issued from every mouth. Ithaca itself was scarcely more longed for by Ulysses, than Botany Bay by the adventurers who had travelled so many thousand miles to take possession of it."

The voyage had taken eight months and one day, and the distance sailed was 15,063 miles. Captain Tench's adventurers, who included 191 women convicts, had not sparkled with joy throughout the trip. "The desire of the women to be with the men was so uncontrollable, that neither shame . . . nor the fear of punishment could deter them from making their way through the bulkheads to the apartments assigned to the seamen," wrote Surgeon-General John White in his Journal.

"The damned whores the moment they got below fell a-fighting amongst one another," wrote Marine Lieutenant Ralph Clark, "and Captain Meredith ordered the sergeant not to part them, but let them fight it out . . . They are a disgrace to their whole sex, b—s that they are." Men convicts, who feared the lash, were easier to manage. "I believe I may say," wrote Surgeon Arthur Bowes, "there was never a more abandoned set of wretches collected in one place. . . ." However, Lieutenant Clark asserted that by and large the prisoners "have behaved very well and quiet."

Captain Phillip took one hard look at Botany Bay, which Cook and Joseph Banks had praised, and moved into neighboring Port Jackson, through the gap

Cook had observed but not explored. On 26 January he broke out the Union Jack on the site of Sydney, overlooking sheltered waters he declared to be "the finest in the world, in which a thousand sail of the line may rest in perfect security." Two days earlier, the Comte de Laperouse's ships *Astrolabe* and *Boussole* had arrived off Solander Point. They entered Botany Bay on 26 January, the day Sydney was founded.

Laperouse had sailed from France in August 1785, nearly two years before Phillip and his ships left Portsmouth. The Comte's sailing orders, endorsed by Louis XVI, included an instruction to "take a closer view of the southern coast of New Holland, the greater part of which has never been visited." He had no instructions to visit Botany Bay or the eastern coast of New Holland but repaired there for wood and water. Phillip received the French ships courteously and gave them what assistance he could. They sailed from Botany Bay on 10 March and were wrecked a few weeks later in the New Hebrides, not a man surviving.

There is no evidence that either Prime Minister Pitt or any member of his cabinet thought of Botany Bay as anything more than a convenient place distant enough for the safe disposal of social waste. Governor Phillip had a greater sense of destiny. "As I would not wish convicts to lay the foundations of an empire," he wrote on 28 February 1787, before sailing for Botany Bay. "I think they should ever remain separate from the garrison and other settlers that may come from Europe and not be allowed to mix with them. . . ."

James Matra, who had been with Cook at Botany Bay in 1770, also had intimations of a more glorious Australian future. He saw Australia as another America, a new jewel in the diadem of Empire to replace the one lost when American patriots declared their independence. As a Loyalist, Matra saw New South Wales as a possible "asylum to those unfortunate American loyalists, who Great Britain is bound by ties of honour and gratitude to protect and support. . . ." Matra had problems himself. On his return from Cook's first voyage he had left the navy and obtained appointment as British Consul in Teneriffe. When the American troubles began he returned to New York to look after the family estate, his father having died. It was a time when American patriots regarded an American Tory as "a thing whose head is in England and its body in America, and its neck ought to be stretched between." Matra not only failed to regain his New York estate but complained that he was denied a share of the British allowance granted to Loyal Americans.

On 28 July 1783, he wrote to Joseph Banks asking for particulars of two rumored plans of settlements in the South Seas, one of them in New South Wales. He said he had "frequently revolved similar plans" and sought advice from an influential man who had been Cook's patron and his own fellow-traveler. Encouraged by Banks, on 23 August 1783, Matra submitted a plan to North's Coalition Government for a settlement in New South Wales. He envisaged a plantation-type settlement of free men—American Loyalists—drawing labor from China and the Pacific Islands. He pointed out that Botany Bay would provide a handy port for trade with China and the fur trade on the Pacific coast of America and made oblique reference to the possible strategic importance of such a settlement for naval operations in the Pacific.

The Coalition Government which concluded the peace with America had no time to consider Matra's proposals, submitted a fortnight before the treaty was signed. Pitt's reconstruction cabinet, which followed the coalition, was more interested. Lord Sydney, Secretary of State for Colonies, gave Matra an interview and observed "that New South Wales would be a very proper region for the reception of criminals condemned to transportation." Matra obligingly amended his plan to include transportees among the settlers but as cultivators in their own right rather than as forced labor. He assumed that as the area was close to the Indies it would be able to produce spices, sugar, tea, coffee, silk and tobacco. He drew attention to the accessibility of flax and timber for naval purposes in nearby New Zealand.

From the Colonial Office Matra's proposal went to the Admiralty, where it was not favorably received. Matra had chosen the wrong time to suggest what was in effect a revival of the mercantile policy that had failed in America. As Matra put it, ". . . the settlement is designed to increase the wealth of the parent country, as well as the emolument of the adventurers." British statesmen had learned to their bitter cost in prestige, manpower and treasure that colonies of free men were more concerned with "the emolument of the adventurers" than with enhancing the wealth of the parent country. The plan had the added disadvantage of cutting across the East India Company's monopoly of trade with India, China and the Indies. Further complications arose from the continued existence of the moribund South Sea Company, which held a nominal monopoly of trade along the Pacific coast of America.

Criticized from two sides, Matra's plan had little chance of success. On the one hand, those who would have liked to strengthen government control over an increasingly corrupt and inefficient East India Company did not like the mercantilist flavor of the proposed settlement. On the other hand, the Company still represented power, prestige and conventional economic wisdom that had not yet yielded to the onslaught of Adam Smith and the classical economists. Matra's interest in the matter lapsed with improvement in his own fortunes. He was almost certainly among the 4,000 Loyalists recompensed for property losses at the hands of the victorious patriots. Meanwhile, most of the Loyalists were rapidly resettled in Canada and Nova Scotia, on land granted by the Crown. Others sailed to England, Jamaica, Bermuda and the Bahamas. In 1787, Matra became Consul-General at Tangiers where, after earning distinction in diplomatic negotiations with the Sultan of Morocco, he died on 29 March 1806.

Lord Sydney's suggestion to Matra that New South Wales might be "a proper region for the reception of criminals" reflected the persistent and increasing problem brought about by the loss of the American colonies. In mid-1783 a contractor tried without success to induce Virginia and Maryland to take as plantation laborers 150 of the thousand or more convicted felons awaiting transportation. Economic distress and the consequent increasing incidence of crime added to a problem which a fifty percent increase in executions did little to allay. The Government could not afford to await the outcome of deliberations and proposals from jail and penal code reformers such as Howard, Blackstone, Eden and Bentham. Some distant jail had to be found quickly.

As early as 1779, Joseph Banks had told a committee of the House of Commons that Botany Bay would make an ideal site for the reception of convicted felons. Distance and isolation would make escape difficult if not impossible. The natives were few and would be easily cowed. The climate was Mediterranean in comparison with the fever coast of Africa. There were no beasts of prey and sheep and oxen would thrive. There were abundant supplies of wood and water. Seven years passed before Banks's recommendation was adopted. Meanwhile, other influential voices had spoken up in favor of New South Wales rather than Gambia, in West Africa, which Edmund Burke condemned as "the capital seat of plague, pestilence, and famine." When Pitt at last acquiesced, Lord Sydney moved with commendable rapidity in despatching Captain Phillip with eleven ships containing 568 male convicts, 191 female (with 13 children) and four companies of marines, 160 men plus 51 officers and N.C.O.s, 27 with wives.

In due course free settlers arrived but no one among them was inspired to prophesy as John Winthrop had prophesied aboard *Arbella*, bound westward across the Atlantic in the spring of 1630 to found Massachusetts Bay Colony: "Wee shall be as a Citty upon a Hill, the eies of all people are upon us; soe if wee shall deale falsely with our god in this worke wee have undertaken wee shall be made a story and a by-word through the world." However, young James Tuckey, lieutenant aboard the ship which took the first unwilling convict settlers into Port Phillip Bay (the future Melbourne) and Hobart Town in October 1803, was not without dreams for the future.

"I beheld a second Rome," he wrote in his account of the voyage, "rising from a coalition of banditti. I beheld it giving laws to the world, and superlative in arms and in arts, looking down with proud superiority upon the barbarous nations of the northern hemisphere." This was Johnsonian rhetoric rather than serious prophesy but before long colonists and native-born from Sydney Town and Hobart Town were not only competing with Americans in the exploitation of southern seas but thinking of themselves as Australians, with a future more akin to the American future than the commonplace and subservient role allotted them by the British Government and Colonial Office panjandrums.

Meanwhile, news passed throughout the Pacific, from China to Peru, from Kamchatka to the Falkland Islands, that the British had settled New South Wales. The news was confirmed for Samuel Shaw in Canton when three of the convict transports—*Charlotte, Lady Penrhyn* and *Scarborough*—arrived under charter to the East India Company to load tea for England. Shaw did not know that officialdom had decreed that His Majesty's Government intended to prevent by every possible means "every sort of intercourse between . . . Botany Bay or any other place . . . established on the coast of New South Wales . . . and the settlements of our East India Company, as well as the coast of China and the islands situated in that part of the world to which any intercourse has been established by any European nation."

This attempt on the part of the British Government to safeguard the East India Company's monopoly was doomed to failure. As in the American colonies so lately liberated, immediate necessity rapidly swamped long-range policy. Nevertheless, more than four years passed before the first American ship, *Philadelphia*, Captain Patrickson, out of Philadelphia and via the Cape of Good Hope, berthed in Sydney on 1 November 1792, with a cargo that was snatched up by a commodities-hungry settlement. By 1800 British traders, kept away from Sydney by the East India Company monopoly, were protesting that American shippers were monopolizing a market that should rightly belong to British enterprise. By then, the American sealer *Hope* of Rhode Island, Captain Benjamin Page, had landed the first cargo of rum and helped start a process that turned a penal colony into a settlement where military officers, emancipated convicts and one or two enterprising intruders demonstrated the virtues and vices of an unregulated free economy in which the richest were usually the most ruthless exploiters of market opportunities and human weakness.

The myopic gaze of George III and his ministers saw nothing in the sun-dazzled seas of the south except a prison that needed no locks or keys and a possible source of flax and stout-girthed pines to stamp with the broad arrow that meant exclusive use as masts in royal men-of-war. Blinking through salt-rimmed lashes, shrewd eyes that first saw the light in Salem, Marblehead, New Bedford, Rhode Island, Martha's Vineyard and Nantucket, discovered much more than the bare outline of a barren coast. They saw possibilities that King, Lords and Commons, in their corporate capacities, had no eyes to see. There were, however, individuals enough in and out of the East India Company with sufficient nous to see that the two new worlds, that had sprung phoenix-like from the smoldering embers of the old, promised ample warmth and stimulus for those with brains and ability enough to benefit. The past was slowly dying but the present, already born, stretched open fingers towards a calculable future, a future in which there was no place for the original occupiers—the Aboriginals and the Indians.

New England's discovery of New South Wales was a by-product not, as Herman Melville romantically suggested, of the search for whales but of the rush to buy tea direct from China. The American brigantine *Philadelphia*, en route to Canton via the Cape of Good Hope, was the first of sixty or more American ships to berth in Port Jackson between 1 November 1792 and the War of 1812 between Britain and the United States. More than twenty, and these mostly in the ten years after *Philadelphia* in 1792, were bound for China. Sealers and whalers came later. Yankee "Tinmen and Sea Captains" had no need to read Adam Smith to appreciate the virtues of free trade. Self-interest and commonsense rather than economic theory directed their course and helped create a new America in the southern hemisphere.

Self-interest and commonsense also prompted British military officers and emancipated convicts in New South Wales to take advantage of American initiative for their own aggrandizement and the incidental creation of what Australian economic historian Edward Shann calls "an exchange economy based on truck wages, with rum as the main item of consumption and motive for exertion." *Philadelphia's* captain, Thomas Patrickson, had called at Cape Town en route to China with a speculative cargo he was ready to unload anywhere in return for cash or credit good enough to buy tea and China goods at Canton.

At Cape Town, then a criss-cross of Dutch houses around a fort huddled under the shadow of Table Mountain and notable for the rancid smell of the grease used by the burghers' Hottentot slaves to dress their hair, Captain Patrickson met thirty-three-year-old Commander Philip Gidley King, R.N., returning to his post as Lieutenant-Governor of Norfolk Island with his new wife, as passengers aboard H.M.S. *Gorgon*. Norfolk Island had been established as an out-settlement of New South Wales. From King, the American captain learned that Sydney periodically suffered near-starvation from lack of essential supplies. Cook's "fine black soil" and Banks's "waving grasses in fine meadows" had turned out to be fine white sand and "high coarse rushes growing in a rotten spongy bog" while the "woods" grew in thin soil on narrow sandstone ridges and along the slopes of steep gullies quite unsuitable for agriculture.

Better soil was discovered at Parramatta and Toongabbie and marked out in free grants of 100 acres for reluctant noncommissioned officers and privates of the prison guard to set up as farmers. Convicts were set to scratch the land with hoes for the establishment of a Government Farm. Governor Phillip confessed before King left for England in 1790 that none of these measures had made the colony "independent for the necessaries of life." Taking advantage of the Roaring Forties and the long free-running eastward-flowing seas of the southern Indian Ocean Captain Patrickson was soon anchored in Neutral Bay, the area of Port Jackson that Phillip had set aside for foreign vessels. He unloaded 569 barrels of American-cured beef and 27 barrels of pitch and tar for King George's commissariat and disposed of most of his cargo of rum, gin, wine and tobacco to the thirsty officers of the new settlement.

H.M. Storeship *Britannia* had arrived on 14 October of the previous year with "9,278 gallons of rum, being the allowance of half a gallon per annum." Phillip was particularly pleased that the convicts, who worked from daylight to dark trying to keep their open prison habitable, had been included in the allowance "for it is a bounty which many of those people well deserve and to the undeserving it will never be given." Maybe Captain Benjamin Page, who arrived from Rhode Island Christmas Eve that same hot antipodean summer, with his small ship, appropriately named *Hope*, packed tight with "7,600 gallons of raw United States spirits" held a similar pious view that his cargo would go to the deserving, leaving the colony's clear cold water for the un-deserving. If so, like Governor Phillip, he reckoned without due consideration for climate and the great Australian thirst or the natural human propensity for what the custodians of Georgia's colonial morals called "the odious and loathsome Sin of Drunkenness."

Patrickson and Page, related by marriage and both from Quaker Philadelphia, must have seen a great difference between Benjamin Franklin's city, with its "pretty Quakeresses, pale in their little bonnets and their light gray gowns", and Sydney Town where scores of half-naked dirty slatterns clamored for custom in the narrow earth streets and stinking lanes crowded about Sydney Cove. True, there were whores enough in Philadelphia's riverbank cellars but the "Quality" did not instal even the prettiest of them as government-rationed mistresses in the manner common among officers and gentlemen in the New South Wales Corps.

Dispensing good rum to good customers was another matter altogether for New England rum, made from West Indian molasses, had replaced beer and cider as the favorite American beverage. There were sixty-three Massachusetts distilleries operating full blast and Massachusetts sea captains were ready enough to spread a knowledge of the virtue and good qualities of New England rum despite the fact, as an early historian of Salem put it, "If the natives of the West coasts of Africa have been temperate, they have been in spite of the efforts of the Salem merchants to supply them with the materials of intemperence. . . ." The merchants of Massachusetts were equally ready to supply "the materials of intemperence" to the natives of New South Wales, convicted or free, immigrant or locally-born.

They did not know that they were at the same time providing a charter of economic freedom for unscrupulous use by rapacious officers and emancipists, in place of the monopolistic mercantilist charter provided by George III and his forebears for equally unscrupulous use by the East India Company. Samuel Adams and his hard-nosed Yankee sea captains provided the means whereby the new America on the other side of the world could take a few first staggering steps towards the initial goal American rebels had set for themselves: the rights of Englishmen.

Lethargic officers and officials soon found the promise of wealth sufficient incentive to turn a creaking official institution into a functioning economic organism. At the same time, energetic and ambitious convicts found a means to lift themselves out of the proletarian swamp that engulfed them even if it meant pushing some of their fellows deeper into the mire. Nor were rewards reserved for the merely ruthless and unscrupulous. The quick and clever found legitimate openings others were too dull or lazy to exploit.

Captain Phillip, a good, well-intentioned man who did the best he could with refractory material, sailed in the *Atlantic* on 11 December 1792, to seek medical attention. With him sailed Bennelong, an Aboriginal favorite who had acquired a taste for English liquor as well as English food and shelter. Bennelong, like the American Indians sent to England to satisfy European curiosity about the New World's "noble savages", returned to his own people "much broken in spirit", foreshadowing the doom of a race which increasingly lost the virtues of its own traditions and succumbed to the vices of white men. The newcomers treated the victims they had corrupted with amused contempt, remaining blind to the human tragedy symbolized by the Aboriginal waifs and strays who squatted in the dust about the outskirts and along the streets of new settlements.

Phillip's departure marked the beginning of a social revolution. Major Francis Grose, commander of the New South Wales Corps and Lieutenant-Governor, inaugurated the new regime when, as he slyly reported to the Secretary of State for Colonies, he allowed Captain Page to unload his rum so that he would part with his flour and pork.

Phillip, backed by the English authorities, had been anxious to prevent rum from circulating freely among convicts. He directed that the trade in liquor should be subject to "the view and inspection of proper persons." Grose had no doubts about who were the most proper persons for this and other advantageous duties. As soon as Phillip had departed he replaced all civil magistrates with military officers, gave the senior military at Parramatta control over the convicts there and appointed able, ambitious Lieutenant John Macarthur as superintendent of works. As proper persons the officers quickly bought the *Hope's* consignment of rum, then banded together and funded their capital to monopolize imports of liquor and goods from Bengal, Batavia, and Rio de Janeiro, as well as from Massachusetts.

The great Australian thirst, like the great American thirst, developed early. Not unnaturally, convicts, like the hard-drinking mountain men of the American Rockies, sought temporary oblivion from a hard life in uproarious drunkenness. Drink-crazed convicts frequently traded a three weeks' allowance of flour for a bottle of rum. Ex-convicts, known as emancipists, who had acquired small farms, traded their stock for rum and tobacco. The few free settlers who arrived in the 1780s soon followed suit, for the soil was hard, the seasons unpredictable and rewards precarious. New England colonists, faced with stony soil and hard weather, took to the sea. New South Wales colonists, except for the shrewd, took to the bottle. Their sons, the native-born first generation Australians, soon saw the folly of their fathers' ways and followed New England example in looking seaward rather than landward, for independence as well as profit.

Even in America, as a correspondent reminded the abstemious moralists who governed colonial Georgia, poverty, distress and frustrated hopes drove men to drink "to keep up their Courage." In England, the same correspondent averred, many people had nothing to choose but either to be "quite Folorn without hopes or Mad with Liquor." With tongue in cheek Major Grose had something to say on the same subject when he excused his excessive importation of rum on the grounds that it was useful to "relieve the soldiers' necessities" and afforded them "Comfort other than the reduced and unwholesome rations served out from the stores." In fact, he issued the rum and docked the soldiers' pay according to the value of the issue.

Lieutenant Anthony F. Kemp, who had traveled in the United States for a year before he was commissioned in the New South Wales Corps, had nothing to learn from the "gander-shanked Yankee peddlars" he met hawking wooden "nutmegs", cornhusk "cigars" and sawdust "pepper". Joseph Holt, an Irish rebel transported for his part in the "troubles" of 1798, had a good deal to say in his *Memoirs* about the shop-keeping methods adopted by Lieutenant Kemp (promoted Captain in 1801) and other monopolizers "who never grew a grain (yet) sometimes would have a thousand bushels of wheat to put in the store."

Amiable and easy-going, Grose, who ruled two years with John Macarthur as his energetic accomplice, laid the foundation for Australia's earliest identity: a Virginia-style plantation society based on assigned convict labor instead of bought negro slaves. Grose began the process when, acting in accordance with Home Office instructions, he provided officers, civil officials, emancipated convicts and a few immigrant settlers with free land to farm for personal profit. He also provided each farmer with ten convict laborers provisioned at government expense, which was directly contrary to instructions. Legal or illegal, the innovation soon made the colony economically viable in a manner no government order had yet managed to do.

Within the next twenty or thirty years the countryside around Sydney was dotted with eighteenth-century English country houses, where those lucky enough to dip deeply into the cornucopia Grose so obligingly provided sought to emulate the lives of the English landed gentry. They built fine houses, imported handsome furniture, promoted race meetings and cricket matches and flogged recalcitrant convict serfs who failed to see on which side their bread was buttered. Ex-naval surgeon Sir John Jamison outdid them all. Regentsville, his estate at Penrith on the Nepean, was a complete manorial domain with 200 assigned servants, woolsheds, workshops for cobblers, carpenters, weavers and harnessmakers. He instituted colonial racing on his estate and rode to the meetings escorted by liveried retainers flourishing staffs, ready to keep down any rowdyism they did not themselves initiate.

Actually, the officers' monopoly was never so complete nor so rapacious as Holt and some later historians have asserted. Rum-stimulated wealth did not stay in favored pockets. Nor was every officer a neurotic sadist always fingering a whip. Nevertheless, the poorer settlers of Parramatta scarcely exaggerated when they complained in a petition to the Secretary of State, that the officers enjoyed "singular advantages." They were advantages that shrewd ex-convicts, soon to emerge as an Emancipist middle-class, were ready enough to share. Emancipists grew rich acting as go-betweens for officers who disdained the dirty work associated with the liquor traffic once Grose's successors tried to crack down.

Like its examplars in the West Indies and the Southern States of America, the new society was not entirely mercenary and cruel. John Macarthur, who with Parson Samuel Marsden introduced Merino sheep and developed an export trade in wool, shared with Captain John Piper, Lieutenant William Cox and others a feudal sense of responsibility towards faithful retainers. To be "one of Macarthur's men" was to be well-fed, well-cared for and almost without fear of physical punishment. James Macarthur, John's son, adopted the old English custom of Harvest Home Dinners during which he and his family waited at table on their convict servants, carefully watering down the brandy when the compulsory guests refused flat English porter, as they invariably did. A beneficiary of "Cox's Liberty" enjoyed almost equal felicity until Lieutenant Cox, who succeeded Macarthur as Paymaster of the New South Wales Corps, overstrained his credit and faced a deficiency of £7,900 in his regimental accounts.

In September 1788, nine months after Governor Arthur Phillip had established "Botany Bay" on the shores of Port Jackson, English whaler Sam Enderby sent his ship *Amelia* round Cape Horn in search of new whaling grounds. *Amelia* returned in March 1790 with more than a thousand barrels of sperm oil lifted off the coasts of Chile and Peru. The news spread. A year later six American whalers, eager to rebuild their war-shattered industry, were working off the Pacific coast of South America.

Enderby, some of whose ships were under charter as transports taking convicts and stores to New South Wales, instructed his captains to keep a weather-eye open for whales. Thomas Melville, master of the Enderby-owned storeship *Britannia*, reported on his arrival at Sydney on 14 October 1791, that he had seen more sperm whales between the South Cape of Van Diemen's Land and Port Jackson than he had seen during six years' whaling in the South Atlantic.

By then Sydneysiders had already had their first experience of whaling. In July 1790, several boats had put out after a sperm whale that appeared in the harbor. Unskilled in the difficult art of harpooning, the amateur whalers met with no success. A few days later off South Head a whale "pursued and upset" the punt belonging to an officer of marines. Midshipman John Ferguson and two marines drowned while the fourth man, a sergeant of marines, found himself clinging to the whale's back. When the mammal sounded the sergeant swam safely ashore.

Meanwhile, Sam Enderby enlisted official sympathy for an easing of the East India Company's monopoly over whaling in Pacific waters east of the Cape of Good Hope. Melville's *Britannia* and four other transports made a foray out of Port Jackson but without much success because of bad weather. When the *Britannia* returned in 1792 her new master, William Raven, had a three years' license from the East India Company to operate in the Southwest Pacific. By 1801, Enderby, backed by other English whaling companies, had opened the Pacific to British whaling and sealing, provided those so engaged delivered their logs to the Court of Directors of the East India Company on their return to England. Colonial sealers and whalers found it easy enough to ignore the proviso: Americans had no reason to know or to care.

Samuel Shaw, pioneer American Consul at Canton, died in 1794 on a homeward voyage from India where he had inaugurated an agreement with the United States permitting direct trade between America and India. Before he died, Shaw had helped John Ledyard's dream come true: a three-way trade in American ships had established itself between fur-rich Nootka Sound, Canton and the East Indies, with New South Wales as a sometimes profitable stopover.

The American ship *Fairy*, which in October 1792 brought news of Louis XVI's execution, had come from Boston via the Cape of Good Hope bound for Nootka Sound to collect sea-otter skins for Canton. She was not the first American ship to fulfil Ledyard's dream. Four years after the *Empress of China* opened the China trade Captain John Kendrick in *Columbia* and Captain Robert Gray in *Lady Washington* reached Nootka Sound, the first American ships to winter there (1788-89). The following summer Kendrick

Bay whaling, Twofold Bay, New South Wales.
Whaling in the South Seas seemed romantic to
artists

loaded *Columbia* with furs and stayed behind with *Lady Washington* while Gray sailed to Canton, exchanged the furs for tea, and returned to Boston via the Cape of Good Hope, thus becoming the first American ship to circumnavigate the globe. Other American ships soon followed.

By 1788, the Russian sea-otter industry was well established along the southern coast of Alaska, and moves by the Spanish Royal Philippines Company to exploit the same area persuaded the British Government and the East India Company to develop the fur trade. East India Company red tape successfully strangled British efforts and within fifteen years American ships, not needing East India Company licenses, had captured the trade.

In the meantime, New South Wales had been drawn into a British scheme to establish a settlement, as a sort of off-shoot from Sydney, on the northwest coast of America. In March 1790, the British Secretary of State for Colonies, Lord Grenville, wrote Governor Phillip that the sloop *Discovery*, under Captain George Vancouver, with the armed tender *Chatham*, was about to leave on an expedition to the northwest coast of America, where the Spaniards had attacked a British fishing vessel in June 1789.

Grenville continued:

> One of the objects of this expedition being to form a settlement on the north-west coast of America [it] is His Majesty's pleasure that you should select from amongst the people with you a proper number of persons to compose it and that you should embark them either on board the *Discovery* or the *Gorgon* [which had brought Grenville's despatch to Phillip]. The extent of this establishment . . . need not at first exceed thirty persons, a moiety of whom at least should consist of drafts from the new corps under the command of a discreet subaltern officer who is to be entrusted with the temporary superintendence of the new settlement. The remainder should consist of two or three of the most intelligent of the overseers . . . together with a few of the most deserving of the convicts, to whom you may offer a remission of a part of their service as an inducement to go.

Nothing came of the project. Phillip, desperately trying to establish the colony of New South Wales with the minimum resources, had no men or supplies to spare for a similar attempt across the Pacific. *Gorgon* sailed, taking with her the marines who accompanied the First Fleet and leaving the specially raised, highly dubious New South Wales Corps in their place. Vancouver, although he surveyed part of the southwest coast of Australia and discovered the commodious King George's Sound in Western Australia, where Albany now stands, did not call at Sydney. Instead of establishing a new convict settlement, Vancouver performed the more useful task of surveying the Tahitian and Hawaiian Islands and completing charts of the vast complex northwest coast of America from San Francisco to the Alaskan Peninsula, much of the work being done in open boats. He returned to England in 1795.

When Captain John Hunter, R.N., arrived as Governor in September 1795, Sydney did not appear much like the capital of a nascent "great colony" although Captain Benjamin Page of the American ship *Halcyon* averred to Captain David Collins, R.N., that all that was required to make it so were "large herds of grazing cattle."

Governor Hunter had more success with colonial fashions than with colonial habits. After a futile attempt to prevent the landing of spirits, he endeavored to regulate the traffic he could not prevent by granting licenses for the brewing and sale of beer and spirits. A woman convict, more respectable than most of her sisters in sin, opened the first decently-conducted house in Sydney. She called her licensed premises *Three Jolly Sisters* and in a letter to her father declared, "I really believe, with the assistance of God, by the time I have paid this forfeit, according to the laws of my country, I shall acquire a little money to return home with, which I have not the smallest doubt of, and to be a comfort to you at the latter end of your days. . . ."

The new licensee of the *Three Jolly Sisters* had a truly Yankee sense of business. "I did a little trade on the passage here," she told her father, "in a number of small articles, such as sugar, tea, tobacco, thread, snuff, needles, and every thing that I could get anything by. The needles are a shilling a paper here, and fine thread sixpence a skein. I have sold my petticoats at two guineas each, and my long black coat at ten guineas, which shows that black silk sells well here; the edging that I gave 1s 8d per yard for in England I got 5s for it here. . . ."

In the United States by this time, signwriters had changed most of the old inn signs from *Royal Standard* to *George Washington* or from *Rose & Crown* to *Three Horseshoes*. In early Sydney, licensed victualers, mostly ex-convicts encouraged by naval Governors Hunter and King, recorded their gratitude with such names as *The Royal Admiral, Governor King, Endeavour, Crown and Anchor*, and the name shrewdly concocted by ex-marine John Redmond for his George Street tavern, *The Keep Within Compass*. Sydney's earliest innkeepers, Simeon Lord, Henry Kable, James Underwood, Edward Wills, Thomas and Mary Reiby, were the first to take a leaf out of New England's book, the first to build ships, the first to trade abroad, the first to develop an export staple: seal oil and seal skins.

Thus New South Wales changed from an open prison to an open society with room at the top for ex-convicts as well as military officers on the make. In due course adventurous sheep and cattlemen followed the money-making example of Sydney's Emancipist and Currency Lad pioneers, although the newcomers looked homeward across the Blue Mountains to the vast open spaces of the wide interior. About the same time, Santa Fe traders and rumbustious mountain men were opening up the American continent across the Missouri to the Rockies and beyond. In both continents, selfish, ruthless and conniving pioneers regarded the aboriginal people either as vermin to be exterminated or as potential serfs to be exploited. Even the righteous saw hope only in the terms laid down by Christopher Columbus when he declared the *Indios* to be a tractable, peaceable people who should be "made to work . . . and adopt our ways. . . ."

3

Officers and Gentlemen

The war in Europe slowed down the flow of convicts into New South Wales but Governors Hunter and King had to contend with new and difficult types of transportees: political exiles. The "Scottish Martyrs" were first and then the Irish "Rebels of '98". William Pitt, seriously concerned about the spread of sympathy for the French Revolution, acted swiftly and ruthlessly against anything that might be interpreted as sedition. Among those arrested and charged were Thomas Muir, Thomas Fyshe Palmer, William Skirving, Joseph Gerrald and Maurice Margorot. Although usually referred to as the "Scottish" Martyrs only two were Scots but all were intellectuals sentenced in Scotland in the years 1793 and 1794 and transported to New South Wales.

Palmer, a Unitarian minister of cultured tastes, served his seven years' sentence and became a close friend of an adventurous naval surgeon, George Bass, who, in 1798 with Lieutenant Matthew Flinders, R.N., opened up Bass Strait between Australia and Van Diemen's Land, soon to become the quarrelsome hunting ground of American and Australian sealers. Palmer died at Guam on his way home. Because of his religious views Spanish friars refused him a Christian burial and his body was interred on the beach amongst pirates. Two years later Captain Balch, of the American ship *Mary*, en route from Sydney to Manila, received permission to remove the body to Boston for burial with a commemorative tablet in a city church. No trace of the grave and tablet remains.

Skirving lived less than two years after his arrival in New South Wales despite George Bass's daily attendance in his last illness. A marginal note on the burial register in St. Phillip's Episcopalian Church sums up his record: ". . . a Seditionist, but a man of respectable moral conduct." Margorot, whose wife accompanied him, was a cantankerous, troublesome man suspected by some of being a government informer. When the first batch of Irish rebels arrived Governor King accused Margorot of helping them to plan an unsuccessful rebellion on 4 March 1804. He was sent to Norfolk Island, the settlement's penal colony for secondary offenders. His seized papers contain bitter denunciations of the officers, rum monopoly and a forecast that Australia would one day succeed America as the world's chief power. Margorot returned to England in 1810, where he continued radical political propaganda until his death in 1815.

Joseph Gerrald, fifth convicted Scottish Martyr, arrived about six months after the others in an advanced state of tuberculosis. Born in the West Indies, he migrated to the United States after the Treaty of Versailles and practiced at the Bar in Pennsylvania for four years, before visiting England to prosecute a law suit. He became active in agitation for parliamentary reform. In New South Wales, Governor Hunter treated him well, allowing him to buy a cottage and garden at Farm Cove where he lived the life of an invalid until too weak to be alone, when he moved in with his friend Skirving. Although regularly attended by George Bass he died early in 1796 and was buried in the garden of his Farm Cove home. His tombstone carried the inscription: "He died a martyr to the liberties of his country, in the 36th year of his age."

Thomas Muir, who had carried a French passport and was on his way to the United States when arrested in Scotland, bought himself a small farm across the harbor from Sydney Cove not far from Neutral Bay, where American vessels anchored. On 18 February 1796, he escaped aboard the Boston ship *Otter*, commanded by Ebenezer Dorr, leaving a letter saying he intended to practice at the bar in the United States. In those days, despite the revolutionary Terror when hundreds of well-born Frenchmen died under the guillotine after condemnation by the "People's Courts", many Americans continued to sing "Ca ira!" and to toast Liberty, Equality and Fraternity in political clubs, established at east coast ports in emulation of the Jacobin Clubs of France. Thus, to Thomas Muir, America appeared the natural place to go. The French Revolution seemed to many Americans a logical development from the American Revolution. Not that Washington and his ministers had much love for the French, but the American public, ignoring mounting French disregard for the rights of American shipping and the looming shadow of Napoleon, persisted in its Francophilia. In 1798, Congress felt compelled to pass Naturalization, Alien and Sedition Acts to protect the country from subversive aliens and seditious Americans. Nevertheless, Tom Paine, Joseph Priestley, Richard Price and prickly anti-American William Cobbett, with many men of lesser fame, found refuge in America.

Thomas Muir was unlucky. Dorr in the *Otter* took the escapee to Nootka Sound, which had been ceded to Britain by Spain. To keep check on foreign ships visiting the coast Spanish authorities at Monterey patrolled the coast regularly. Learning from the Spanish gunboat *Sutil* that H.M.S. *Providence* was in the area, Muir transferred to *Sutil* for passage to Monterey where he hoped to persuade the Spanish Governor of Upper California to permit him to proceed to Philadelphia to join Joseph Priestley.

The *Sutil* arrived at Monterey on 5 July 1796, where the Governor, Don Diego Borcia, treated Muir with every consideration, although he was an illegal immigrant in a country where foreigners of all kinds, especially Protestant foreigners, were officially unwelcome. Upper California at that time consisted mostly of missions in a land occupied to forestall Russian fur traders moving south. Before long, Spanish-Mexican ranchos and presidios stretched in a wide arc from San Francisco to Texas. In theory, all intercourse or trade with foreigners was banned, a restriction Americans and Californians were ready enough to flout.

Thomas Muir wrote eight letters from Monterey, all radiating confidence that he would obtain a passport from the Viceroy of Mexico to proceed to the United States. The first of these letters, dated 15 July 1796, was addressed to General George Washington, President of the United States. After relating his adventures since first setting out, with a French passport, to reach America, he continued, "Sir, I have claimed the protection of your name. I hasten to Philadelphia to solicit it in person . . . I have likewise presumed to draw upon you for what expenses may attend my journey. Needless to observe that these bills will be joyfully reimbursed in Europe."

The Spanish authorities intercepted Muir's letters which are now in the Archives of the Indies, Seville. Instead of willingly acceding to Muir's petitions, the Viceroy ordered that he be conducted "without outward signs of arrest" to Vera Cruz and there await transport to Spain. Consequently, Muir found himself in Vera Cruz and then in Havana, where he was imprisoned for several months before being shipped aboard the frigate *Ninfa* to Spain.

At this time, Britain and Spain were at war. According to William James's *Naval History of Great Britain*, at six o'clock on the morning of 26 April 1787, the British seventy-four-gun ship *Irresistible* and the thirty-six-gun frigate *Emerald*, being on a cruise off the coast of Spain, chased two Spanish frigates, the *Santa Elena* and the *Ninfa* of thirty-six guns. The pursuit lasted until four o'clock in the afternoon, when, after a sharp action, both Spanish ships struck their colors. A severe wound in the face, which resulted in the loss of an eye, left Muir unrecognizable and he was sent ashore with the Spanish wounded to hospital at Cadiz. News of his plight reached Paris where Talleyrand, the French foreign minister, intervened and had Muir transferred to Paris.

At first the Directory made much of Muir and consulted him on proposals for the invasion of England. A highly propagandist account of his adventures was prepared and published in 1798 under the title *Histoire de la tyrannie du gouvernement anglais exercé envers le célèbre Thomas Muir, écossais*. However, Muir himself was soon forgotten in the upheavals of French politics and he died in obscurity at Chantilly, near Paris, on 26 January 1799, the eleventh anniversary of Botany Bay.

Herman Melville, whose classic *Moby Dick* spread the saga of the Pacific throughout the literate English-speaking world, described Australia as, "That great America on the other side of the sphere. . . ." Furthermore, he declared that after "its first blunder-born discovery by Dutchmen" the whalemen of New England opened the new continent to "the enlightened world." If we center the enlightened world in Massachusetts, as many nineteenth century Bostonians would have done, Melville was right. The whalers and sealers of New England discovered Australia more precisely than Captain Cook, for Cook took a peep and drew part of an outline, whereas, in the first decade of the nineteenth century, Yankee whalers and sealers investigated every river mouth and cove along the southern and southwestern coasts, which Cook had not seen.

Britain's war with Spain, which had such disastrous effects on the fortunes of Thomas Muir, prompted British whalers to renew their attack on the East India Company's monopoly in the Pacific. The temporary respite, which permitted them to round Cape Horn and fish off the Pacific coast of South America, did not extend to Australasian waters, although an occasional ship, either an interloper or armed with a temporary license, tried its luck in the turbulent Tasman Sea.

The appearance of Spanish cruisers, in search of British whalers, changed the situation. The war began in October 1796 and the following year, Sam Enderby and other British whalers petitioned the Board of Trade asking for permission to operate in Australasian waters. A minute of the Board of Trade dated 26 December 1797, stressed that the closure of South American ports made it absolutely necessary to provide a new port of refreshment. Sydney, already attracting a good deal of favorable attention throughout the East, was the obvious answer.

In July 1798, a British whaler named *Cornwall* anchored in Port Jackson. Her captain reported that a Spanish warship, attended by two armed brigs, had driven him from the Peruvian whaling grounds. In the same month, a despatch from Britain informed Governor Hunter that the East India Company had granted a temporary concession permitting British whalers to operate west of the previous limit, the 108th degree of longitude. They were not, however, permitted to carry merchandise for sale in New South Wales nor were Sydney-based ships to be allowed to load whale products for sale in England. Two other British whalers, *Eliza* and *Sally*, followed the *Cornwall* and before long these and other ships opened up the new ground, with sufficient success to attract American whalers whose activities were un-hampered by East India Company restrictions.

The advantages which New England adventurers enjoyed over British was demonstrated early. The American ship *Mercury*, which opened up the New Zealand sealing rookeries, called into Sydney to refit. The following year two

American ships, *Argo* and *Semiramis*, berthed in Port Jackson on their way to China. The *Semiramis* from Rhode Island made the run to Sydney in 101 days, about half the usual time. Her skipper disposed of his cargo in Sydney, loaded seal oil and skins in the Tasman Sea, sold these in Canton and took home a shipful of tea and China goods. Fifteen years passed before British ships enjoyed the same advantages. Although the East India Company, under government pressure, yielded privileges, it yielded so slowly that American sealers and whalers were able to dominate the new sealing ground, soon extended to Bass Strait, despite attempts by Governor King to restrict activities in the interests of British whalers and colonial sealers.

On 7 October 1798, the day the *Semiramis* sailed from Sydney, George Bass and Lieutenant Matthew Flinders left Port Jackson in the *Norfolk*, a twenty-five-ton sloop built at Norfolk Island, accompanied by Captain Charles Bishop in the brig *Nautilus*. Bass and Flinders were intent on proving whether or not a strait ran between the Australian mainland and Van Diemen's Land. Bishop, who had heard from survivors of a shipwreck that seals abounded among islands south of the mainland, accompanied them to try his luck. He had already suffered losses from an ill-timed trip to the northwest coast of America and was anxious, as he assured Sidenham Teast, the Bristol merchant who backed him, to redeem "all the failures of a sad five years' adversity." While Bass and Flinders sailed around Van Diemen's Land and home again, Bishop, in two forays, lifted 5,000 seal skins, worth a guinea apiece, and several tons of seal oil.

Bishop and George Bass formed an ambitious partnership to reap the reward for opening up the southwestern Pacific to commercial enterprise. They were unlucky. Bishop, too mentally ill to join Bass on the last of his many ventures, returned to England. Nothing more is known of him. Bass, whose partnership with his afflicted friend was never formally dissolved, sailed from Sydney on the brig *Venus* on 5 February 1803, on what was destined to be his final voyage. Nothing certain is known of his fate or the fate of the twenty-four crewmen who sailed with him. The chief of the Division of Manuscripts of the Library of Congress in Washington made an exhaustive search of South American records to check stories that Spanish warships had seized the *Venus* and sent Bass and his men to slavery in the mines. Nothing tangible emerged beyond the fact that the Spanish authorities were not in the habit of sending captured seamen to the mines. Dr. K. M. Bowden, who wrote a biography of Bass, believes that the *Venus* ended up one of the many unknown wrecks off the southern shores of New Zealand.

Charles Bishop's pioneering trips to the Bass Strait sealing grounds provided the colony of New South Wales with an export staple and a temporary economic base. Shrewd ex-convicts like Henry Kable, James Underwood and Simeon Lord joined the merchant Robert Campbell, who arrived from Cal-

Rival whaling crews often met on and off the
Australian coast

cutta in 1798, in the new and highly profitable business of sealing. They bought up Spanish prize ships and built forty and ninety-ton vessels locally to send sealing gangs to Bass Strait. The colonial boats remained among the islands for long periods and when they brought back full cargoes Sydney merchants sold oil and skins to American skippers for disposal in Canton, where Sydney traders were excluded by the East India Company monopoly. By 1803 more than two hundred men employed by Sydney traders were killing seals and sea elephants at a prodigious rate.

Sydney sealers soon had competition from American, British and French gangs in the bloody task of exterminating an animal species for quick profit. It was not a trade for the queasy or the soft-hearted. Gangs of rough men, often left on the islands for two years at a time, beat the animals to death with nail-studded clubs until the stench of oil and blood and rotting carcases drove them to defile fresh areas. Sydney men earned five shillings for each skin procured and soon extended the carnage to mating females and their young. The pelts brought twenty-one shillings each at Canton so the sealing masters, with no eye to the future, encouraged wanton slaughter. Numbers declined drastically in Bass Strait and the sealers moved across the Tasman to New Zealand or south into the lonely wind-whipped vastness of the Southern Ocean, where there was less competition among the rocky barren islands of the sub-Antarctic. By the 1830s fur seals were virtually extinct in the Southern Ocean and sea-elephants were on the way out.

From the beginning violence and murder were rife among the sealing islands and mostly went unpunished. Disputes between American and colonial sealers were frequent. Joseph Murrell, master of the colonial sloop *Surprise*, reported a typical instance to his employers, Kable & Underwood of Sydney. He alleged that gangs from the *Pilgrim* and *Perseverance*, sealers belonging to the well-known Delano brothers of Duxbury, Massachusetts, seized him by the hair and dragged him to the beach where they belabored him with clubs. He broke away and ran into the water, "determined rather to be drowned than tortured to death. They then sent into the water after me a Sandwich Island native, who overtook me and gave me a desperate blow on the head with a club, which club I have now, and shall bring to Port Jackson, please God I live." Dragged ashore with a broken arm and a badly battered head Murrell was warned that other American ships on their way to Bass Strait were likely to be even rougher towards "Port Jackson gentlemen."

Amasa Delano, rugged French-descended Massachussets sea-captain and forebear of Franklin Delano Roosevelt, was a remarkable man who wrote a book about his adventures in the South Seas. He blamed Murrell and the Sydney gangs for trespassing on his claims. He admitted to Governor King that Murrell was "beaten-up a little" but claimed that he had himself intervened and provided medicines from his ship to salve Murrell's wounds. King

Illinois Chief, Black Hawk, was placed on public show

*Aboriginal Chief, Bungaree, a prisoner of rum
and a uniform*

came to the conclusion there were faults on both sides. When the Delanos finally quit Bass Strait for Juan Fernandez they took with them seventeen escaped convicts. They were Kable and Underwood employees who, according to an advertisement in the *Sydney Gazette* of 11 November 1804, had "unlawfully absconded and deserted, by entering and engaging themselves on board an American vessel called *Perseverance* said to be commanded by Delano." Kable and Underwood may have felt themselves unjustly done by but it was generally supposed that some owners were in league with American sealing masters and sent men by arrangement to Bass Strait, at so much a head, to be abducted by foreign vessels.

When the Americans moved on to other and richer grounds, escaped convicts and other dubious characters moved into the islands to scrape a living hunting the few seals left. They lived on kangaroo meat, mutton birds and wombats and abducted Aboriginal women from Van Diemen's Land and from the mainland to live with them. "They have a Custom of getting the Native Women of Van Diemen's Land among them," a complaint to the Colonial Secretary stated in 1815, "who they mostly obtain by force and keep them as Slaves or Negroes, hunting and foraging for them, who they transfer and dispose of from one to another as their own property, very few of whom ever see their Native Home, being away for a number of Years, they by way of punishment half hang them, cut their heads with clubs in a Shocking Manner, or flog them unmercifully with Cats made of Kangaroo Sinews."

In America at this time, following the defeat of the mid-Western and southern tribes under Tecumseh of the Shawnees, white settlers were flooding into Illinois territory with as little regard for Indian rights as the Australian and American sealers of Bass Strait had for Aboriginal rights. The Indians were more resolute and warlike and, under a chieftain known to history as Black Hawk, the Illinois tribes attempted to stem the tide of Western expansion. Betrayed by his own people, who sold him into captivity for a hundred dollars and twenty horses, Black Hawk was put on public show until he died. Even then his skeleton was kept on view in the office of the Governor of the newly-created Iowa Territory.

In Australia, while Black Hawk was a sight for the curious, native-born John Batman "bought" 100,000 acres of the best sheep land in southern Port Phillip (site of the future Melbourne) from local chiefs for "20 pair of blankets, 30 knives, 12 tomahawks, 10 looking glasses, 12 pairs of scissors, 50 handkerchiefs, 12 red shirts, four flannel jackets, four suits of clothes and 50 lbs of flour" plus the promise of similar yearly tribute. The British Governor disallowed Batman's "treaty" but news of new lands open and waiting for commercial exploitation soon spread and as a later Governor expressed it, the sheepmen of Australia were what the backwoodsmen had been in America—the pioneers of civilization. "Wherever they find good

Rebels at Castle Hill, near Sydney, 5 March 1804, dispersed by Major Johnston

The battle of Bunker Hill. The rebels were
ultimately successful

pasturage they fix themselves, and do not become known, even to the Commissioner, until some accidental occurrence (perhaps an unfortunate collision with the aborigines) brings them under his notice and ultimately under that of the government." In short, to almost all colonists "Australia Felix" was a British possession in which men could grow rich. Even benevolent Governors, who insisted upon the equality of both races under the law, never thought of the land as belonging to the people who had occupied it for thousands of years.

Captain King, who had been promoted from Lieutenant-Governor of Norfolk Island to Governor of New South Wales, strove in vain to stem abuses among the islands of Bass Strait. From his point of view they were within Australian territorial waters and in 1803 he established a settlement in Van Diemen's Land on the present site of Hobart to forestall a possible French attempt at annexation. To American sealers Bass Strait islands were simply unclaimed islands in the Pacific, like New Zealand, among which ships from Massachusetts roamed as their masters willed. The Lords of the Admiralty were too busy fighting the French to pay much heed. Nevertheless, King succeeded in keeping American sealers from using Sydney as a base by refusing clearance to all foreign vessels bound for the sealing grounds. Foreign ships had to pay a bond of £200 (later increased to £500) to prevent illegal trading and the "seizure of convicts."

Meanwhile, American whalers were already active in the Pacific although it was not until after the British-American War of 1812-14 that they expanded into the dominant position they held for the rest of the nineteenth century. By this time, Hobart Town had replaced Sydney as the most popular whaling port. Ships from New Bedford, Salem, Brest, Cherbourg and other ports shared the grounds with colonial whalers. At one time during the 1840s forty American and twenty French whalers were anchored in the Derwent River at Hobart. "In those days Hobart was the New Bedford of the Southern Seas," wrote an old colonist in the *Hobart Mercury*, 3 February 1890. "I can remember the time when fully 30 whalers were registered there. There used to be roaring times along the wharfs when a number of these came into port about Christmas time. Like returned diggers who had been fortunate, they spent their money freely, and the industry undoubtedly gave great impetus to trade." The chief colonial effort, however, went into bay whaling which lasted well into the twentieth century.

Whaling and sealing were much more than picturesque episodes in American-Australian relations. As Australian historian Thomas Dunbabin reminds us, in every Australian State except New South Wales and Queensland, whalers and sealers played an important part as the pioneers and forerunners of settlement. At a time when no one had penetrated more than fifty miles inland, whalers, sealers and sandalwood traders had explored and exploited the vast recesses of the Southern Ocean and provided the first important articles of Australian export. Sydney, and the surrounding County of Cumberland, was born of the sea and the first forty years of Australia's history was the history of a seafaring people. Sydneysiders shared fortunes with New Englanders, another seafaring people, whose rocky fields and craggy shores also provided a hard school of experience which gave color and character to a new type of man.

Captain William Bligh, R.N., who had been honorably acquitted at a court-martial in 1790 inquiring into the mutiny on the *Bounty*, enjoyed the favor of Sir Joseph Banks, now President of the Royal Society. Banks kept in touch with the affairs of New South Wales and knew the need for discipline. He was sufficiently high in government counsels to recommend Bligh as Governor of New South Wales in succession to Governor King. The new Governor arrived in Sydney during August 1806, and was soon reporting to Banks that "this sink of iniquity Sydney is improving in its manners and its concerns." On 1 January 1808, 833 settlers signed an address thanking him for improving their lot and pledging themselves "at the risque of our lives and properties" to support his government.

The officers of the New South Wales Corps, under Major George Johnston, a veteran of the revolutionary war, continued to work in secret to undermine Bligh's authority. John Dorr, captain of the American ship *Jenny*, revealed in a letter to the authorities how Johnston and his fellow-officers tried to use him to evade Bligh's regulations against the trade in liquor. Dorr described how Captain Kemp came to him, when he was dining at Bevan's, the auctioneer's, to take him in a chaise to Major Johnston's seat at Annandale. They found Lieutenant William Lawson with Johnston, who welcomed Dorr cordially and asked him if he had obtained permission from the Governor to land his cargo of liquor.

When Dorr said no, Kemp asked, "Do you not intend to smuggle?" and, according to Dorr, Johnston added, "By God! the Governor must look sharp otherwise we will take it from you in spite of him." When Kemp and Dorr were returning to Sydney, Kemp explained that Johnston, as commander of the New South Wales Corps, had given permission for purchase of the spirits but "wished that his name might not be brought in Question." Dorr added: "I have been continually harrassed by these Gentlemen Officers and Men employed under them to undertake the smuggling of Spirits: the temptation offered and such frequent applications would be almost impossible for any man to withhold."

Bligh's attempts to put down the traffic in liquor, which included the arrest of the incorrigible Lieutenant John Macarthur, led to the famous "Rum Rebellion" on 26 January 1808, the twentieth anniversary of the colony's founding. With colors spread and marching to the tune of "The British Grenadiers", 300 men of the New South Wales Corps, led by Major Johnston, Captain Kemp and Lieutenant Lawson, marched "in battle array" to seize the person of Governor Bligh and instal Johnston as Lieutenant-Governor according to "the people's will." This illegal procedure prompted the British Government, whose lethargy and mercantilist notions had contributed to the crisis, to make the effort necessary to reorganize the settlement as a colony open to free and enterprising men.

Johnston, who had been promoted Lieutenant-Colonel before news of the rebellion reached London, was court-martialed and cashiered but provided with a free passage back to the supervision of his extensive properties in New South Wales, where the new Governor, Major-General Lachlan Macquarie, was instructed to treat him as he would "any other ordinary settler." He died in 1823. Kemp and Lawson, who escaped court-martial, returned to the colony after the disbandment of the New South Wales Corps and its replacement by regular regiments of the line. Kemp lived to be ninety-five and flourished as a merchant and grazier in Van Diemen's Land. Lawson, never enthusiastic in the cause of rebellion, continued to live in colonial style near Sydney. In 1813, he accompanied William Charles Wentworth and Gregory Blaxland on the first successful exploration of the Blue Mountains. Widely known as "Old Ironbark" he became a widely popular figure, remembered as a man who helped open the interior to settlement.

Oddly enough, although the eastern coast of America was settled more than one hundred and fifty years before America's independence forced Great Britain to establish a penal colony in New South Wales, the sister continents were opened up about the same time. Once British and colonial troops, with their Indian allies, had subdued the French in America, George III and his government barred the way west. Thomas Walker, an English doctor with an itch for land speculation, entered Kentucky from Virginia in 1748 and two years later discovered a gap through the Appalachians which he named after the Duke of Cumberland. The Cumberland Gap became and remained the southern highroad into the American interior but in 1763 the British Government ruled that the American colonies should remain east of the mountains. In the interests of the fur trade, developed by Indians and French-Canadian *voyageurs*, a Royal Proclamation sealed the west to settlement and to land speculation.

The Peace of Versailles, which ended the American War of Independence, extended the United States westward to the Mississippi but Louisiana, which then embraced the whole watershed west of the Mississippi all the way up to Canada, remained with Spain. In August 1798 Nelson defeated the French fleet in the Battle of the Nile and ended Napoleon's dream of restoring the French Empire in India. The First Consul and Emperor-to-be turned his attention to

America and obtained Louisiana from Charles IV of Spain, in return for creating in Tuscany a petty Bourbon kingdom for the Duke of Parma, Charles's imbecile son-in-law.

What Napoleon intended to do with Louisiana, a huge wilderness inhabited by a handful of trappers and missionaries, nobody now knows. When he followed up his acquisition with the despatch of a French expeditionary force to subdue the "black Jacobin" Toussaint L'Ouverture, in West Indian Santo Domingo, Jefferson, newly-elected President of the United States, took fright. "The cession of Louisiana and the Floridas . . . to France works most sorely upon the United States," he wrote to the American Minister in Paris. If France actually occupied the territory which Spain had so neglected, the President added, then "we must marry ourselves to the British fleet and nation." This was the last thing Napoleon wanted to happen. In 1803, hard up for money and forced to withdraw from Santo Domingo, Napoleon sold Louisiana to Jefferson for $16,000,000, equivalent to about four cents an acre for the richest lands in North America and possibly in the whole world.

While Jefferson was concluding, without seeking the advice or the consent of the United States Senate, a deal which doubled the size of America's domain, Massachusetts sealers and whalemen were helping to open up the nooks and crannies of Australia's eastern and southern coastline. From the sea much of it looked as their native New England looked, a bleak land without beauty, sparse trees clinging to gray rock. Most Englishmen, like Colonel Godfrey Mundy, Deputy Adjutant-General of the Australian colonies, found "the leaden tint of the gum-tree foliage" as repulsive as "the dry and sterile sandstone from which it springs." The Americans, if they thought about the matter at all, were possibly more aware that a hard soil often produces sturdy growth and twisted beauty more invigorating than the smooth lawns and neat hedgerows of a disciplined landscape.

Yet, though Cook had charted the coast north of Port Jackson to Possession Island, and Bass and Flinders had done the same for much of the shoreline south of Botany Bay, what lay behind the stubby, rugged coastal mountains and the sand dunes of the southern coast remained a mystery. Captain Pendleton of the patriotically-named New York ship *The Union* landed at Kangaroo Island and stayed among the sand dunes during the summer of 1803-4, building a thirty-five-ton schooner, the *Independence*, the first vessel built within the limits of what is now South Australia, but he saw nothing beyond the coastline of what was a vast unknown.

Jefferson was better informed about what lay beyond Cumberland Gap and the Missouri. Months before he bought Louisiana from the French he had "spun an espionage network across the west." Jefferson knew what he was buying although not even he realized the enormous extent of the bargain he had made. In one stroke he added all or most of thirteen states to the Union:

a third of the United States we now know. No white man had set foot on a large portion of this new territory. There was no time to be lost. British fur traders were already penetrating south from Canada and Spanish raiders moving north from California. Rumor had it that the British planned to raise the Union Jack at the mouth of the Columbia River. If they did so, the whole northwest could easily fall to them.

"An intelligent officer with ten or twelve chosen men, fit for the enterprise and willing to undertake it . . . might explore the whole line, even to the Western Ocean," the President told Congress; "have conferences with the natives on the subject of commercial intercourse, get admission among them for our traders as others are admitted, agree on convenient deposits for an interchange of articles, and return with the information acquired in the course of two summers." An intelligent officer willing to undertake the expedition was not far to seek. Jefferson selected his secretary, twenty-nine-year-old Virginian Captain Meriwether Lewis, experienced frontiersman and Indian-fighter, strong, able and eager to be the first to cross the continent from east to west.

Lewis nominated his best friend, artillery Lieutenant William Clark, thirty-four, as second-in-command. Lewis spent several months in Philadelphia buying scientific instruments and learning how to use them before going to St. Louis to pick up all the information he could from rivermen about the Indian nations living along the Missouri, which there joined the Mississippi.

Clark spent his time enlisting and drilling men for the march westward. The total company of forty-five greatly exceeded Jefferson's "ten or twelve chosen men" but all were found necessary. They included Irish, Scots, Dutch and French Americans and Clark's negro servant, York; Virginian hunters, Vermont farmers, Pennsylvanian tradesmen, a corporal and six soldiers and nine rivermen to help row the heavy boats upstream. The party left its river camp on 14 May 1804. Twenty-eight months later Lewis and Clark brought home all but one of their men, having accomplished their mission and remained as fast friends as when they set out.

Disappointingly, the boundless Missouri proved no highway to the Pacific but ended in a small stream a man could straddle. Away to the west lay "an immense range of mountains . . . their tops partially covered with snow." The Shoshone Indians showed the explorers the way over the mountains. In the Clearwater valley of Idaho, on the other side, the Nez Percés Indians be-friended them and after resting to recover from the struggle through snow-blocked passes they constructed six canoes and began the journey along the Clearwater and Snake rivers that led to Columbia. On 7 November 1805, Lewis and Clark first sighted the Pacific. Building a fort on the south bank of the Columbia, near present-day Astoria, the Americans spent a dreary winter before beginning the long trek home. They had beaten the British in

*Lewis and Clark's expedition often stopped to
parley with Indians on their westward march*

the race for the mighty Columbia and opened the Oregon Trail, although Canadian fur-trappers were not far behind.

It could be said that Australia's Cumberland Gap was Macquarie Pass through the Blue Mountains, opened in 1813, and that the River Murray, discovered in 1824 by native-born Hamilton Hume, became Australia's Mississippi. But the comparisons are misleading. A vastly different geography produced parallel but diverse national destinies. As Australian historian Geoffrey Blainey reminds us in *The Tyranny of Distance* (Melbourne, 1966), inland waterways were vital in opening up much of the interior of the United States whereas Australia lacked inland rivers despite the fine appearance intermittent streams make on the map. Furthermore, from the early nineteenth century on, man-made canals, including the famous Erie life-line between New York, New England and the Midwest, provided cheap barge transport for American produce.

Australia, on the other hand, possessed no terrain suitable for canals. Once they had crossed the mountains the colonists of New South Wales found it cheaper to bring grain by sea from Van Diemen's Land than to transport it on bullock waggons over the Dividing Range. Sydney merchants could send a barrel of whale oil to London more easily and cheaply than they could send it 100 miles inland. This, quite apart from different qualities of soil and the slow growth of population, is the essential difference between Australian and American development although both nations opened the way to the west within the same decade. Once Australians looked inland from the sea, sheep not grain provided the staple export, and the Murray River, in its long, leisurely course through some of the finest country in Australia, flowed from stony mountains to salt sea marshes unsuitable for porterage or harbor facilities.

For many years, Australian historians reiterated that the Blue Mountains, thirty miles west of Sydney, barred the spread of settlement because tangled westward-running valleys ended in steep unscalable cliffs and nobody thought of following the stony ridges across the watershed to the gentle slopes on the other side. More recently, Australian geographer Dr. Tom Perry has dismissed the argument that for twenty-five years the mountains, really the broken tip-tilted edge of an inland plateau never rising much more than three thousand feet, presented an unsurmountable barrier to westward expansion. Nobody crossed the mountains, he says, because nobody had sufficient economic incentive to do so. Only convicts and the curious looked longingly at the line of blue that could be seen on clear days from the low hills overlooking Port Jackson.

Thus, for the first quarter-century of Australia's existence, Cumberland County, the variegated coastal plain that comprises Sydney's hinterland, provided sufficient growing space to meet the colony's needs, once the regular appearance of American ships had allayed the fear of starvation. Short rivers draining from the mountains to the sea provided cheap and easy transport for agricultural settlements around Parramatta and along the Hawkesbury River flats. Between mountains and sea and from Broken Bay in the north to Bulli Pass in the south there was room enough for John Macarthur, Parson Samuel Marsden and other members of what became satirically known as the "Ancient Nobility" to establish their Virginia-like plantations with convicts instead of negro slaves and fine wool instead of cotton as a staple product. Nor did a succession of naval and military governors wish to add to their problems by opening the prison gates for men desperate enough to attempt unmapped paths to freedom. No one without a permit from the governor was supposed to cross the Nepean River, which wound along the outer edge of the rugged plateau.

The first organized attempt to cross the Blue Mountains was more akin to Dr. Thomas Walker's excursion into the Appalachians than Lewis and Clark's historic expedition across America and back. Escaped convicts and curious colonists had earlier crossed the Nepean and penetrated into rocky tree-crowded narrow valleys, which took days and even weeks to negotiate and always ended in vertical cliffs. There were no flats for agriculture, no pastures for sheep or cattle, no practical droving paths leading to the inland on the other side. The curious soon turned back while escaped convicts either died of exposure and starvation or turned bushranger and exacted tribute by force of stolen arms from the coastal plain below.

Aboriginals appeared and disappeared like dark ghosts in the mountain fastnesses, making occasional forays from hidden mountain valleys to open cultivated plain, fleeing pursuit along narrow, secret tracks where bare feet found swift footage impossible to clumsy-booted soldiery or mounted colonists. In May 1813, Blaxland, Lawson and Wentworth, three free colonists with a kangaroo hunter as guide, determined to avoid the valleys and follow the ridges. The path they found is still the main route followed by road and rail.

Gregory Blaxland, a friend of Joseph Banks and a well-born, educated settler "of responsibility and capital", was a speculating individualist who had plagued a succession of governors by his hard-headed pursuit of commercial opportunities. Restless and dissatisfied with the extent of their land grants, he and his brother refused to grow grain as requested, and continued to increase their flocks and herds. By 1813, these had expanded beyond the resources of their coastal grant and Governor Lachlan Macquarie could not be persuaded to give them more. Macquarie agreed, however, that Blaxland should attempt to cross the mountains although he made no extravagant promises about rewards if the attempt succeeded.

William Lawson, former officer in the now disbanded and discredited New South Wales Corps, had returned to New South Wales without giving evidence at the Rum Rebellion court martial. Turned pastoralist he was anxious to rehabilitate himself in colonial estimation. Colonial-born William Charles Wentworth, destined for political fame as the colony's "Liberator" from British leading-strings, had recently returned to Australia after failing to win a place in the military academy at Woolwich or in the East India Company.

Despite their chosen route the explorers did not find the going easy but had to force a path "through brake and briar", skirting "really terrific gullies . . . nearly perpendicular for several hundred feet", edging along narrow ridges "in some places not exceeding fifteen yards in breadth", surrounded by the crash of waterfalls and stealthy rustlings that might have been night winds or watching Aboriginals. It took twenty days of difficult traveling before the party burst through to the "boundless champaign" they sought: forest and grassland, Blaxland reported, "sufficient in extent to support the stock of the Colony for the next thirty years." Wentworth, with uncharacteristic caution, wondered whether they had crossed the watershed (they had not) but quite rightly concluded, "admitting that we have not traversed the mountains, we have at all events proved that they are traversable, and that, too, by cattle. . . ."

No fanfare of excited congratulation greeted the explorers on their return and they themselves were reticent about their accomplishment. The Governor, although he reported the achievement with some show of satisfaction, was not altogether happy. Like his predecessors, he found it hard enough to control the speculative spirit he found all around him and like the British after their defeat of the French and the Indians beyond the Appalachians, he had no desire to encourage expansion of settlement or speculation in land beyond the existing boundaries of his already difficult domain. The kangaroo hunter had to wait five months for his £10 reward and the Governor's edict continued to prohibit movement of stock across the Nepean River and the occupation of land beyond the mountains.

Once the mountains were crossed and inland occupation began the Aboriginals, who had been there for perhaps 30,000 years, were doomed.

"In all parts of Australia," says James Collier in *The Pastoral Age in Australasia* (Melbourne, 1911), "the advance of white settlers was in the nature of an invasion, and was resisted by the blacks as invasions are resisted. Wave after wave of settlement flowed along the shores of rivers and the banks of creeks, and occupied ground where the nomadic blacks dwelt, and drove away the game on which they fed. Can we be surprised that the plundered and expelled natives had recourse to acts of war? All the records are full of such facts and events that belong to a state of war . . . Real and deep provocation there doubtless often was . . . There is abundant evidence to show that the black women were taken and kept, their husbands being sometimes murdered to facilitate the rape. On the other hand, the settlers asserted that the women either voluntarily offered themselves or were offered by their relatives in exchange for presents."

4   Wide Open Spaces

Within Cumberland County, New South Wales, the summer of 1813 was desperately dry. Fires swept the parched herbage and leapt from treetop to treetop in bushland between orchards and grazing paddocks. Farmers and graziers alike faced ruin and looked to the government to save them. Macquarie, who came from the island of Mull and preferred industrious ex-convicts to trading military men or greedy land-owners, decided that the time had come to open up the passage to the west and provide a new field of endeavor for the hard-working. Governor Macquarie, like Matra, Phillip and Bligh before him, had dreams of an Australian Arcady but they were different dreams from those of the colony's Ancient Nobility or, as things turned out, of the authorities "at home."

For Lachlan Macquarie, Australia was a sanctuary in which the outcasts of civilization could begin life anew—under strict Macquarian supervision. Macquarie was at heart a Highland laird and he believed in benevolent autocracy. He had been commissioned ensign in Canada, the year after the Declaration of Independence, and served with the 71st Highland Regiment in New York and Charleston, before returning to Scotland where he found his family struggling with their farm at Oskamull after the hard famine years of 1781-3. After a further seventeen years' active service in India, he had reached Australia as Governor of New South Wales in December 1809.

According to his own account, Macquarie found the colony "barely emerging from an infantile imbecility; the country impenetrable beyond forty miles from Sydney, agriculture languishing, commerce in its early dawn, revenue unknown, famine threatening, and (everything) mouldering to decay." With the help of the talented convict architect Francis Greenway, he transformed Sydney from a few "nasty, dirty-looking houses", a squalid dumping ground for convicts, into a dignified maritime Georgian town where decent men and women could lead decent lives if they had the will to do so. "This country," the Governor wrote, "should be made a happy home to every emancipated convict *who derserves it. . . .*"

52

The Aboriginals, he commanded, should not be molested in their persons or property but should be treated with kindness and attention so as to conciliate them to civilized government in a settlement where, Macquarie was sanguine enough to hope, "all the dissensions and jealousies which had unfortunately existed . . . would now terminate for ever, and give way to a more becoming spirit of conciliation, harmony, and unanimity among all classes" and both races. Before long, says M. H. Ellis in *Lachlan Macquarie: His Life, Adventures and Times* (Sydney, 1947), "Buckshot flew about like rain in the wind. At the rising of the moon in Appin, in June 1814, blood curdling shrieks in the night suggested to the gathered settlers who clutched their blunderbusses the possibility of open battle with the tribes. Luckily it did not come. But there was soon more blood upon the corn and the Governor, after holding a magisterial inquiry, lamented that any cause should have been given on either side for "the sanguinary and cruel acts which had been reciprocally perpetrated by each party."

With the New South Wales Corps disbanded and the liquor traffic squashed there seemed no reason to Governor Macquarie why respectable settlers should not be allowed to farm the new country glimpsed beyond the Blue Mountains by Blaxland, Wentworth and Lawson. Consequently, he ordered George Evans, the Government Surveyor, to follow Blaxland's route and explore the country that lay beyond. In December 1813 Evans crossed the main dividing range that marked the true boundary between the eastern and western watersheds and entered open country where pouring rain and "the finest grass mixed with the white daisy as in England" presented a cheerful contrast to the burnt-out paddocks of Cumberland County. On 9 December he camped on the banks of "a glorious stream", which he named the Macquarie, now the site of Bathurst, Australia's first inland township.

Evans returned to Sydney on 20 January 1814. This was three months before Napoleon abdicated and seven months before, in the War of 1812 (which continued until late 1814), British forces burned Washington's main official buildings. Less noted but ultimately more important, it was the year John Jacob Astor established Astoria on the Columbia River, blazing the way for the great westward-rolling wagon trains with their pioneering families that led to America's eventual possession of Oregon despite British counter-claims. Australia's inland pioneers, on the other hand, were men without women, sheep-herders and cattlemen, not the neat family groups Macquarie hoped to establish.

"O strange New World, that yit wast never young," wrote American poet and essayist, James Russell Lowell, in *The Biglow Papers*, lapsing into the vernacular used by the "stern men" he celebrated, men "with empires in their brains." Australia, too, was new, yet old and opened to civilization by men

The Omeo Track, Victoria. Settlers and gold-seekers had to cross the mountains on their way to the plains or the diggings

Right: *The Ute Pass, Colarado. American venturers faced similar rigors of travel*

who saw beckoning visions along distant horizons. There was room enough for human expansion in both continental domains, each almost exactly three million square miles, if we exclude Canada and assume, as Thomas Jefferson assumed, that American man's destiny embraced the continent from Atlantic to Pacific, from the Great Lakes to the Gulf of Mexico. Room enough, indeed. There the likeness ended.

Well beyond the Mississippi the forest ended and prairies of waving grass began, spread endlessly under a high wide sky, where herds of buffalo ranged and Indians rode and hunted. The fertile treeless plains merged at last into scraggy semi-desert that humped again into high mountains enclosing deep valleys where bear and beaver awaited the exterminating hand of man. Daniel Boone and fellow-frontiersmen, with long rifles cocked and ready, snaked through Indian country among forested Appalachian ridges. Once they had crossed the mountain barrier, and Jefferson had bought the right to prairie and mountain lands beyond, the way west lay open, save for the Indians and, for most pioneers, the only good Indian was a dead Indian.

In time, the prairie plains comprising Indiana, Illinois and parts of Wisconsin east of the Mississippi, Iowa, Minnesota and the Dakotas between the Mississippi and the Missouri, and the wide rich farmlands of Nebraska, Kansas and Oklahoma beyond became the Garden of America, surpassing in its original fertility perhaps any other area of the world. West and southwest of the prairie plains lay what was known as the Great American Desert, an area early explorers dismissed as a treeless, grassless arid waste of cactus and sand, a region of savages and wild beasts useless to civilized man.

During the great movement westward, when pioneers moved across the Missouri in endless columns, the editor of the Methodist *Christian Advocate*, whose church already had a mission far west along the Oregon Trail, declared the Great American Desert as unfit for human emigration as Botany Bay. The missionary editor's comparison was apt for, beyond the hard line of the Blue Mountains on the western horizon of Sydney's coastal plain, rolling savannah grasslands sloped westward to the dead heart of an arid continent more akin to the Great American Desert than to the Garden of America. The harsh Australian interior, like the Great American Desert, grew less forbidding as men learned to adapt to its physical conditions. But from the beginning, the pitiless challenge of a hard, drought-prone land molded men and society differently from the men and societies that developed west of the Mississippi. There was, however, little difference between the Australian and the American attitude to the native peoples. For most Australian pioneers, also, the only good black was a dead black or one so subdued that what one pastoralist regarded as "a beautiful harmony" could be set up between exploiters and exploited on the Christian principle that there was a place for all men provided all men knew their place.

Macquarie named the newly-discovered country beyond the ranges West-moreland County, and proceeded to establish a town on the south bank of Evan's Macquarie River. He devoted a page of the Government-sponsored and Government-censored *Sydney Gazette* to publicity for the promised land —promised to "particularly selected, sober, industrious men, with small families from the middling class of free people." In February 1818, the first ten selected, sober and industrious settlers plowed the soil of the Bathurst Plains.

Half of the new settlers were Australian born, the Currency Lads and Lasses, so called to distinguish them from "Sterling", those who still bore the stamp of the Old Country. Macquarie encouraged the use of "Australia" in place of "New Holland" and did all he could to promote Australian consciousness and Australian enterprise. According to contemporary observers, the locally-born were already noticeable in a still predominantly immigrant community for their lean frames, bleached hair and nasal drawl. In 1819, when Mr. Commissioner John Bigge came to investigate the colony, convicts still made up 38.3 percent of the total population of New South Wales, then about twenty-five thousand. The free population was made up largely of ex-convicts and the native-born. Bigge, who was not partial to ex-convicts or Governor Macquarie's policies towards them, nevertheless agreed that the native-born were a distinct improvement on their parents. "They are generally tall in person, and slender in their limbs," he wrote, "of fair complexion and small features." A few years later, ex-naval surgeon Peter Miller Cunningham, who had served in North America, likened currency lads to Americans. They are "tall and slender," he wrote, "generally remarkable for that Gothic peculiarity of fair hair and blue eyes . . . for the most part easily distinguishable —even in advanced years—from those born in England."

Before long, accent and vocabulary marked off locals from new arrivals or from officials who cultivated accents which, in England, unlike Australia and America, have always possessed a class rather than a mere regional significance. Nor was Australian colloquial speech, as rich, varied and vigorous as American colloquial speech, confined to the native-born. As Peter Cunningham put it, "A number of slang phrases current in St. Gile's Creek bid fair to become legitimised in the dictionary in this colony . . . the dross passing here as genuine, even among all ranks." In both instances, local circumstances produced a significant variation of the parent tongue which initially owed more to the mixture of former regional accents and the general break-up of old associations than to the accident of birth.

As early as 1828, Noah Webster put the crux of the matter in the introduction of his *American Dictionary of the English Language:*

Language is the expression of ideas and if the people of the one country cannot preserve an identity of ideas [with the people of another country], they cannot retain an identity of language. Now, an identity of ideas depends materially upon a sameness of things or objects with which the people of the other two countries are conversant. But in no two portions of the earth, remote from each other, can such identity be found. Even physical objects must be different.

As Sidney J. Baker points out in *The Australian Language* (Sydney, 1945), this statement holds for far more than flora and fauna. It encompasses the whole physical and mental environment—in fact everything that makes an American recognizable as an American and an Australian recognizable as an Australian and an Englishman different from both. Writing in 1829, an Australian commentator noted that the English of the United States and Australia was not the same as that of England. He saw sufficient reason for the increasing differences of language between the three countries in their different physical conditions, their intercourse with different nations and their differences of occupations and habit.

In New South Wales, differences in physical conditions and differences of occupation and habit were already sufficient to shatter Macquarie's vision of a contented peasantry in a colonial reformatory. Farms, not plantations or ranches, were his preference; stationary agriculture, not moving flocks and herds, his objective in sending families with "a cow, rations from the King's store and four bushels of seed wheat for sowing" to occupy the free grants of fifty acres of wheat land near the new township of Bathurst.

The lure of wide open spaces began early. Neither William Lee nor the Blackman brothers, three of the five native-born pioneers among the ten farmers settled at Bathurst in 1818, had the stay-put temperament. With a continent spread wide open around them they were not content to sow and plow and scrape a living growing wheat for a Sydney Town whose merchants could buy cheaper and better grain from Van Diemen's Land, where there were already waving fields of corn and orchards heavy with fruit.

Lee, son of a convict woman in one of the irregular unions Macquarie frowned upon, soon became noted for introducing horned cattle into the Bathurst Plains. Both he and the Blackman brothers were cronies of William ("Old Ironbark") Lawson, who had accompanied Blaxland and Wentworth on the first cross-mountain expedition. Macquarie rewarded each of the three explorers with 1,000 acres west of the ranges. Lawson lost no time in driving stock into the new country. Lee and James Blackman joined him in searching out even better country west and north-west of the Bathurst Plains.

By 1828 Lawson owned 84,000 sheep, 14,750 head of cattle and 100 horses. When he died in 1850 his estates covered more than 200,000 acres and his sons were successful inland squatters. Lee died in 1870, leaving an estate sworn at £41,000 and including 18,509 acres, apart from the sheep and cattle station occupied by four of his six sons. Even James Blackman, who started as a small farmer on Macquarie's grant of fifty acres, soon turned government official in Bathurst. He was largely responsible for opening up Wellington County, northwest of Bathurst. When he died at Mudgee in 1868 he owned some 2,000 acres and had developed a pastoral property rather than a farm.

Lawson's horned cattle were the beginning. Stockowners pushed out in all directions from Cumberland County, raising superb fat creatures, says J. H. Roberts in *The Squatting Age in Australia* (Sydney, 1935), "compared with the mediocre beasts of the settled districts." Meanwhile, John Joseph Oxley, Macquarie's Surveyor-General, had discovered the rich Liverpool Plains to the north of Bathurst and crossed the New England Ranges to Port Macquarie on the coast. In the south, Charles Throsby and Hamilton Hume had reached the Goulburn country.

Against all Macquarie's inclinations, Bathurst soon became a frontier post, a jumping-off place for explorers and pioneers in search of runs, rather than a placid agricultural community. The "new country" now lay along the Lachlan, the Goulburn, the Castlereagh and the Peel, rather than the Macquarie. Within five years of the first herd reaching Lake Bathurst, settlers had set the bounds of what later became known as the Nineteen Counties: "from the Manning to Moruya, from the coast to the Lachlan. Here, official Sydney took its stand. These were the limits of colonization, and only within them would settlement be tolerated."

The War of 1812 did not leave New South Wales unaffected. To begin with, there was a complete cessation of American shipping between the departure of the *Ann* to the whale fisheries on 19 September 1812 and the arrival of the *Ontario* from Boston on 30 January 1816, en route to Macao with merchandise, with our old friend Ebenezer Dorr as skipper. Between these two events the colony suffered a mild scare arising from rumors that a Franco-American naval squadron intended to attack Sydney.

Jorgen Jorgenson, a Dane with colonial experience as a seaman in Australian waters, had in 1809 "liberated" Iceland from Denmark and declared himself "Democratic King" of the island until ousted by the British Navy. In June 1813, Jorgenson wrote the British Foreign Secretary, Lord Castlereagh, to say that he had wind of a joint French-American plan to make two flanking landings in New South Wales to seize Port Jackson: one on the Hawkesbury River and the other at Botany Bay. Jorgenson, who had been a sealer and whaler in New Zealand after leaving the British service, commanded a Danish privateer when Denmark became Napoleon's ally. After taking three prizes he struck his colors to H.M.S. *Sappho* and declared himself a British subject on the strength of his British and Australian experiences.

Jorgenson claimed that Count Dillon, a French secret agent, had approached him and offered him a command in a French flotilla of four frigates, carrying 1,000 troops, due to slip out of Rochefort in November 1813, to link up at the Falkland Islands with an American frigate and storeship carrying 300 American soldiers for a joint descent on Port Jackson. Two Americans named Kelly and Coleman, whalers with an intimate knowledge of the Australian coast, were to act as guides and it was proposed to arm any convicts who were prepared to join in the assault on Sydney. Lord Bathurst passed the information to Macquarie with the comment that, in view of the "doubtful character of this individual", His Majesty's Government did not give much credence to the report.

Despite these doubts, the Colonial Office drew up "Suggestions for defeating an attempt reported to be in preparation against N.S.W. by a squadron of four French and one American Frigates" and forwarded the memorandum to the Admiralty for consideration.

The Colonial Office proposed that two ships of the line be sent to the Falklands to intercept the French-American expeditionary force. If there was no sign of any enemy in the South Atlantic or Pacific the ships were to proceed to Port Jackson to repel any attack there. There is no evidence that the Admiralty attempted to implement these suggestions. His Majesty's Navy had work for "two line of Battleships" in nearer waters and could not spare time for the protection of a distant penal colony of no immediate strategic importance from a largely hypothetical attack. Macquarie, in his reply to Bathurst, acknowledged that a person "under the name of Johnson or Jansen did serve for some little time in this country on board the *Lady Nelson* and other vessels, and may therefore be supposed to be tolerably well acquainted with its several ports and harbours." Nor did the Governor dismiss the possibility of attack as chimerical. "It has been generally supposed," he wrote, "that the *Géographe* and *Naturaliste*, French ships of war under Captain Baudin, came solely for the purpose of ascertaining how far it might prove expedient for the then Ruler of France to establish a Colony on some part of New Holland."

Jorgenson, after a spell in the Fleet prison for debts due to his inveterate gambling, acted as a British spy on the continent for two years before drinking and gambling brought him into further trouble. Transported to Van Diemen's Land in 1825 he was assigned to exploration activities and eventually became a police constable noted as a tracker of Aboriginals and bushrangers. In contributions to the *Van Diemen's Land Annual* in 1835 and 1836 he claimed that two French vessels under Count Dillon did sail on the secret expedition he exposed but were wrecked near Cadiz. He said the American vessel proceeded to the Pacific, after the French frigates failed to keep the rendezvous in the Falklands, and occupied itself capturing British whalers.

There is no evidence, other than Jorgenson's statement, that the French contemplated an attack on Port Jackson.

The United States however, did carry the war into the Pacific. Captain David Porter, of the U.S. frigate *Essex*, rounded Cape Horn in mid-1813 and established a base at Nukahiva in the Marquesas Islands where he used prisoners-of-war from captured British whalers to build a fort and harbor defenses. On 6 May 1814, while *Essex* was away in search of fresh prizes, fourteen prisoners seized the storeship *Seringapatam*, a 370-ton ex-whaler, secured the prize crew aboard, spiked the guns of the fort, and set sail for Sydney although they were all ordinary seamen with little knowledge of navigation, their officers having been taken by the *Essex* to South America. A few weeks later the Sydney merchant Joseph Underwood came across the *Seringapatam*, off the Australian coast, short of food and water, and guided them into port.

With Underwood's help the fourteen men, half of whom could not sign their own names, petitioned Sydney's Vice-Admiralty Court for possession of the *Seringapatam* as a lawful prize. They told the court that they had set the prize crew afloat, with adequate provisions and arms, at a safe distance from Nukahiva before attempting to navigate the captured vessel to Port Jackson. Judge-Advocate Ellis Bent decided to send the ship to England for adjudication. As the escapees felt incapable of navigating her safely on the long voyage, Governor Macquarie prevailed upon veteran whaler Captain Ebor Bunker to come out of retirement and take command. Bunker took the *Seringapatam* to England where it was suggested that the captors had served with rather than rebelled against Captain Porter, a proceeding for which there were many precedents on both sides.

Six weeks before the scratch crew of the British ex-whalers had "captured" *Seringapatam*, H.M.S. *Phoebe* and H.M.S. *Cherub* caught up with the *Essex* outside the South American port of Valparaiso, where Captain Porter had gone for supplies. After a fierce fight the British ships sank the American frigate which in less than a year had destroyed British shipping to the value of $2½ million.

In Sydney, meanwhile, Governor Macquarie's strict new measures were making him many enemies. It was no longer possible to buy another man's wife for four bottles of rum or to pay a laborer's wages in gallons of raw spirit. Macquarie imported Spanish dollars to provide an effective medium of exchange and had the middles stamped out of the coinage to provide small change and to prevent the "holey dollars" flowing out as fast as they came in, as had happened previously.

Colonial usurers and employers concerned with the cost of labor were restless under the Governor's benevolent dictatorship and some officials were concerned at his disregard for the strict letter of the law. A true Highland chieftain, Macquarie tended to make his own laws. Ellis Bent, colonial Judge-Advocate, inquired of the Colonial Office whether the Governor, "under the pretence of local circumstances requiring it, can abrogate Acts of Parliament which he is sworn to inforce?" Meanwhile, Supreme Court Judge Mr. Justice Jeffrey Bent, Ellis Bent's brother, kept his court closed rather than admit ex-convict attorneys to practice even though at that time there was only one free lawyer in the colony.

The arrival of the American ship *Traveller* from Canton en route for Timor gave Macquarie's enemies an opportunity to challenge his authority. The *Traveller* was the second American ship to berth in Port Jackson since the end of the War of 1812 although before that they averaged four or five a year. The East India Company had cleared the *Traveller* from Canton, issuing a pass for her to visit Port Jackson with goods consigned to a Sydney merchant. Macquarie, strongly in favor of the "restoration of trade formerly carried out by American shipping," granted the *Traveller* entry, all the more happily since Sydney was short of the tea and sugar she carried. The Governor then left for a planned country tour, inadvertently giving the Bent brothers and their associates an opportunity to challenge his authority.

When Macquarie was well clear of Sydney, the Reverend Benjamin Vale, chaplain of the 46th Regiment, and W. H. Moore, a government solicitor, proceeded from Mr. Justice Bent's house with papers made out authorizing them to arrest the *Traveller* as a lawful prize under the British Navigation Act, the Act which had contributed so greatly to the American revolution by attempting to restrict all trade between England and her colonies to English shipping. Having arrested the ship the two conspirators called on the Lieutenant-Governor, Colonel George Molle, commanding officer of the 46th Regiment and an intimate friend of the Bents, to convene an Admiralty Court to confirm their action.

Molle was too cautious to take any risk. Thus, Vale and Moore were left to face the Governor. Nobody had much doubt but that their action had been motivated by spleen against the Governor rather than patriotic indignation against a renewal of American trade with the colony. Nevertheless, as Macquarie was to discover, it was spleen backed by sound mercantile law, spleen that eventually led to the Commission of Inquiry which ended Macquarie's New Order and inaugurated a "New Deal" based on capital investment and private enterprise rather than "a merciful and enlightened jurisprudence" aimed at providing a happy home for every ex-convict who deserved it.

On his return to Sydney, Macquarie was incensed. He denounced the arrest of the American ship as an example of "factious and illiberal principles" and ordered the liberation of the *Traveller* and a resumption of trade. He made Vale stand court-martial for "insolent and highly insubordinate" behaviour and dismissed Moore from his government post, which meant the loss of £300 a year perquisites. The court-martial ruled that Vale had acted in a manner unbefitting his position as Assistant Colonial Chaplain and ordered a public and severe reprimand. Macquarie contented himself with private admonishment.

Vale left the colony to continue his vendetta in England. Meanwhile, the Bent brothers smiled behind their hands for they were well aware that Macquarie would soon learn that it was the Governor not Vale or Moore who had contravened the law. Before long His Excellency found himself, in view of the "obstinacy and contumely with which Mr. Vale and his abettors perservere", submitting to Lord Bathurst's "superior wisdom and kind consideration", asking for "an *Act of Indemnity for me*, in the event of the Navigation Act having been thus unknowingly violated. . . ."

In defense of his actions, Macquarie pleaded that it had been the uniform practice of previous governors to admit American vessels. He submitted a list of forty-one vessels "which had been brought to entry and cleared out from Port Jackson since the formation of this colony under Governor Phillip." Eight of these vessels had entered the port during his own governorship and no one had previously raised the question of illegality. The British Government admitted that Macquarie's actions with respect to the *Traveller* had been justified by precedent but informed him that in future the Navigation Act would apply to New South Wales.

Henceforth, ships of any nationality were to be forbidden to trade, "except in cases in which the necessities of the Colony may require the relaxation of this general rule." As a result regular trade between the United States and New South Wales virtually ceased in 1816 until the Navigation Laws were relaxed in the 1820s during the general abandonment of the mercantile system, although they were not formally repealed until 1849. Meanwhile, a certain amount of indirect trade occurred through the transhipment of American goods into British vessels. Whalers continued to use Australian ports to refit and for "refreshment", that is to say, wine, women and song.

Macquarie's benevolent despotism and Highland disregard for the letter of the law led the Colonial Office to appoint John Thomas Bigge, an experienced London barrister, to investigate the affairs of the colony. Bigge arrived in Sydney in September 1819, and a few months later Macquarie resigned. He was succeeded by Major-General Sir Thomas Brisbane, an amateur astronomer of note, who had commanded a brigade in the United States in 1814. Macquarie, who had viewed New South Wales as "a Penitentiary or Asylum on a Grand Scale" left for England "with an arkful of Australian wild life" for friends and patrons at home, cheered by a "Harbour full of People".

Despite his amiable despotism he had been the colony's most popular Governor, especially among ex-convicts and the native-born.

Mr. Commissioner Bigge, sent to discover whether Macquarie's "ill considered compassion for convicts" had ceased to make transportation "an object of real terror" to wrongdoers, was not impressed by the humanitarian despot's achievements. He considered the ex-Governor's building program wastefully expensive, his "insensibility to the controlling power of law" dangerous, and his concern for the rights of convicts and emancipists excessive. These were the opinions of a penny-pinching pedant. Bigge's constructive suggestions were vastly more important than his disparagement of Macquarie's outstanding contribution to colonial welfare.

The Commissioner's recommendations changed New South Wales from a penitentiary for the rehabilitation of the convicted to a colony for economic exploitation by free men. Macquarie had converted the colony from a prison to a reformatory and, in the words of Australian historian Arthur Jose, "somewhat to his disgust, he expanded it from a forty-square-mile collection of small farms to a vast region capable of holding great estates." What the colony now needed, Bigge concluded, was an influx of "really respectable settlers—Men of real capital—not needy adventurers."

So it came about. Free land grants were virtually abolished. Good grazing land was parceled out in accordance with the amount of capital a new settler brought into the country. "So Macquarie's little river-flat farms and all his and Simeon Lord's schemes for fostering small independent industries went into oblivion, and the whole colony devoted itself for the next seventy years to exporting wool in sufficient quantities to pay for the import of everything else." The "New Gentry", as they came to be called, wandered with their sheep and cattle over yet untapped goldfields, for in those days nobody gave much thought to recurring stories of gold in the hills. Up to 1851, "every phase of Australian life was valued or disparaged in accordance with its bearing on the wool industry."

In Australia, as in America, it is true, as Ray Allen Billington says in *The Western Frontier: 1830-1860* (London, 1956), that "mass migrations occurred only when attracting and expelling forces operated in conjunction; not until people were unhappy at home and assured of greater prosperity ahead were they willing to risk the uncertainties of a new land." In America, the way for the mass movement westward in the 1840s was prepared by fur-traders in the northwest, Santa Fe merchants in the southwest, an increasing number of American interlopers into Mexico, which declared its independence of Spain in 1821, and by the hard times associated with the economic panic of 1837.

Texas, rather than Oregon or California, provided the first goal for footloose Americans. Despite efforts by the American Government to control the rush from the Mississippi across the Sabine into what was then Mexican

*Weapons of the frontier were much the same for
lawmen, bandits and bushrangers*

territory, more than thirty thousand Americans entered Texas between 1821 and 1836, when Sam Houston became President of the Republic of Texas after the battle of San Jacinto. Most of them were simply in search of new land and a fresh start. Others, like Sam Houston, were political activists eager to end Mexican rule and bring the province into the United States.

The Mexican Government's vacillating policies and increasingly harsh measures against the intruders offered plenty of excuse for hotheads like Houston, Jim Bowie and Davy Crockett to rebel. Bowie and Crockett died at the Alamo, when a Mexican army massacred the small garrison occupying an old abandoned mission, providing the rebels with a rallying cry and America with an heroic legend. Less than ten years after Sam Houston became President of the Republic of Texas, U.S. President James K. Polk annexed Texas to the United States of America.

In 1836, the year Texas became a republic, Samuel Colt took out a patent for the weapon that enabled the Texas Rangers to dominate the Southwest Indians. As Walter Prescott Webb pointed out in his classic *The Great Plains*, it took American pioneers in Texas at least a minute to discharge and reload the early unwieldly pistols they carried and the old long rifles were useless to a mounted man. In the time a Texan was reloading, the Comanche warrior could ride three hundred yards and discharge twenty arrows. Australians are familiar with pictures of white men and women huddled behind the shelter of their wagons on the trans-Plains trails leading from Missouri to Oregon, California, and Santa Fe, while plumed and mounted Indian braves ride in a narrowing circle "drawing the white man's fire" hoping to exhaust the defenders' ammunition before the exterminating rush. In all such encounters the agility and rapidity of Indian movements offset the longer range and greater accuracy of the white man's weapons. Experienced Indian fighters practiced the platoon system of rotation firing to overcome the disadvantage of the long and clumsy methods of reloading.

The quick firing Colt revolver and the Winchester rifle, like Britain's Gatling gun, robbed the "savages" of all their former advantages. It was no longer possible for them to resist effectively the inroads of white men into tribal lands. Gatling guns and semi-automatic weapons were not necessary to subdue the Australian Aboriginals, who succumbed to the white man's vices and diseases rather than the white man's weapons. There was sporadic violence on both sides but no organized resistance or planned extermination, except in Tasmania where the Aboriginals were taken from their homeland. They were put into a concentration camp on Flinders Island, where they pined away. In Tasmania, neither the humanitarian edicts of British Governors, nor scientific interest, nor Christian charity, could save the native race from extinction. Much the same is true of southwestern Australia. In the rest of the continent the Aboriginal race survived despite what nineteenth-century historian

G. W. Rusden condemned as the lust, fear, hatred and revenge of settlers. Even James Collier, early panegyrist of the pastoral age in Australia, does not gloss over atrocities perpetrated by white man against black although he gives equal space to depredations by Aboriginals, who speared sheep and cattle, raided isolated stations and committed many murders.

By the mid-1820s, Spain and Russia had dropped out of the competition for the Oregon country of northwest America. Neither the United States nor Britain wanted another war to settle the question. Consequently, they agreed on a treaty of joint occupation which allowed British and American nationals to trade or settle "on the North West Coast of America, Westward of the Stony Mountains." As many Americans saw it, this meant if they were first to occupy the area it would be American.

On the Columbia itself Dr. John McLoughlin, the British Hudson Bay Company's factor at Fort Vancouver, behaved like the governor of a colonial territory. He sought to mollify inhabitants and freeze out intruders. "We opposed him as much as was Necessary," he wrote to the Company after he had politely but relentlessly opposed one American enthusiast who had secured Boston backing for a Columbia River Fishing and Trading Company. When the American Methodist Mission Society despatched a pastor and three helpers to envangelize the forest Indians, Dr. McLoughlin turned out the white population to greet them. He did not mind missionaries or farmers but interference with the British-dominated fur trade he would not brook. McLoughlin soon persuaded the Methodists that mission work among fur-trading Indians would be wasted effort. Instead, he steered them into the Williamette Valley, south of the river in an area useless to the fur trade, where he could keep them under observation. The sheltered valley proved ideal farm country and American settlers soon outnumbered the British.

Meanwhile, Mexico had opened California's long-closed ports to foreign shipping. British and American ships were soon exchanging manufactured goods for tallow and hides. By the end of the 1820s, Yankee traders from New England ports were dominant. The arrival of an American ship at Monterey was the occasion for a gala week. "From all the country round," says Allen Billington, "came friars and rancheros and natives, to be rowed to the ship in small boats manned by the crew. What marvels awaited them there! The main deck was fitted out like a store, with cases of goods temptingly displayed and freshly scrubbed clerks standing about awaiting to bargain. 'For a week or ten days,' one observer of such a scene wrote, 'all was life on board. The people came off to look and to buy—men, women, and children. . . .!' "

Nor was the display confined to Monterey. The ships moved along the coast, stopping to trade at each harbor or inlet, while the holds were gradually filled with tallow and hides. Trading in this fashion a New England vessel

Aboriginals attack a cattle drive. Australian
overlanders fight off an Aboriginal assault

Indians attack an emigrant train

often spent a year or eighteen months on the Californian coast before returning around the Horn to Boston, Salem or New York. Later, when the missions were secularized and credit arrangements difficult, shippers established shore agents to buy hides ready for shipment. These were the first permanent American residents in California.

Among the shippers who traded with California in the 1830s was an American-Swiss named John A. Sutter, whose enterprise had already been tested in a Santa Fe trading caravan and as an employee of the American Fur Company in Oregon. He saw potentialities in California beyond the trade in tallow and hides. Presenting impressive credentials to Don Alvarado, the Governor of California, he offered to police the wild Sacramento border. For the most part, the Spaniards had stayed in the coastal cattle country and the ports; and inland among wild valleys and rugged mountain slopes, fur traders, outlaws and untamed Indians held almost unchallenged sway. Don Alvarado was happy to grant Sutter some fifty thousand acres and soldiers to help him in his task.

Sutter sailed to the head of navigation on the American River, a tributary of the Sacramento, and established Fort Sutter, a redwood fortress with cannon mounted at the corners, as capital of the unofficial principality named New Helvetia. The hunters and outlaws and Indians were soon intimidated and Fort Sutter became a Mecca for westward-moving Americans who had heard about the rich prizes to be won in California. By the early 1840s, its towering accommodation was sufficient for 1,000 men and women and Sutter could write, "I was everything—patriarch priest, father, and judge."

Compared with the rough pioneering bear and beaver hunters who opened the West, the new arrivals' were mild, middle-class men. Some obtained grants of land from the local authorities and became rancheros, others settled in the towns as traders, merchants, storekeepers and schoolteachers. These busy merchants and traders were a greater threat to Mexican California than the rough mountain men had ever been. Even the indifferent hidalgos began to look uneasily at each other when an American Consul (Thos. O. Larkin) settled in Monterey as an efficient watchdog over Yankee rights in a leisurely, tomorrow-will-do outpost of Latin-American civilization, where men had time to be dandies and women lived according to the age-old rituals of a complex etiquette.

Thos. O. Larkin kept westward-looking President Polk fully informed about what was happening west of the mountains. Then, late in 1844, John Charles Fremont, an ambitious, intrepid American explorer, arrived on the Sacramento from across the Sierras. Fremont's party of sixty men rested at Fort Sutter while the engaging young leader visited Monterey and begged permission to bring his men into California proper to replenish their ragged outfits. He told the Governor they were engaged in surveying the best land route from the Atlantic to the Pacific, in the interest of science, commerce and civilization.

Reluctantly, the Governor gave the required permission. Sixty armed men were a big intrusion into an isolated province where the army counted its manpower in hundreds rather than thousands. Fremont's men settled down comfortably on a rancho near San Jose. Neither they nor their leader showed any hurry to go home. When 1846 dawned the Americans were still in California. Fremont was popular wherever he went; he dined with notabilities, acted graciously towards the ladies and avoided aggravating discussion. His followers were not always so well-mannered nor so discreet. "There are 10,000 Americans waiting to move westward in the spring," they boasted.

Early in 1846 trouble flared between Fremont's men and the Californians following a quarrel over a woman. General Jose Castro, the local comman- dant, ordered all Americans out of his area. Fremont chose to interpret this as an insult to the United States. He moved his men onto a hilltop camp and defiantly unfurled the American flag. Three American warships, the *Ports- mouth*, the *Cyrene* and the *Levant*, moved into Californian waters. At New Helvetia, "King" Sutter, who was now a Mexican citizen, openly showed his American sympathies and expressed hostility to the new Governor, Manuel Micheltorena.

Meanwhile, the American Congress had offended Mexico by admitting revolutionary Texas, a former Mexican province, in the Union. President Polk tried to settle the matter amicably and offered to buy California and New Mexico. The Mexicans refused to bargain away the outlying edges of their sprawling inefficient empire. In May 1846, American troops moved into disputed Texan territory and war with Mexico began. In June, General Castro issued a proclamation in California ordering all Americans in the province to swear allegiance to the Mexican flag or to leave the country at once. This provoked resident Americans into an opéra bouffe uprising known as the Bear Flag Revolution.

Bear Flag revolutionaries kidnapped the fiery General Mariano Gaudalupe Vallejo, self-styled Lord of the North, and locked him with other prisoners in Fort Sutter. The revolutionaries had vague ideas of setting up a self- governing Californian Republic but before their plans were realized the current of the Mexican war swept them into the main stream of American history. On 7 July 1846, Commodore Solat, of the U.S.S. *Portsmouth*, ran up the Stars and Stripes over the Customs House at Monterey without opposition from the lackadaisical townsfolk. Soon after, General Kearney with a small American force arrived overland and linked with Fremont. After a short almost farcical campaign the Americans completed the conquest of California and established a military government which soon had to cope with gigantic social and economic problems arising out of the Californian gold rush.

Like the newly independent America before the Louisiana Purchase, the newly expanding Australia had no established right to unoccupied lands west of the shifting bounds marked by settlers seeking fresh pastures for their flocks and herds. Cook and Phillip had annexed New South Wales for George III but New South Wales was no more than a geographical expression for the eastern coast of New Holland, from Wilson's Promontory to Cape York Peninsula. How far west New South Wales extended was anybody's guess. The British Government decided that the 135th meridian would serve as well as any, which left two-thirds of the continent no-man's-land. In 1825, Imperial authority extended the boundary to the 129th meridian so that the new Governor, Sir Ralph Darling, would have jurisdiction over Melville Island, north of what is now Darwin, where, at the instigation of the East India Company, the British Government established an ill-sited, short-lived settlement to provide a treaty port for dealings with the Malay Peninsula.

Even so, New South Wales comprised hardly more than one-third of the continent and of that one-third only about one-twentieth was actually occupied. The other two-thirds were open to any nation that cared to stake a claim, for there was nobody except a handful of Stone-Age Aboriginals to oppose movement inland from the southern, western or northern coasts. With the French again showing an active interest in the area, it seemed prudent to take some pre-emptive action.

Acting under instruction from the British Government Governor Darling sent Major Edmund Lockyer, of the 39th Regiment, to establish a settlement at King George's Sound. In the event of American or French visitors to the Sound, site of the town of Albany, Lockyer was under instructions to "regulate his communication" and that of his officers and men "so as to avoid any expression of doubt of the whole of New Holland being considered within this government." Although beset by initial difficulties, especially from local Aboriginals who had been molested by sealers, Albany persisted. By the 1840s the port had become an important whaling center frequented by American and French ships.

In May 1829, Captain Charles Fremantle, R.N., took formal possession of the whole of New Holland westward of New South Wales. Before doing so, he was instructed to ask the Aboriginals if they objected! At about the same time President Andrew Jackson was negotiating a Bill through Congress, empowering the Army to shift all the Indian tribes in the eastern states west of the Mississippi. When Chief Justice Marshall of the Supreme Court ruled in favor of the Cherokees, who appealed against the proposal, President Jackson declared the decision "preposterous" and ordered the Army to get them out.

Most Australian colonists would have agreed with President Jackson. Despite the good intentions of the British Government, the efforts of humanitarians in England and attempts on the part of colonial governors to apply the law impartially to black and white alike (including a readiness to hang stockmen found guilty of murdering Aboriginals), the popular colonial view was expressed by squatter John Cotton: "the worthless, idle aborigine has been driven back from the land that he knew not how to make use of, and valued not, to make room for a more noble race of beings, who are capable of estimating the value of the fine country. Is it not right that it should be so?"

Throughout, the British Government, far from the scene of actual conflict, tried to treat white and black as equals under the law. In rare cases where white men were tried for killing Aboriginals they usually claimed they were not aware that in killing blacks they were breaking the law. As Collier observed, the admission was itself a condemnation of the state of society in which such a sentiment could be cherished. Australian Aboriginals were so completely submerged by the conquest of the continent between 1830 and 1850 they made no contribution to the historical record. What is known of their history is seen through the eyes of white men and although the Imperial Government and missionaries tried to cushion the impact between the two races few if any among humanitarian-minded observers and workers saw any value in the Aboriginal way of life *per se*. Collier expressed the educated nineteenth-century point of view when he wrote: "There can be no question of right or wrong in such a case. The only right is that of superiority of race, and the greater inherent capability on the part of the whites; the only real wrong on the part of the blacks is their all-round inferiority and their inability to till the ground or even make use of its natural pastures . . . Their disappearance was a natural necessity. It came about in obedience to a natural law. It was effected by natural processes, and followed on the lines of the substitution of vegetal and animal species all over the world."

Few thoughtful or educated people nowadays subscribe to such a crude interpretation of the Darwinian survival of the fittest. Now that it is almost too late, contemporary Australians, like contemporary Americans, have a conscience about the original inhabitants of the continents they settled. There were an estimated 300,000 Aboriginals in Australia when white settlement began. There are now about 140,000, including people of Aboriginal descent. Few live a nomadic life unaffected by contact with Europeans. In the center and north, Aboriginals mostly live and work in reservations or on pastoral properties. In the southern states, where most are of mixed descent, they struggle against odds for social equality, although, in theory, they enjoy equal citizenship. In 1967, a continent-wide referendum vote gave the Australian Federal Government power to legislate for Aboriginal affairs. Previously,

Aboriginal welfare was primarily a matter for State Governments. The Federal Government now supplements State expenditure on programs of Aboriginal welfare and advancement.

There is much talk about helping the Aboriginals maintain their cultural identity. This attitude has replaced the former policy of assimilation. For most Aboriginals assimilation meant assimilation on the ground floor and nowadays most Aboriginal spokesmen assert the right of the Aboriginal people to their own way of life. Certainly, neither Indian nor Aboriginal has disappeared altogether into the "great White swamp" of urban life and both have begun to reappear in literature and folklore not as exotic local color but as heroic figures symbolizing a new underground mythology. What lies in the future nobody knows. All we can decently say of the past is to echo Robert Frost's grim irony in his cruelly literal poem, "The Vanishing Red". . . .

> You can't get back to see it as he saw it.
> It's too long a story to go into now.
> You'd have to have been there and lived it.
> Then you wouldn't have looked on it as just a matter
> Of who began it between the two races.

Although two Sydney ex-convicts, Solomon Levey and Daniel Cooper, put up most of the money, the new Swan River settlement in what is now Western Australia, was to be a colony of free men. Lured by the sort of publicity Dickens condemned so heartily in his castigations of America, the first shipload of colonists, with Captain James Stirling, R.N., as Lieutenant-Governor, arrived in June 1829. Ships could not cross the bar at the mouth of the river and the colonists were dumped on the beach, pianos, carriages, wives, children and all, and left to shelter under crude bough lean-tos on "the Plains of Lombardy", which turned out to be fine sand almost as white as snow and quite unsuited to depasture stock or cultivation.

Ten years after the first landing the colony was hardly self-sufficient. In his influential book *The Art of Colonization* (1849), Edward Gibbon Wakefield, the English colonial reformer, dismissed the experiment in two stinging lines: "There are one or two colonies, like West Australia, so stagnant, tame and torpid, as to have no politics." Progress was almost minimal until the introduction of convict labor in 1849.

Meanwhile, in eastern Australia, explorers and squatters in search of fresh grazing land had moved steadily inland from Cumberland County and the Bathurst Plains. The Government Surveyor, John Oxley, traced the rivers running north and west of the Blue Mountains until they lost themselves in salty marshes. Native-born Hamilton Hume and retired sea-captain William Hovell undertook at their own expense to explore what lay beyond the Murrumbidgee, discovered by wide-ranging stockmen in 1821.

Starting from Hume's station on Lake George, near the present site of Canberra, they crossed the flooded river on a raft, worked their way through the snow-covered Dividing Range and reached the sea at Corio Bay, on a western arm of Port Phillip Bay, near the present town of Geelong. Having read the published notes of this journey, native-born John Batman organized the Port Phillip Association in Van Diemen's Land for the purpose of developing the mainland territory described.

In the drought-stricken summer of 1828-9, Captain Charles Sturt of the 39th Regiment, accompanied by Hamilton Hume, penetrated westward beyond Oxley's marshes and discovered the Darling River, undrinkable because of salt springs. This was saltbush country, a vast forbidding region of red earth and low rocky hills, the semi-arid belt between the comparatively well-watered east coast and the central deserts, a legendary country like the Great American Desert.

Sturt and Hovell brought sheep to the Darling and found they thrived on Chenopodiaceae, the family name of the saltbush genera that flourished in this outback region as they do in semi-arid regions of America. In those days, sheepmen were looking for grasslands with sweet water within reasonable hauling distance of a port. Sturt's Darling River was salt and 500 miles west of Sydney, with no usable water transport between.

So far as the pastoral pioneers were concerned, this was the edge of beyond, out where the dead men lie, the river they could not pass. In the same decade, U.S. Army Major Stephen H. Long traversed the area between the Missouri and the Rocky Mountains, describing it as "the Great Desert at the Base of the Rocky Mountains." For years, eastern mapmakers continued to label this territory "The Great American Desert" although westerners soon learned differently. Australians were similarly convinced that their continent had a "Dead Heart", although once Adelaide became a port and the Darling River's saltiness was known to be localized, pastoralists were able to utilize saltbush country. Indeed, Australian saltbush was found so good that it was soon acclimatized in California.

At the end of 1829, Sturt led a second expedition from Warby's station near Gundagai, on the Murrumbidgee River, then the limit of settlement. Using a whale boat brought overland from Sydney Sturt and seven men from his party spent twenty-six days floating down-river into the Murray, which the explorers named. They continued along the Murray, past its junction with the Darling, to Lake Alexandrina where the river disappointingly petered out among sands impracticable for shipping. Sturt and his men now faced the appalling task of rowing 900 miles the way they had come, against a strong current and on rations reduced to half-a-pound of flour a day. The base camp party had left when they arrived but Sturt sent two men in search of relief and they returned a week later with supplies. This was exploring

William Penn's treaty with the Indians set a precedent in Australia

John Batman's treaty at Port Phillip. His purchase of the future site of Melbourne was disavowed by the Governor

comparable with the efforts being made in the United States during the same decade.

Sturt succeeded in knitting together all the threads of a vast river system draining a territory as great as France and Germany combined. When he reached the junction of the Darling and the Murray, he rowed some way up the broad clear river which on his previous expedition, 300 miles upstream, he had found a desolate salt ooze seeping through drought-stricken wilderness. "An irrisistible conviction impressed me," Sturt wrote, "that we were now sailing on the bosom of that very stream from whose banks I had been twice forced to retire. I directed the Union Jack to be hoisted, and giving way to our satisfaction we all stood up in the boat and gave three distinct cheers. It was an English feeling, an ebullition, an overflow, which I am ready to admit that circumstances and situation will alone excuse."

From then on, so far as New South Wales was concerned, explorers and sheepmen simply had to fill in the gaps. Major Thomas Livingstone Mitchell, the colony's Surveyor-General, set out to prove Sturt wrong. Instead, he confirmed the existence of the river-system Sturt had disclosed. He discovered that the succession of salt pools the Darling at first appeared to be, became after a good season, a free-flowing river of sweet water which joined the Murray, as Sturt had claimed. The Darling River Aboriginals proved hostile. "Implacably hostile and shamelessly dishonest" Mitchell called them. Several were killed or wounded in an affray. On his third and most important expedition Mitchell again had trouble with Aboriginals. His party killed seven in an affray near the Darling. On his return journey, south of the Murray, he not so much discovered as revealed the Western Districts of what is now Victoria, calling the area "Australia Felix", so great was the contrast with the watershed of the Darling.

"A land so inviting and still without inhabitants!" he exclaimed in *Three Expeditions into the interior of Eastern Australia*. "As I stood, the first European intruder on the sublime solitude of these verdant plains, as yet untouched by flocks and herds, I felt conscious of being the harbinger of mighty changes, and that our steps would soon be followed by the men and animals for which it seemed to have been prepared . . . Here was an almost boundless extent of the richest surface in a latitude corresponding to that of China, yet still uncultivated and unoccupied by man. A great reserve, provided by nature for the extension of his race, where economy, art, and industry might suffice to people it with a peaceful, happy, and contented population."

From the top of a high mountain, on his way home, Mitchell saw, in the heat-haze of an Australian summer, what he fancied to be a mirage, "white objects which might have been tents." It was no mirage. The "white objects" were indeed tents, the encampment of John Batman from Van Diemen's Land who had just landed near the present site of Melbourne to bargain with the Aboriginals on behalf of the Port Phillip Association.

The Port Phillip Association was indeed the forerunner of mighty changes especially for the peaceful, happy and contented population already in possession—the Aboriginals whom John Batman considered should by God's grace be prepared, for a down payment of blankets, knives, looking-glasses, tomahawks, beads, scissors and flour, to hand over 600,000 acres to those whom Mitchell considered God's chosen people, John Cotton's "more noble race." In 1827, John Batman and Joseph Tice Gellibrand, settlers in Van Diemen's Land, had written to Governor Darling on behalf of what they called the Port Phillip Association asking permission to move their sheep and cattle across Bass Strait to the fertile mainland areas described by Hume and Hovell. In keeping with the British Government's policy of restricted settlement, the Governor refused, although Van Diemen's Land was admittedly fully grazed, and the Lieutenant-Governor welcomed the proposal.

Batman, sometimes called Australia's William Penn, proceeded to Port Phillip nevertheless. Penn's treaty with the Indians was Batman's model for the elaborate parchment he presented to the tribe of Dutigalla, in exchange for the right of occupancy, signed, sealed and delivered with due ceremony. The new Governor of New South Wales, Sir Richard Bourke, declared the treaty null and void but could do little to change the fact that Port Phillip was now occupied not only with settlers from Van Diemen's Land but by a mounting flood of overlanders from New South Wales. Bowing to the inevitable, the Governor recognized the fact of the matter and sent down officials and a military detachment to act as midwives for the birth of Melbourne.

5 Democratic Vistas

In the eyes of thirty-year-old Edward Gibbon Wakefield, a student of public affairs temporarily incarcerated in London's Newgate Prison for an injudicious attempt to get rich quickly by stampeding a fifteen-year-old heiress into a clandestine Gretna Green marriage, Australia's pastoralists were too many and too scattered to provide a firm foundation for what Blue Mountains explorer William Charles Wentworth, in his prize-winning poem "Australasia" (1823), had called "A New Britannia in Another World. . . ."

Wentworth, whose antecedents were dubious although he came from the best Whig stock on his father's side, had been rejected as suitor for the hand of John Macarthur's daughter, Elizabeth. Macarthur had survived his leading role in the Rum Rebellion to become the doyen of the Ancient Nobility. The Ancient Nobility were the Australian equivalent of the great New York families—the Coopers, the Platts, the Ogdens and others—who had moved up-state to establish landed estates reminiscent of the great Whig manors of eighteenth-century England.

In New South Wales, Colonel George Johnston's Annandale, Alexander Riley's Burwood, Sir John Jamison's Regentville on the Nepean River, and Macarthur's Elizabeth Farm at Parramatta were famous seats from which the colonial aristocracy exercised power and exuded status. Wentworth initially dreamed of a great Wentworth-Macarthur alliance acceptable to his father's patron and kinsman, the great Whig Lord Fitzwilliam. It was not to be. Wentworth's father had been exiled (though not convicted) for his family's good and his mother had been a convict. The Macarthurs were clean-skins. The disparity might have been overcome had it not been that Wentworth's notions were too Whiggish for John Macarthur, who had no wish to share power with an urban middle-class, especially a middle-class including many ex-convicts.

Wentworth had already announced his Whiggish credo in an epoch-making book, the *Statistical, Historical and Political Description of New South Wales* (London, 1819). With Edmund Burke's great American speeches ringing in

*Thomas Jefferson was an inspiration to Aus-
tralian Emancipists*

William Charles Wentworth saw Jefferson's
America as an ideal society

his ears, the aspiring young colonial had endeavored to do his country justice in the eyes of the English-speaking world. John Macarthur was not impressed although the book provided a manifesto for those who wished to see English liberties extended to colonial Australia. Instead, Wentworth found himself the champion of the Emancipists who formed a new middle-class become rich by all sorts of respectable and unrespectable means.

Wentworth's book was part exposition and part rhetoric. He outlined the potential wealth and future prospects of the colony in factual terms down to practical details of how much land and how many head of stock would be needed to prosper in the new land of opportunity. Then, in rolling Burkean periods more fitted to the platform than the study, he launched into an impassioned plea for the rights of Englishmen to be extended to the free inhabitants of New South Wales and Van Diemen's Land. He admitted that such a plea would have been unwise earlier but reminded his readers that thirty years had passed since the colony was founded and that the old authoritative form of prison government was no longer applicable. The Macarthurs would not have quarreled with this. The crucial matter was the interpretation of the word "free". Wentworth meant "freed" as well as "free". The Ancient Nobility would have none as legislators and magistrates of the New Britannia but those who had arrived free.

The United States represented for Wentworth what Australia should aspire to become but Wentworth's America was the America of Thomas Jefferson and the "Virginian Dynasty", already crumbling at the edges as easterners and migrants percolated into the new western states (via Kentucky and Tennessee as well as New York and New England) of Ohio (1803), Indiana (1816), Mississippi (1817), Alabama (1817), Illinois (1818), and Florida (1819). Jeffersonian America was eastern America, seaboard America, republican America, deriving inspiration from the Roman Republic and the French Enlightenment. What became Jacksonian America, democratic America, was already rising behind the Alleghenies and the Appalachians where two streams of migrants, one from the Southern states and the other from New England, mingled along the Mississippi and in the Middle West, the heartland of the new America.

The new America was inward-looking, westward-looking, indifferent to European ideas, hating Indians, suspicious of foreigners, an America peopled by small farmers, rivermen, mechanics and the laboring poor, who saw in Andrew Jackson their champion against banks, big business, landlords and an interfering government. "The wind of democracy blew so strongly from the West," said Frederick Jackson Turner in *The Frontier in American History* (New York, 1920), "that, even in the older states of New York, Massachusetts, Connecticut and Virginia, Conventions were called which liberalized the constitutions by strengthening the democratic basis of the state."

An ambitious young colonial, writing a book in London ten years before Andrew Jackson became President of the United States, could not have been expected to know all this, however well read he might be in Burke, Franklin, the Federalist Papers and the Declaration of Independence. In any case, Wentworth, for all his seeming democracy, was no Andrew Jackson. He played for the support of the new middle-class, including ex-convicts, for whom he fought in the courts and through his newspaper the *Australian* but he remained a Jeffersonian Whig to the last. The revolution he cited was the American Revolution not the French and certainly not the Chartist. His threats were rhetorical rather than genuinely threatening. Unless the British Government had the foresight to see that the colonists of New South Wales and Van Diemen's Land would not submit indefinitely to "the present system of injustice and oppression", he said, they would be faced with a situation such as that which had arisen in colonial America.

In short Wentworth was a "patriot", one of the founders of the Australian Patriotic Society, whereas, in his eyes, the Macarthurs and their kind were "Loyalists". Almost certainly, he threatened, unless the loyalist "Exclusives" were prepared to lift political and economic restrictions from Emancipists and the native-born, the patriots would be driven into making overtures to the United States, if only with the intention of placing themselves "under the government of more just and considerate rulers." Should the colony be "goaded into rebellion", as the American colonists had been, an Australian Declaration of Independence was neither "problematical nor remote." Nor did he fear the outcome of an Australian War of Independence. "If the colonists should prudently abandon the defence of the sea-coasts, and remove their flocks and herds . . . behind these impregnable passes [of the Blue Mountains] what would the force of England, gigantic as it is, profit her?"

These were fighting words which General Andrew Jackson, then commander of the U.S. Army's Southern Division, might have used against England or Spain although, as an experienced soldier, he might have wondered where the colonists, behind the barrier of the Blue Mountains, would have obtained their powder and shot. "Old Hickory", after virtually forcing the United States to take over Florida, was elected Senator. "Everybody expected to see me with a tomahawk in one hand and a scalping knife in the other," he said. Instead, he turned on his Southern charm and took care not to commit himself until he saw how the land lay. Wentworth, a hulking young man with a cast in his eye, was too young and too ambitious to remain uncommitted. Had things turned out differently with the Macarthurs he might have emerged as a Whiggish spearhead of the Old Families. Instead, he became the Liberator. Either way, he would never have been, nor ever was, a democrat like Andrew Jackson, even though Jackson was more democrat by circumstance than through passionate conviction.

General Andrew Jackson—some remarkable similarities with Wentworth

Despite the vastly different social and economic circumstances that helped condition Jackson and Wentworth there were remarkable similarities between their political careers. Both were *arrivistes* in so far that each had to fight his way up against entrenched social and political privileges. Both found the law a convenient ladder of ascent. Both relied on overwhelming popular support to maintain them in places of political power. Both were ardent and sincere nationalists whose policies sometimes smacked of self-aggrandizement but always contained elements of genuine political idealism. Both initiated policies which changed the course of national development. Initially, at least, both rode the crest of the tide of change. Finally, both saw the progressive economic interest they represented crumble away into mere sectional self-interest. Andrew Jackson did not live long enough to see Jacksonian democracy replaced by the gilded age. Wentworth saw with despair the passions of colonial equality he had evoked turn into what he considered rancorous leveling class conflict which denied the essentially Burkean principles he had from the beginning maintained.

Wentworth's book appeared at the right time and ran into several editions. Together with Mr. Commissioner Bigge's reports on Macquarie's world, and Peter Miller Cunningham's *Two Years in New South Wales* (London, 1828) it provided stimulating reading for a restless post-Napoleonic era. "I thank God," said Goethe, "that I am not young in so thoroughly finished a world." The Messianic promise of the American and French revolutions, which had flared to a holocaust of the young and ardent under Napoleon, now spluttered among dying embers in a blackened grate. Those who had applauded and those who had opposed were left without a purpose in bleak times of rising prices and falling employment. Ex-officers, who had stormed the heights of Badajoz or rallied the red-coated squares at Waterloo, counted sparse guineas in London or provincial lodgings. Old soldiers begged in the streets or, like Wentworth's father in earlier less poverty-stricken times, took to the road. With oatmeal at ten shillings a stone even proud and frugal Scottish husbandmen like Carlyle's father were reduced to thin gruel and plain water.

Wentworth, in prose and verse, had uttered a paean of praise about Australasian possibilities once the dead hand of prison officialdom had given way to self-government by a people capable of obliterating their convict birth-stain in a flood of free immigration. Cunningham's descriptions of colonial Sydney had a pastoral quality compared with the grim statistics of rural England and the Stygian squalor of London's back streets and dark alleys: "generally speaking, the better sort of houses in Sydney are built in the detached cottage style, —of white freestone, or of brick plastered and white-washed, one or two stories high, with verandahs in front, and enclosed by a neat wooden paling, lined occasionally with trim-pruned geranium hedges. . . . At the corners of the streets, and before many of the doors, fruit-stalls are to be seen, teeming, in their proper season, with oranges, lemons, limes, figs, grapes, peaches, nectarines, apricots, plums, apples, pears, &c., at very moderate prices."

Bigge's reports, although Wentworth hotly condemned them for raking together "all the dirt and filth, all the scandal, calumnies and lies that ever circulated in the colony", pointed the way to the Arcadia Wentworth and Macarthur desired: a wool-exporting pastoral society, with convict labor providing a cheap and effective way of establishing free settlers and reforming as well as punishing criminals. Bigge, Wentworth and the Macarthurs shared a Rousseauistic and Jeffersonian faith in the healing virtue of rural simplicity and the country life. It was a faith widely shared in Britain among hard-working yeomen farmers, demobilized naval and army officers, younger sons, the surplus offspring of fecund parsonages and among sensitive Romantics fearful of the social consequences of a developing industrialism. As the poet Robert Southey saw it, England was becoming a country in which stark industrial barracks, set row on row and back to back, were replacing rose-embowered cottages and winding country lanes.

Caught up and swirled about by the tides of change, the people of England looked America-wards, where republicanism and democracy seemed to promise more immediate and tangible rewards than a reconstructed rural England in the Antipodes. Respectable settlers, impressed by Bigge, Wentworth and Cunningham, preferred the promise of hard cash and vast estates to democratic vistas. The New Gentry, who succeeded the Ancient Nobility as economic pacemakers, made the long and difficult journey to the far side of the globe in search of economic opportunity. For the most part, they possessed no vision of a New Jerusalem nor entertained any hope of building, as John Winthrop had hoped to build in Massachusetts, "a Citty upon a Hill" with "the eies of all people upon us. . . ."

Thus, the first wave of free immigrants into Australia was composed of minor gentry, yeomen farmers, disgruntled middle-class expatriates, plus a sampling of Scottish "mechanics", rather than the "redundant poor", who came later. The staple of what became known as the New Gentry was formed from people such as the Hentys of Tarring, who pioneered the breeding of Merino sheep in Sussex before migrating to Australia, the McIntyres of Tomcairn in Perthshire, the Widow Bussell and her nine children left fatherless in a Hampshire parsonage, Peninsular War and Waterloo veteran Colonel John Molloy, and those a later Governor (Sir George Gipps) described as "young men of good family and connections in England, officers of the army and navy, graduates of Oxford and Cambridge, &c."

Meanwhile, from his cell in Newgate, where he absorbed all that Wentworth, Cunningham, Bigge and others wrote about Australia, Edward Gibbon Wakefield wrote a series of eleven anonymous "Letters from Sydney" to the

Morning Chronicle, beginning 21 August 1829. Although he had never been to Australia, nor to America about which he had so much to say, his "letters" started a revolution in British colonial policy and almost provoked Australian colonists into the Declaration of Independence that Wentworth had reluctantly prophesied. As the brilliant, acidulous, temporary colonial Robert Lowe afterwards admitted, to shake the complacency of Englishmen at home it was sometimes necessary to exacerbate and exaggerate colonial feeling. Wakefield believed as firmly as Wentworth in colonial self-government but he did not at any time visualize a self-governing Australia as an independent Australia. Rather, he believed implicitly in the civilizing virtues of the British connection and saw the southern continent as a new America but an America retained as one of the brightest jewels in the diadem of Empire.

Wakefield did not like the new Australia any more than he liked the new America. As he saw things, Australia's New Gentry were likely to be as great a threat to civilized values as America's New Democrats. Mr. Wentworth, Wakefield said, had informed people in England that land in New South Wales was more than an exercise yard for Botany Bay criminals: colonial land was valuable land and a colonial estate could be had almost for the asking. Here was a place where government could reward the friends of government and the relatives and hangers-on of government. The result was that in New South Wales there were now more landlords than tenants, more absentee owners than careful husbandmen, more sheep and sheep-cotes than people and houses. The whole system would have broken down, Wakefield argued, had not Australian settlers possessed the equivalent of American slaves: convict labor.

In Wakefield's view the inhabitants of new rich lands, where gains were comparatively easy, experienced a well-nigh irresistible desire to scratch the surface over as wide an area as possible, thus developing an uncouth, shambling, provincial society, similar to that created in America by the opening of the West, compared with the neat, orderly, civilized society of colonial and Jeffersonian America:

. . . . the migrating habits of the Americans opened my eyes. I saw a people without monuments, without history, without local attachments founded on impressions of the past; without any love of birthplace, without patriotism—unless constantly roaming over immense regions may be called a country. I saw Europeans the only visitors to the grave of Franklin, and heard Americans titter at Englishmen for admiring the other founders of America. I learned that, with a new people, restlessness is a passion, insatiable whilst any means of indulging it remains; a disease, incurable but by cutting away its source. "What a blessing," I exclaimed, "for the present race of Americans, if the Pacific should overflow all the land that separates it from the Mississippi!"

In short, Wakefield believed in concentrated settlement, slow, steady expansion, the recreation of British civility in distant lands. In Australia and America, by contrast, the frontier and easy access to frontier land created carelessness, squalor, ignorance and indifference to the fate of native peoples such as Aboriginals and Indians. Even Van Diemen's Land, that agricultural jewel set in a silver sea, faced a commonplace unprogressive future unless the rest of Australasia was swallowed by the sea, for Bass Strait was not wide enough to prevent Van Diemenians spreading to the mainland (as John Batman and others were soon to do), a mainland so vast that stored dams of literature and art, law and learning, manners and morals, soon spread out into thin muddy trickles that held no refreshment or replenishment for the spirit although sustaining the full vigor of sensual life.

The solution, as Wakefield saw it, was to *sell* land, not give it away, and to sell it at a price sufficiently high to prevent every new settler from becoming at once a landlord or a Wool King. Thus, newcomers without great reserves of capital would be compelled to work long enough to learn to work the land under different conditions from the old. At the same time they would provide a pool of labor more efficient and more reliable than convict or slave labor, labor buoyed by the hope that they, in time, would be landowners and employers in their own right. Instead of a wide brown land peopled by wild colonial boys, Wakefield envisaged compact green settlements grown up about courthouses, churches, guildhalls and libraries, and settlers grouped in proper hierarchial order, with aspiring free laborers working for skilled approving farms, a tidy administrative and marketing superstructure topping all.

Two essentials were necessary to make this Arcadian dream come true: land must be sold at a price sufficient to compel immigrants to work in order to save enough to become landowners, and wages must be sufficiently high and sufficiently steady to give the right type of immigrant laborer real hope of becoming—not too quickly but in time—an employer and landowner himself. In addition, the sale of land at "a sufficient price" would provide government with a "Land Fund" with which to subsidize and regulate an adequate stream of selected immigrants. By this means only could the spirit of British civilization be preserved from the leveling tendencies of frontier societies. This was Wakefield's answer to what many British people saw as the dangers of "Americanization" and it was an answer that appealed to a number of influential people in the British Imperial Establishment.

In due course, an influential lobby of colonial reformers and humanitarians partially convinced the British Government that Wakefieldian principles were basically sound. Here was a way of preserving Crown Lands of the colonies for posterity instead of allowing, as Wakefield put it, the profusion of government in land disposal to equal the greediness of colonists in acquiring more land than they could use. Here, too, was a means of solving the Malthusian problem of an increasing number of mouths for a decreasing amount of food, clothing and shelter in what now appeared to many political economists as an overcrowded island beset with social problems of growing magnitude.

Ironically, honest reformers like Lord John Russell, descendants of those English Whigs who had applauded the American patriots in their defiance of George III and his friends, soon found themselves in the position Farmer George and his Ministers had found themselves: objects of colonial obloquy and contempt. If mercantile principles and taxation without representation were anathema to most American colonists, a high upset price for land, concentrated settlement and the cessation of assigned convict labor were equally anathema to many Australian colonists, especially to the spearhead of colonial economic development—the flockmasters and squatters of New South Wales.

In each instance, simplistic theory, administrative convenience and sheer ignorance of local conditions came face to face with practical experience, contempt for red tape and the restless pursuit of wealth by new men in a new country unhampered by conventional restraints and indifferent to the rights of the aboriginal cultures they were about to replace. The Pilgrim Fathers may have emigrated to America seeking a political asylum and "those durable riches, and that better country, in comparison with which all the possessions of the world are a bauble." Their descendants, like the first wave of free Australian colonists, were more intent on acquiring wealth or bettering their condition in the world as they found it. The frontier, in both countries, offered more immediate chances than any scheme of systematic colonization. Thus, the essential conflict was between colonists who knew what they wanted and an Imperial Government which thought it knew better.

To begin with, the interests that held the colonists together in opposition to Great Britain were more important than the things that kept them apart. The conflict between Emancipist and Exclusive stemmed from questions of pride and prestige and did not represent a struggle for power. Political power lay overseas, in the British Parliament and the Colonial Office. When colonists realized this, Wentworth had no difficulty in achieving a temporary unity of purpose, including support from the Macarthurs, in pursuit of representative rather than responsible self-government. Meanwhile, the new Governor, Sir Ralph Darling, expressed the prevailing Establishment view when he dismissed Wentworth as "a vulgar, ill-bred fellow, utterly unconscious of the common civilities, due from one gentleman to another."

In a letter to the Colonial Office, Darling added, ". . . he speaks as he wrote when compiling his book, of the independence of the colony, and compares it to the situation formerly of America and the probability of being driven, as America was, to shake off the yoke. In short, he is anxious to become the 'Man of the People' and he seems to think the best means of

*King's Tableland, New South Wales, the open-
ing of a new road. Augustus Earle records the
opening up of the Western Plains of New South
Wales*

The Oregon Trail. Albert Bierstadt commemorates the westward march of settlement in the United States

accomplishing this is by insulting the government." As things turned out, Wentworth had indeed chosen the best means of becoming a Man of the People. The Old Country distinction between Whig and Tory meant little in colonial Australia. Almost everybody, in some degree or other, was against the Imperial Government, and the class that in England was the greatest support for the Establishment—the landowners—was, in the colony, the class that had defied Governors King and Hunter, deposed Bligh and challenged Macquarie. In championing the Emancipists, Wentworth did no more than seek legal and social recognition of a colonial "interest" that would help strengthen the demand for self-government.

In an Anniversary Day speech on 26 January 1827, Wentworth told his audience they should continue "in that degraded condition" in which they found themselves rather than assist in the creation of a legislature "of such circumscribed extent as would leave them the name of popular representation, whilst in reality it delivered them into the hands of an oppressive and rapacious oligarchy." A dozen years later he was himself accused of advocating just such an oligarchy. In fact, he remained consistent throughout his political career: it was not the government of the people, by the people for the people that he advocated, but government by men of talent, education and responsibility who represented the best interests of the people. Such men, he contended, must be men of property with a stake in the country. Emancipists represented such an interest. So did the squatters. When representative government was at last achieved a new contradiction emerged: town against country, propertied Australian against propertyless Australian, the little man against the big.

In America, the voice of the people was initially the voice of the small farmer and the small town, expressed through state legislatures which rapidly spread universal suffrage throughout the West. In Australia, on the other hand, the voice of the people was first heard among immigrant townsfolk. Thus, in America, the tide of democracy may be said to have flowed from the rural areas until it flooded the strongholds of privilege along the eastern seaboard, whereas, in Australia, the springs of democracy started first in towns along the seaboard from whence egalitarian waters seeped slowly into an arid interior, to be dammed and hoarded by a militant few before it irrigated the many. In both cases, the result was bourgeois democracy, the democracy of the respectable, rather than class war or, as Wentworth feared, the mob dictatorship of socialists and levelers.

In his fear of democracy, Wentworth did not realize that political development occurs as much through mutual assimilation of principles as from the conflict of opposites. In England, the landed classes preserved their privileges for another generation and more by absorbing the bourgeoisie, just as in the twentieth century, the bourgeoisie absorbed the proletariat in a liberal-

Henry Parkes, one of the founder-fathers of the
Australian Constitution

socialist mish-mash which constituted the affluent society before inflation brought fresh challenge. Thus, twentieth-century conservative parties exist politically by advocating policies which to Wentworth and others in the nineteenth century would have appeared to be extremist radicalism and socialism. Before he gave up the struggle, Wentworth attempted to create a landed class in Australia that would preserve intact property under attack. The attempt failed, as it was bound to fail although it was not so absurd in the circumstances of the time as it appears now.

Basically, Wentworth was moved by the same fears that moved not only Jonathan Edwards and Alexander Hamilton but James Fenimore Cooper, America's literary giant in the Jacksonian era, to say nothing of Mark Twain, the West's first and finest literary genius. All four Americans, in their different ways, dreamed grandiose dreams of different ends for their homeland than the utilitarian "countries of the common man" that America and Australia eventually became.

In contrast to Wentworth, whose liberalism turned sour, the line of liberal democracy in Australia runs through Dr. John Dunmore Lang and immigrant Chartist Henry Parkes. Lang, a Scottish Presbyterian cleric who sniped left and right from the perimeter of his own powerful ego, had no doubts about himself or the way the world was going. From the beginning he saw the America of President Andrew Jackson as the hope of the common man and, for all his contempt of morally contaminated Emancipists and shiftless Irish immigrants, Lang believed in the common man—provided they had un-common men like himself to lead them. He arrived in Sydney in 1823, at the age of twenty-four, the first Presbyterian minister in New South Wales. Shocked by the immorality he found all about him, an immorality he attributed to transportation and the birthstain, he set himself to promote the immigration of carefully-chosen Scottish tradesmen and to provide education facilities for all classes of the community. He succeeded, partially at least, in both these objectives.

Waspishly intransigent against all authority, including the authority of his own church, incorrigibly disputatious in all matters personal and public, Lang failed to make the political and social impact that was his due because he was too much a peregrinating one-man-band. Through sermons, articles, speeches, books and the columns of the several newspapers he founded, and in turn neglected, he fulminated against human selfishness and folly and reiterated his faith in the greatest happiness of the greatest number through democratic self-government especially democratic self-government represented by Ulster Irish and Lowland Scots. In the fifty-five years of his colonial career he made twenty-one voyages overseas, including two to America, and almost always came back to find his affairs in chaos and his enemies on the verge of triumph. His enemies were many, most of them earned. There was hardly a colonial official or politician or a British institution that did not come under virulent, if often deserved attack. His saving grace, oddly enough, was a sense of humor which took some of the sting out of his sharpest barbs.

Lang's excuse, if excuse were needed, lay in the times with which he had to grapple. He shared the spirit of a period, in Australia as in America, crystallized by Daniel Webster, when he said, "Society is full of excitement; and intelligence and industry asks only for fair play and an open field." The *Australian Quarterly Journal*, in the year of Andrew Jackson's election as President, saw it rather differently: "This must be allowed on all sides to be a most pugnacious colony—a very centre of jealousies and fears—squabbles and contention—libel and litigation." John Dunmore Lang was in the center of it all. He might doubt, as he confessed in a letter to a Scottish friend, the capacity of the masses to command but he had no doubts about his own capacity for leadership in the sectional conflicts that bedeviled society and which, in Australia, tended to coalesce in mounting opposition against the military autocracy of colonial governors however benevolent, for Lang was no admirer of the recently departed Macquarie.

Lang's first important book, *An Historical and Statistical Account of New South Wales* (2 vols., London, 1834), displayed all his idiosyncrasies. A reviewer in the Benthamite *Westminster Review* suggested that its title should have been "A History of Doctor Lang, to which is added A History of New South Wales." If the book had been less vigorously personal nobody would now read it. Unlike Wentworth and his American contemporary George Bancroft, who adopted a full-blown rhetorical style better suited to the plat-form or the pulpit than the written page, Lang was vigorous, colloquial, hard-hitting, delighting in anecdote and personal reminiscences of people and places. He saw at once the essential differences between the American back-woodsman and the Australian squatter, a difference which Wentworth missed. In the second edition of his *History*, published after his first visit to America, he wrote:

The American squatter is a backwoodsman who travels westward, in the van of advancing civilisation, with his axe on his shoulder, and his wife and children (if he happens to be married) and all his other property on a dray or light cart. On finding an eligible spot in the wilderness, he halts for a time, builds a log house, clears, fences and cultivates a few acres of land. He embraces the first opportunity to sell his "betterments" as he calls them, together with the right of pre-emption to which they entitle him, to some bonafide settler from the eastern states, or from the old country or Germany. Then he shoulders his axe again, replaces his family on the light cart or dray and moves further west to repeat the process. The Australian squatter is a gentleman, it may be, of birth and education. He goes into the great Australian wilderness with his flocks and herds, his stockmen and

The Reverend Dr. John Dunmore Lang, admirer of President Jackson and fighter for freedom

shepherds. He erects a temporary house, generally of large sheets of bark in the first instance, in the first eligible and unoccupied tract of pastoral country which he finds; he there lives, like one of the ancient patriarchs, depending for present subsistence on the wool of his flocks and for his future fortune on their rapid increase. . . .

In America, when the movement west began during the 1840s, it was the movement of a people: a migration of frontier folk who took their folkways with them. The wagon trains that crossed the Missouri were communities in embryo. Wagon-masters administered agreed community laws; preachers reminded men and women of their duties to God and their fellows; wives and children tempered the rough edges of untutored men. When the pioneers settled they settled as neighbors and small townships grew up around them with what the Sydney *Colonist*—always alive to what was happening across the Pacific—called "an almost talismanic rapidity"—tavern, gristmill, store, court-house, post-office following in quick succession and, finally, printing press and bank.

Nothing like this happened in Australia. The men who possessed the wide new world Macquarie opened across the mountains were lone horsemen with lean dogs and bleating flocks or herds of lowing cattle. They flowed through the narrow passes and along twisting ridges until they reached the fine grass-lands beyond. There they fanned out north, south and farther west, until the grass failed and they could see nothing ahead but endless miles of stony flats and tufted spinifex, streaked with dry river beds which flooded after rare cloud-bursts, then shrunk to meandering veins of coarse sand.

The wagons that brought supplies to the stations they established, and freighted coastward the fine wool they shore, were sturdy vehicles with wide-rimmed wheels that made the tracks they followed. This was no country for four-wheeled shop wagons filled with "Yankee notions" or covered farm wagons with a driver's seat fit for sunbonneted wives and daughters. The men who drove the Australian wagons were bullockies, squat, hard men with lashing long-thonged whips and a range of expletives beyond the compre-hension of ordinary humans. The cow punchers, who pioneered semi-arid southern Texas with long-horned cattle in the 1830s, were akin to the mounted squatters who inaugurated Australia's pastoral age. The plodding bullockies had no kin, in Australia or anywhere else. They were the unique products of a unique land.

Lang saw the effects of new countries on the habits and manners of Aus-tralian and American youth although he would not have subscribed to the opinion of Washington Irving who, when he returned to the United States after a long stay in Europe, complained at what he called an "all-pervading commonplace." "The youth of Australia," Lang wrote, "is giddy and frivolous, impatient of restraint, apt to fancy himself of more importance to society than he really is. He has a blustering and somewhat offensive affection of liberty and independence, somewhat similar to the usual demonstrations among the lower classes of Americans. Such a feeling operates in rendering the Australian youth impatient . . . of parental restraint, and subsequently leads him . . . to boisterous assertion of rights which nobody ever thinks of calling into question."

Whatever else they might be, in Lang's opinion, the native-born were anything but commonplace. "The Australian intellect comes to maturity earlier than the British," he wrote. "I have known instances of boys making much greater progress . . . in a given time than I have witnessed in Scotland . . . The Scotch boy compared with the Australian is like a steady-going draught horse compared with a hopping kangaroo. Application is not the forte of the Australian youth and he is apt rather to be cast down at the sight of difficulties than roused to exertion." Lang might easily have been writing of Tom Sawyer or Huckleberry Finn whose creator, Samuel Langhorne Clemens, was born at Florida, Monroe County, Missouri, on 30 November 1835, the year after the appearance of Dr. Lang's *History*. Young Sam was still short of four when his parents, a Virginian father and a mother from Kentucky, moved to Hannibal, Missouri, bounded by the woods and lapped by the Mississippi, the post-frontier settlement he immortalized.

Lang had been impressed by American democracy long before his first visit and the publication of *Religion and Education in America* (London, 1840). His newspaper, the *Colonist* (1835-40), regularly reported American affairs in articles lifted from the English and American press. "Proceedings of the Senate of the United States" (from the New York *Working Man's Advocate*) occupied almost as much space as "Reports from the House of Commons". References to West Point were as frequent as those to Woolwich and the newspaper ran a regular column of miscellany from America under the peculiar title "American Statistics". Readers of the *Colonist* were thus kept fully informed on American politics, economics, literature, agriculture, morals and religion—especially the temperance movement, which had many followers in Australia and was later regularly invigorated by visiting American lecturers.

As a Calvinist, Lang did not believe in the possibility of human perfection. He did, however, approve of nationalism and democracy as he saw them during his three months' visit to America in 1840. Nor was he without prevision. He predicted that state rights, not slavery, would lead to conflict between North and South and he favored state rights, although when the Civil War ended he paid a glowing tribute to Lincoln, "the martyred President". After his second visit he forecast that America and Russia would one day be the two dominant world powers. Approving America's "manifest

destiny" to occupy the continent from the Atlantic to the Pacific he nevertheless warned against imperialistic ambition: "Ever since the fall of the Roman
Empire . . . divine providence has set its face against every attempt at a
universal empire in any part of the earth."

An earlier visitor to the United States, Alexis de Tocqueville, had probed
more deeply into the world's first experiment in democracy. He took it for
granted that America had set the standard other nations would follow and
sought to discover how America's democratic disciples could benefit from the
democratic principle without succumbing to the social and cultural defects
already apparent in the American structure.

De Tocqueville saw that majority rule threatened liberty as surely if more
subtly than despotism. Lang entertained "no fears whatever from universal
suffrage . . . provided it is always accompanied . . . with universal education
and entire freedom of rule . . . In the ordinary course of events, something
like universal suffrage will ere long become the law of the land in New South
Wales . . . From what I have observed in the actual working of that system
in the United States, I have no hesitation in saying, 'the sooner the better'. . . ."

This was a time in England when Liberals of the Manchester School were
prepared to see colonies "drop like ripe fruit from the parent tree." If Lang
had remained in the colony, instead of darting hither and thither like a water-
beetle skittering over the surface of a pond, he might have brought his mind
to concentrate on colonial affairs and made real impact with republican ideas.
Instead, his energies were dispersed over too wide a field; bitter sectarian
feeling, church politics, education, personal quarrels, journalism, poetry and,
above all, anti-Catholicism. Nevertheless, he never compromised on what he
declared to be his three fundamental principles: universal suffrage, political
equality and popular education. As he saw it, all three "stemmed from that
word of God that endureth for ever." If God were supreme, John Dunmore
Lang never had any doubts about who was His prophet. So far as republicanism was concerned, though it later became a major interest, initially he
had doubts about a young colony displaying too much "nursery valour."

Certainly, in his initial political forays, Dr. Lang did not fly the Stars and
Stripes, even when advocating secession of the Port Phillip District, which he
represented, from the parent state in the first partially-elected Legislative
Council of New South Wales. Nevertheless, he applauded the "splendid
banner" designed by some of his Melbourne supporters which showed the five
stars of the Southern Cross against a blue satin background and on top the
words "Australasian League", foreshadowing what was to become his
cherished "United States of Australia". He made no objection, however, to
the Union Jack in the top corner of the new banner, which soon became the
emblem of Australian nationalism, an indication that thus early many of
Lang's followers interpreted freedom and independence differently from

American patriots and British republicans. At this stage of his career, Lang himself warned against "youthful presumption" and thought that an Australian Declaration of Independence was a matter for future, a distant future, consideration.

The "spirit of commercial enterprise", as the *Colonist* termed it, which carried American ships into the newly-opened harbors of Mexican California, also took them across the Pacific to Australia. During the 1830s, twenty American whalers made Port Jackson their permanent Pacific base and by 1833 several American merchants had appointed agents in Australia. Kenworthy and Company, the first American firm established in Sydney, quickly secured a virtual monopoly of trade between the two countries.

In May 1836, President Jackson appointed J. H. Williams as the first American Consul in Australia. Mr. Williams arrived by the *Draco* from Boston on 10 January 1837. "And so we have an American Consul!" the *Colonist* exulted on the nineteenth.

> We welcome his arrival with unfeigned goodwill, regarding it as a pledge of increasing intimacy between the two countries, from which mutual advantages may be expected to flow. The spirit of commercial enterprise was never perhaps, more energetic, adventurous, and persevering, in any nation, than it is now in the United States of America. It is the presiding genius of all their maritime towns, shaping their plans, animating their exertions, moulding their laws, polishing their manners, expanding their intellect, and raising them to municipal wealth and national eminence. Scarcely is there a sea which their ships do not plough, or a port in which they do not ride. . . ."

Ice was among the amenities Sydney gained from the reopening of American commerce. Southern planters had been using ice since the seventeenth century, storing it in specially constructed pits under their houses for cooling wine and preserving butter and meat. As early as the 1790s people in Baltimore were drinking "ice water", a term Mark Twain deplored although he did not subscribe to the British superstition that "iced water", as he preferred to call it, was "frightfully unhealthy". Frederic Tudor of Boston was the first man to turn the use of ice into a paying export business, as it had become by the time Mr. Williams reached Sydney in the *Draco*. Lang had already picked up the catch-phrase, common in the United States at that time, that New England produced "nothing but granite and ice", though he was probably unaware that in the year he left Australia for his first trip to America, the Boston ship *Tartar* had already brought the first ice and iceboxes for use in Australia. After a second experimental cargo in 1840, the trade was discontinued until the American influx during the 1850s gold rushes.

Charles Wilkes. As Commodore of the U.S. Surveying and Exploring Expedition he brought the U.S. Navy to Sydney for the first time

In December 1839, Sydneysiders had their first visit from the U.S. Navy—a peaceful one. From 29 November four ships of the United States Surveying and Exploring Expedition under command of Commodore Charles Wilkes, U.S.N., (nephew of "that devil Wilkes" who had been huzzahed by a London mob when Cook sailed) berthed in Port Jackson until 26 December to refit and enjoy Christmas in what they discovered, rather to their surprise, to be a civilized country. The flotilla, *Vincennes, Peacock, Porpoise* and *Flying Fish*, had left the United States in August 1837 and passed round Cape Horn on a leisurely investigatory voyage through the whaling grounds to Sydney before attempting "new discoveries within the Antarctic Circle." Wilkes found many resemblances between Australians and Americans: ". . . the acquisition of wealth seems to be the only object of all exertion here, and speculation was as rife as we had left it in the United States. . . . Cutting down hills, filling up valleys, laying out and selling lots . . . [are] particulars in which the people of Sydney resemble those of America."

Commodore Wilkes and his civilian scientists, geologist James Dwight Dana, philologist Horatio Hale and the Curator of the American Academy of Sciences, Dr. Charles Pickering, went everywhere and saw everything. When Wilkes sailed for the Antarctic the three scientists remained for three months to make a thorough study of New South Wales. Besides his official report, Dana published an *Atlas* containing fourteen plates of Australian fossils. He considered the Illawarra District, south of Sydney, "a perfect gem of a place for Geology . . . one of the loveliest spots of the globe." Hale, who visited mission stations run by the Reverend William Watson and pioneer Australian philologist the Reverend L. E. Threlkeld, published the first American field study on the Australian Aboriginals. Pickering, chief zoologist of the expedition, included a section on the Australian Aboriginals in his *Races of Man* (London, 1850).

Besides contributing to the scientific study of Australian geology, anthropology and zoology, the Wilkes Expedition created remarkable good feeling. The *Colonist* attributed the absence of bad language and drunkenness among the American crews to the example set by "good and pious captains and officers" and remarked that many of the men, offered the choice between a free issue of grog or the cash equivalent, preferred to take the money. Wilkes, on his part, was shocked by the "open practice of the vice of drunkenness" he observed in Sydney and could not refrain, in his account of the visit, from repeating an old and by then discredited quip: "There are only two classes of persons in New South Wales, those who have been convicted and those who ought to be."

The Governor, Sir George Gipps, gave the officers and scientists an official reception, and the exclusive Australian Club entertained them at dinner, adopting the American habit of printing the toast list with appropriate song titles and comment. When it was all over, Gipps reported to the British Secretary of Colonies: "I am happy to be able to inform your Lordship that the most friendly intercourse prevailed between the People of this Colony and the Officers and men of the Expedition during the whole of their visit."

6 *California, Here We Come!*

In California in 1848 James Wilson Marshall, a taciturn, bearded carpenter from New Jersey, began a train of events which changed the history of Australia. Marshall was building a water mill for John Augustin Sutter on the south fork of the American River, among the tangled foothills of California's Sierra Nevada. Towards the end of January, Marshall tested his mill race and found that the lower end needed deepening. He put his men onto digging and blasting during the day. At night he turned in the water to scour the channel.

On the morning of 24 January 1848, Marshall took his usual stroll along the bank to inspect the tailrace. He saw something glitter in the early morning sunlight. He took a second look. The bedrock of the washed-out channel sparkled with tiny points of golden light. Marshall jumped down and picked up a handful of flakes and grains of pure gold. He put the specimens into the dented crown of his slouched hat and, jolted out of his customary moroseness, rushed back to the mill buildings, shouting "Boys, I believe I've found a gold mine."

For hundreds of years Spanish Conquistadors had followed will-o'-the-wisp rumors from Mexico over all the southwestern plains looking for the fabled Seven Cities of Cibola. Credulous friars and lying Indians told of cities, here and there, where the dwellings shone with precious stones and the inhabitants ate off gold plate. Always the sought-for fabulous city turned out to be a miserable mud village where primitive Indians eked out a precarious existence. When at last Spanish missionaries established permanent missions in California at San Diego and Monterey they did not know that they had reached El Dorado.

Sutter and Marshall tried to keep the discovery a secret. Sutter, quite rightly, thought that a gold rush would destroy his pre-eminence. But on 24 March the California *Star* reported that gold had become "an article of traffic in New Helvetia" and the editor was warning his fellow Californians to build their future on the sound foundations of plowing and planting rather than on insubstantial dreams of easy money. Even so, there was no rush to Coloma and the American River. This was not California's first gold mine and people refused to get excited. It was not until Sam Brannan, a San Francisco newspaper proprietor, had been to Coloma to see for himself and had published the news throughout California that men began to flock to the valley.

The news soon began to spread up and down the coast and across the Pacific. Seamen from Lima and Valparaiso who saw gold dust and nuggets in the grog shops of San Francisco spread the news. Miners from Peru, Chile and Mexico reinforced the congregating crowds of Californians. Whaling and trading skippers from Nantucket who called along the Californian coast, carried the news to the Sandwich Islands (Hawaii), New Zealand, Australia and Van Diemen's Land. South Sea Islanders, Maoris, free-born Australians, lash-scarred old lags and smooth-tongued Emancipists were soon on their way to the rich new world.

In terms of travel Sydney and Hobart were nearer to San Francisco than New York. Whaling barques and trading brigs took eight months to sail round the Horn from the eastern seaboard of the United States. Overland travelers struggled against incredible hardships either along the Santa Fe trail from Independence, on the Missouri, or across Arkansas and through the desert into New Mexico, or over the Oregon trail from Kansas to the Platte, through Fort Laramie, over the main pass of the Rockies, along the Snake River and down the Columbia to the Pacific coast. Between the Missouri and the Pacific lay 2,000 miles of prairie, arid desert and towering mountains. A fast ship could cross the Pacific from Sydney to San Francisco in seventy days or less. In 1849-50, there were more than two hu ,dred sailings from Sydney, carrying some seven thousand Australians and New Zealanders.

News of Sam Brannan's dramatic announcement reached Sydney within four months. But Australians, in the late 1840s, were more interested in local affairs. A severe depression had reduced the price of wool and led to a spate of business bankruptcies. English migrants preferred unemployment in the towns to hard and lonely work in the bush for Wool Kings who grumbled at having to pay £20 a year, with keep, for shepherds and stockmen. Sheep-farming, compared with American pioneering, was essentially a highly-capitalized industry, the perimeter of British capitalism rather than a frontier, in Frederick Jackson Turner's sense of a democratic safety-valve for an increasingly urbanized colony.

Turner believed, although subsequent research has not borne him out, that the magnet of free land out West attracted unemployed eastern workers in times of economic depression and delayed the growth of aggressive trade unionism in the cities. In Australia, on the other hand, the early pioneers were mostly aristocratic younger sons, middle-class "drop-outs", ex-army and navy

The escaping slave. Slavery became an over-shadowing political problem

Irish convicts sometimes escaped on visiting whalers, often reaching America to live in safety

officers, displaced English and Scottish yeomen and the more enterprising among the native-born. Unemployed or malcontent workers usually did not "go bush". Australian frontiersmen were squatters with money to invest in sheep runs and a squatter needed capital for often he had to wait three years before receiving any income from his efforts.

Despite repeated challenge, the germ of Turner's frontier thesis remained true: democratic institutions in both America and Australia were not due to "imitation or simple borrowing" of European democratic ideas but to the "evolution and adaptation of organs in response to changed environment. . . ." Consequently, democracy in the United States developed into Jacksonian democracy, the democracy of small farmers and small towns, rooted in state rights rather than in federal institutions, whereas democracy in Australia originated in coastal ports and remained consistently urban and class-conscious, encouraging the early growth of radical labor unions. In 1848, democratic emphasis in Australia was directed against a renewal of convict transportation, which the squatters favored as a source of cheap labor.

In Australia, as in America, slavery provided the catalyst which clarified the turbulence of a changing society and separated backward-looking traditionalists from forward-looking democrats. As the *Sydney Morning Herald* put it on 29 November 1848: "Rights clash with rights, interests with interests, ill-feeling is everywhere engendered." From the middle of the 1840s the question of slavery grew to be the over-shadowing problem of American politics. In Australia, the question of transportation was of equal if less devastating importance. The Californian gold rush, when it came, was almost equally distant, in both countries, from the main focus of political and social agitation.

To the Jeffersonian democrats of the Virginian Dynasty that guided the United States from its revolutionary beginnings to national stability, slavery was an awkward but inescapable concomitant of independence, an institution humanized by a sense of feudal responsibility on the part of a plantation aristocracy nurtured on the tenets of the European Enlightenment. The Ancient Nobility of New South Wales had something of the same attitude towards transportation and assigned labor. With the growth of Benthamism and the new economics the emphasis changed in both countries from feudal responsibility to frank exploitation.

Southern planters stressed the economic necessity of slavery and its national utility. Australian landowners contended that they and the economy would be bankrupted unless convict or imported coolie labor continued to keep wool-growing profitable. Northeastern Whigs may well have borne with Southern slavery if Southern leaders had not developed what Vernon Louis Parrington called "an imperious desire to spread it westward to the Pacific." In Australia, an emergent urban middle-class saw an initially radical and working-class antitransportation movement as a means of challenging the political supremacy of the landed interest. In both instances, abolitionists came from similar class and humanitarian backgrounds and acted on a wide gamut of motives, from fervid emotionalism to reasoned self-interest.

Australian antitransportation agitation was sparked off in 1846 when the Secretary of State for War and the Colonies, W. E. Gladstone, partner in a Port Phillip sheep station, proposed a revival of transportation which had been suspended in 1840 in response to pressure from influential and ardent colonial reformers. The Legislative Council of New South Wales, dominated by wool-growers, was happy enough to concur. A Select Committee, under the chairmanship of William Charles Wentworth, duly reported in favor of convict labor. The proposal raised howls of protest in Sydney and Melbourne. Anti-transportation mobs, encouraged by the brilliant Sydney lawyer and politician Robert Lowe, later Viscount Sherbrooke and Chancellor of the British Exchequer, threatened to repel convict transports by force.

A new Governor, Sir Charles FitzRoy, judiciously diverted convict transports from Sydney and Melbourne, thus averting riotous Australian equivalents of the Boston Tea Party. As Robert Lowe put it: "The injustice forced upon the Americans was not half so great as that forced upon this colony. I . . . remind you that this is only the beginning of a struggle, that you must be prepared to meet any emergency, any difficulty, if you would free your necks from the yoke of the odious domination to which you have been subjected and put yourselves in the position of Englishmen and freedom." Most influential antitransportationists, on the other hand, emphasized that they wanted the colony to remain an integral part of the British Empire and deplored comparisons with the American Revolution as both unfortunate and erroneous.

In America, the Californian gold rush became a test case in the slavery question. Before Congress could establish an organized local government for the region the problem whether it was to be a "free" or "slave" state had to be decided. Senator Henry Clay, "hero of the new West . . . spokesman of the new ambitions", suggested a compromise. On the one hand, he proposed that California be admitted to the Union as a free state. On the other, he suggested the establishment of effective machinery for catching runaway slaves and returning them from California and elsewhere to their masters. Clay's Compromise did not last long. As one commentator put it, "the thin crust laid over the rupting lava was continually cracking." In the end, as everyone knows, the issue had to be decided by force.

Acting on FitzRoy's sensible estimate of local opinion, the British Government defused the situation in Australia by allowing the question to lapse despite the squatters' continued demand for cheap labor. Earl Grey, the Colonial Secretary, was not prepared to grant responsible government on colonial terms. Nevertheless, his Australian Colonies Act of 1850 established Victoria as a separate colony and opened the way for all the Australian colonies to rewrite their own constitutional futures. This diverted the debate from the colonies versus the Imperial Government to a wrangle between colonial privilege and an aspiring colonial middle-class, backed by workers who favored an Australian version of Jacksonian democracy rather than class war in the Marxian sense of the term.

With all this excitement simmering, the first news of the Californian gold discoveries made no immediate impact in Australia. Things were different early in 1849, when the *Sydney Morning Herald* published four closely-printed columns of news from "the New Gold Country." "There are no poor in California," said one item. "Once at the gold mines, the most indolent man can easily procure his ounce or two per diem, and hundreds obtain two or three times that amount. . . . The people of California now look upon this region as a bank upon which they have only to present a check, to draw what amount they wish, the acquisition is so rapid. . . ."

In January 1849, when squatter Simpson Davison rode into Sydney to arrange a shipment of wool to England, placards on the wall of the Old Imperial Barracks proclaimed: "Gold! Gold! Gold! in California!" Below this startling announcement were lists of ships advertising impending departures for San Francisco. Davison rode thoughtfully back to his station, Goodgood, near Canberra, and went carefully over the quartz veins on his run but, as he reported afterwards, "not a speck of gold was there to be found in them. . . ." Disappointed, he decided to try his luck in California where he was not very successful as a gold-seeker. However, he did reasonably well as a merchant in San Francisco before returning to Australia to back the claims of Edward Hammond Hargraves as pioneer Australian gold-digger.

Davison's initial prospect of his own property was based on more than hope of discovering the foot of an Australian rainbow. As early as 1823, Government Surveyor James McBrien had found "numerous particles of Gold in the hills convenient to the Fish River" on the western slopes of the Blue Mountains. In the mid-1830s, John Lhotsky, an impecunious Polish scientist, returned with valuable specimens from the Australian Alps. In 1839 the Polish explorer Paul Edmund de Strzlecki found gold in "the Vale of Clyyd, South Coxe's River", less than a hundred miles from Sydney. In 1841 the Reverend William Clarke, an able geologist, was equally successful in the Blue Mountains. In 1843 a shepherd named McGregor was regularly selling small quantities of gold to Sydney jewellers, "enough for his needs but never enough to excite public interest."

When the Reverend William Clarke showed his specimens to the Governor, Sir George Gipps, His Excellency grumbled, "Put your gold away, Mr.

Clarke. Put it away or we shall all have our throats cut." Neither Sir George nor the squatters saw gold as a way out of their economic troubles. There was as yet no Californian precedent to suggest that immense riches lay in Australian earth. It was public knowledge that miners had worked rich gold-bearing areas in Russia, South America and the Appalachian Mountains in the United States but the little known about these workings was not calculated to reassure conscientious officials in a remote ex-penal colony with unruly mobs of unemployed clamoring for assistance. In the Appalachians, in particular, miners were notorious as lawless individualists always in trouble with each other and the Indians. Sir George, with a colony of similar rough-and-ready individualists, feared that the news of a gold find would bring more trouble to his already burdened administration.

By 1849, with Sir Charles FitzRoy in Government House, an exodus to California was not so serious in the eyes of the Establishment as the development of an Australian gold rush. They did not see that, given the known presence of gold in the Blue Mountains, the one would soon lead to the other. Meanwhile, between January and February 1849, at least seven ships were laid on in Sydney with passages "For California Direct . . . the New Gold Country!" They included the *Eleanor Lancaster*, 480 tons, which sailed on 21 January and arrived 2 April, a passage of seventy-one days, the first Sydneyside ship to arrive in San Francisco with gold-seekers from Australia. She carried fifty-two passengers packed tightly in tiers above a cargo of liquor and merchandise. The passage cost £30 for cabin, £10 for steerage and freight was carried at £5 a ton. By the end of January, six ships had sailed, carrying a total of ninety-three passengers. Before the initial excitement ended the total had swollen to more than seven thousand.

Initially, Melbourne was less enthusiastic than Sydney. Carried on the overland mail the news from California reached the southern capital on 30 December 1848. At the Commercial Hotel a public meeting was called to arrange passages to California but the *Argus* warned workers to be "careful how they exchange health, competence and security here for a feverish dream in California. . . ." The barque *Thomas Lowry* advertised passages but there was no response and she eventually sailed for Hong Kong. The first ship direct from Melbourne to San Francisco did not leave until June although many Port Phillip gold-seekers went from Sydney, as it was cheaper to travel by packet or overland to Sydney than to sail direct to California from Melbourne.

Fares and freights from Hobart were also high but the 118-ton schooner *Eliza* sailed on 31 January and three more schooners were on their way by the time the first ship left Melbourne. Before long Lady Denison, wife of the Governor of Van Diemen's Land, where transportation of convicts continued, was writing to her mother in England, "We have now eight or ten vessels loading for San Francisco and as each will take a full cargo of emigrants, we shall lose the persons upon whose labour we depend to get in and reap the crops." Nor were all the emigrants legitimate. A group of convicts pirated the Anglican (Episcopal) Bishop's schooner and sailed for California. Adelaide, capital of the distant free colony of South Australia, received the news much later. Three ships were advertised immediately but there was no rush of passengers until the middle of 1849 and by the end of the year about 140 had sailed on three ships.

In mid-March, the *Spencer* and the *Sabine* arrived from California with more enticing news. Mr. Kingsbury, supercargo and part-owner of the 175-ton American brig *Sabine* told the *Herald* (no doubt with an eye to a profitable return trip to San Francisco) that reports from California had not been exaggerated. "One man dug up 1200 dollars in six days and three others obtained in one day 36 lbs of pure metal," he said.

Diverse characters were aroused by Mr. Kingsbury's news. "Fortune had not smiled on me so favourably during a 22 years' residence in New South Wales," wrote Edward Hammond Hargraves, who had made an unsuccessful bid at cattle-raising in Australia, "as to make me proof against the contagion; and, after a little consideration, I took my passage for San Francisco." James ("Happy Jim") Esmond, who drove a country coach between Geelong and Buninyong in the Port Phillip District, threw up his job to try his luck in California. A decent, industrious Irish-Australian, he may have heard tales, already circulating around Buninyong, that William Campbell of Strathloden had found gold in quartz at Burnsbank and that Donald Cameron of Clunes had seen specimens on his farm. Like most squatters, Campbell and Cameron had no desire to broadcast news that might start a gold rush in a district where rural labor was already sparse and expensive.

Those who took part in the exodus were not all so respectable as Davison, Hargraves and Esmond. Among the Sydneysiders who made an early departure was a notorious rogue named Thomas Belcher Kay ("Singing Billy"). Sam Whittaker, a neat young man who had arrived under hatches at fourteen for some trivial offense; a lumbering, loud-mouthed bully named John Jenkins; a tall, handsome forger, "Gentleman Jim" Stuart; George Adams ("Jack the Dandy"), a metallurgist with a flair for cutting duplicate keys; a semi-respectable couple named Michael and Mary Ann Hogan and a dozen or so more who in California rapidly became ringleaders of a notorious, loosely-organized gang known as the Sydney Ducks. Tom Kay quickly wangled himself a strategically useful job as Port Warden at San Francisco while Michael and Mary Hogan opened Port Phillip House, a clean, respectable boarding place on Sansome Street.

By this time there was no shortage of passengers for San Francisco. Charles Bateson, an Australian maritime authority who has checked all the records, estimates that 7,000 Australians and New Zealanders migrated to

JAMES STUART HUNG BY THE VIGILANCE COMMITTEE ON MARKET ST. WHARF, ON, THE 11ᵗʰ OF JULY 1851. — IMMENSE MULTITUDE PRESENT. — 500 OF THE VIGILANCE COMMITTEE ON DUTY AT THE EXECUTION. — *His confession & evidence proved him guilty of the murder of Chas. Moore, Sheriff of Yuba County, — of the murderous assault & robbery of Mr. Jansen in this city, & of the Captain of the brig Jas. Caskie in this harbor — of the robbery of the Custom house at Monterey — besides numerous other robberies & murders. No criminal was ever more daring or successful — more reckless or cold blooded. He was a Sydney convict, transported for life for forgery. His last words were "I die resigned — my sentence is just."*

VIEW TAKEN FROM THE STORESHIP BYRON.
Foot of Market St Wharf San Francisco.

Publ. & Lith. by Justh Quirot & Cᵒ Calif Corn. Montg. Sᵗˢ S. F.

James Stuart was hanged in San Francisco. Not all escaped convicts bettered their situation in America

California between 1848 and 1851. Out of 2,123 sailing from Sydney in this period only 279 were known to have been convicts, roughly 12.5 per cent. The percentage from Port Phillip would have been lower still. In Van Diemen's Land statistics were not kept but Bateson estimates that of the 763 people who left Hobart for "other places" in 1849 not more than 161 were ex-convicts. There were enough bad characters however, to earn the Australian colonies an evil reputation in San Francisco where the *Californian Courier* and Sam Brannan's *San Francisco Star* soon began to thunder against Sydney criminals who, the newspapers alleged, had brought the settlement to a crisis "where the fate of life and property are in immediate jeopardy."

The *Courier's* solution was simple and drastic: "There is no alternative now but to lay aside business and direct our whole energies as a people to seek out the abodes of these villains and execute summary vengeance upon them. . . . Where the guilt of the criminal is clear and unquestionable, the first law of nature demands that they be instantly shot, hung, or buried alive. . . . We must strike terror into their hearts. . . ." Sam Brannan, acting on the *Courier's* and his own initiative, was soon chairman of a San Francisco Citizens' Committee which checked the credentials of every passenger on every ship that berthed from Sydney, Melbourne or Hobart. Brannan's impromptu Vigilante Committee was soon rounding up "Hounds" and "Regulators", who frequented Little Chile, a shanty town of thieves and harlots on the slopes of Telegraph Hill, and handing them over to the Alcade, or local justice, for trial.

When Sydney Ducks took the place of Hounds and Regulators as the most flagrant of San Francisco's trouble-makers, Sam Brannan organized a regularly-constituted Committee of Vigilance to rid the town of undesirables. One of the Committee's first acts was to hang ex-convict John Jenkins for alleged theft. David C. Broderick, leader of the Democratic Party and president of the recently-constituted California Senate, tried to stop the execution but was shouted down. Policemen who struggled to rescue the Committee's prisoner were hustled aside. Jenkins was strung up in the central plaza and men fought to tug on the free end of the rope when Brannan yelled, "Every lover of liberty and good order lay hold."

In Sydney, when news of Jenkin's hanging became known, democrat Henry Parkes wrote furiously in his newly established *Empire*: "The bloody thirsty mob cannot fling calumnies against Australia when guilty of such acts as this. . . . When the infuriated citizens of San Francisco strangled the thief whom they had caught in the streets, they hanged liberty which they seemed to think they could preserve. . . ." What Henry Parkes did not know was that politics and crime were already so intermingled in San Francisco that the properly-constituted courts, with elected judges, frequently discharged notorious criminals. Even when jailed, the convicted usually found it easy enough to escape. The Vigilance Committee, on the other hand, endeavored to give accused Ducks a fair trial and a quick sentence, a return passage home more often than a hempen noose.

"Gentleman Jim" Stuart was next to go; a handsome plausible rogue, transported to New South Wales at sixteen for forgery, already notorious on the diggings as a man quicker with a knife than a gun. When the goldfields became too hot for him he rode into San Francisco with two Ducks intent on robbing ships in harbor while the crews were carousing ashore.

Gentleman Jim was unlucky. The Vigilance Committee arrested him in mistake for somebody else. His true identity soon emerged. The Committee promised to hand him over for legal trial (a virtual acquittal with his known connections) if he would name his accomplices. This he did in a full confession, naming twenty-six, including Sam Whittaker. Breaking the agreement to hand Stuart over to the sheriff, the Committee hanged him at the Market Street wharf, using a loading derrick as a gallows.

Whittaker, an ex-convict of twenty-nine, tried to make a break for it with his mistress Mary Hogan. Mary took passage on the *Cameo* for Sydney, hoping to smuggle her lover aboard. The Vigilantes escorted her from the ship and held her as decoy. She did nothing to help and was soon released. By arrangement, Whittaker met her at San Diego but luck was against him. At Santa Barbara, Sheriff V. W. Hearne recognized Whittaker as a wanted man and arrested him. Hearne took his prisoner to San Francisco aboard the steamer *Ohio*, intending to hand him over to the police, but a Vigilante posse met the *Ohio* at the wharf and took charge of Whittaker, handing Hearne the cost of the trip from Santa Barbara.

In his confession, Whittaker admitted that the Ducks bribed policemen and assisted in soliciting the Australian and non-American vote to elect Americans to local office. By this time, San Francisco had a mayor, a treasurer, a city marshal, a state attorney, a commissioner of streets, nine aldermen, a superior court judge, a sheriff and five deputies, thirteen police officers, and twenty-two policemen, nearly all elected in true democratic fashion. Whittaker and his associate, Bob Mackenzie, were rescued from the hands of the Vigilantes and placed under the protection of the Governor and the Mayor, but in a well-planned raid on the jail the Vigilantes kidnapped them and hanged them seventeen minutes later before an estimated crowd of fifteen thousand.

Politically-minded Californians were not prejudiced against all ex-convicts from Australia. When Terence Bellew MacManus, one of seven Irish rebels of '48 transported to Van Diemen's Land for treason, arrived in San Francisco on 5 June 1851, Southern Democrat bigwigs, mindful of the Irish vote, arranged a demonstration of welcome. Breaking parole, MacManus had taken advantage of gold-rush confusion and boarded a ship for California. Instead of lynching him, Sam Brannan joined with Senator David C. Broderick and Mayor John Geary in organizing a lavish dinner and presented an engraved silver pitcher to the sea captain who had brought the escapee safely across the Pacific.

Three more of the Irish "exiles"—Thomas Francis Meagher, Patrick O'Donohue and John Mitchel—broke parole and escaped to America. Meagher, a hard-drinking swashbuckler who called himself "the O'Meagher", wrote to the police informing them he intended to escape and would consider himself absolved from his word of honor if they failed to catch him. He then rode within musket-shot of the nearest police station and shouted, "I am O'Meagher. Catch me if you can." The police, who reputedly favored the Irish, failed to apprehend him. Meagher became an American citizen, married an American girl and fought for the North in the Civil War as a Brigadier-General in command of the Irish Brigade. After the war President Andrew Johnson appointed him Governor of Montana Territory.

O'Donohue, after various adventures, reached Tahiti where the captain of an American barque, the *Otranto*, agreed to take him to San Francisco for a down payment of £1,000. From California he made his way to Boston where he was arrested for challenging the chairman of a festival held in honor of Meagher, with whom he disagreed. Mitchel reached Sydney disguised as a priest and was smuggled aboard an American vessel bound for San Francisco, where the Governor of California, with the Irish vote in mind, attended a banquet in his honor. Unlike Meagher, Mitchel joined the South and two of his sons were killed fighting for the Confederacy.

With the Sydney Ducks effectively disbanded the Vigilance Committee of California ceased operations. Some of its members no doubt by now agreed with counsel in a current court case against a member of the Committee, who had sent an armed posse to collect what he erroneously believed to be stolen goods in the house of an Australian who kept a respectable public house. During the trial, counsel for the defense denounced the Vigilantes as a greater threat to law, order and civil government than all the Sydney rascals put together. The original committeemen may have had good intentions at a difficult time, he said, but hell was paved with good intentions and the Committee had brought San Francisco to a hellish state and made the name of California a scandal to the civilized world.

In all, the Vigilantes cross-examined ninety-one suspected criminals, hanged four, whipped one, forcibly deported fourteen, ordered fourteen others to leave town, handed fifteen over to the legal authorities and discharged forty-one. In each instance, the Committee constituted itself a court, took careful notes of evidence and brought down decisions by majority vote. It called this procedure "democratic justice". According to Henry Parkes's *Empire* many respectable Australians, who had left the colony for California "untainted with any tendency towards democracy" were members of San Francisco's Committee of Vigilance. They were now returning, together with American gold-seekers, to take part in the Australian gold rush which, despite all official attempts to stem it, had now set in and soon grew to Californian proportions.

"Let no door be opened to receive blood-stained wretches," thundered Henry Parkes in the *Empire*, for Parkes, as a good Chartist Englishman, disassociated himself from American precedents for Australian social and political developments. Dr. Lang, on the other hand, still preached freedom and democracy for Australia on American lines. The *Sydney Morning Herald* and other newspapers, meanwhile, had reported Californian "mob law" in gruesome detail, strengthening already existing Australian suspicion of American democracy which Harriet Martineau, Frances Trollope and even Charles Dickens found too crude and familiar for English middle-class taste. Nevertheless, a flood of returning "Californians", as Australians who had joined the American rush called themselves, soon changed the pace and direction of Australian development.

On 7 January 1851, Edward Hammond Hargraves and James ("Happy Jim") Esmond arrived back in Sydney aboard the barque *Emma*. Neither had done particularly well in California but both had learned the basic business of "placer" or alluvial mining. In California, Hargraves had teamed up with the squatter, Simpson Davison. They had earned reasonable "wages" but never made a big strike. During the long winter evenings in the Sierras they spoke often of the possibilities of a gold strike in Australia. Both men were impressed with the similarity between the Sierra foothills and the parts of Australia with which they were familiar. Unlike Hargraves and Davison, "Happy Jim" Esmond did not write his reminiscences but he must have thought the same way. Meanwhile, in Sydney, Sir Charles FitzRoy and his Colonial Secretary, Deas Thomson, were staving off local enthusiasts who reported minor discoveries in the Blue Mountains and elsewhere.

Hargraves arrived back, as he wrote later, intent "on making that discovery which has so long occupied my thoughts." Esmond, the ex-coachdriver from Port Phillip, kept his thoughts to himself. However, like Hargraves, he lost no time prospecting an area in the Buninyong district that looked to him remarkably like California. Although, as we have seen, geologists and prospectors had discovered gold in Australia well before Hargraves and Esmond returned, these two were responsible for the finds that triggered off gold rushes which soon turned eastern Australia, especially Victoria, into an El Dorado richer than California and a magnet for gold-seekers from all parts of the world. Hargraves, who had a flair for publicity, was first to break the colonial Establishment's taboo on gold discoveries but Esmond discovered the richest and most lasting goldfield.

*Wells Fargo gold shipment out of Deadwood.
In Australia, police troopers took the role of
these Wells Fargo guards*

Without waiting to go home to Brisbane Waters where his wife and family lived on an income from rented cottages, Hargraves persuaded a Sydney alderman to provide the grubstake for a prospecting trip beyond the Blue Mountains. Esmond took a job on a Victorian station and bided his time. Hargraves was first in the field. With Johnnie Lister, twenty-three-year-old son of a former acquaintance, he decided to pan the sands on Lewis Ponds Creek not far from Yorkie's Corner, where an old shepherd had earlier reported gold. On 12 February 1851, Hargraves found colors in all but five pans. The net result was enough gold dust to cover a threepenny bit. This, as things turned out, was all the gold Hargraves discovered in Australia. It was sufficient, so sure was his sense of publicity, to secure him £10,000 and more in rewards, a well-paid job as a Gold Commissioner, an audience with Queen Victoria and a disputed place in history as the discoverer of gold in Australia.

"This," he shouted when Johnnie Lister came to see what he had found, "is a memorable day in the history of New South Wales. I shall be a baronet, you shall be knighted, and my old horse will be stuffed, put in a glass case, and sent to the British Museum."

Hargraves's jubilation did not last long. Search as he might no more gold showed in Lewis Ponds Creek sands. After a fortnight's fruitless search he decided to return to Sydney to report his find fearful least "some miner from California" should beat him to the post with a similar discovery. Before leaving, he showed Johnnie Lister and Johnnie's friend, William Tom, how to make a California cradle for gold washing. "We'll be partners," he said. "If nothing comes of it perhaps we can all try our luck in California."

Back in Sydney, Hargraves waited three hours to see Deas Thomson, the Colonial Secretary. The great man was not impressed. "Mr. Hargraves waited on me with only a few grains of gold," Thomson said later. "They were almost the minutest quantity that could be conceived; so minute that I could hardly see them without putting on my spectacles." Yet the times were more auspicious than even Hargraves could have conceived. Economic and political troubles crowded the Establishment. In the few weeks since Hargraves had arrived home more than a thousand eager gold-seekers had left the colony for California. The separation of Victoria from New South Wales threatened to leave the home state with no more than a rump of the golden fleece. Thomas Sutcliffe Mort, a leading wool merchant, was already in cahoots with ex-Californian Enoch Rudder planning to offset the exodus to California with talk of gold in Australia. The immediate problem was to keep Australian labor, and gold brought back from California, where it could do most good—in Australia.

Hargraves tried again. This time he called on the Governor, Sir Charles FitzRoy, who blandly waved him back to Deas Thomson. Thomson told Hargraves to put his proposition in writing. Before he did so Hargraves persuaded his old Californian friend Rudder to write a letter for publication in the *Sydney Morning Herald* announcing that "a gentleman recently returned from California" had discovered gold west of the Blue Mountains. Hargraves's letter outlining his belief that a rich auriferous region existed in the Lewis Ponds Creek area reached Deas Thomson the morning Rudder's letter appeared in the *Sydney Morning Herald*. Impressed, Sir Charles instructed Deas Thomson to send Hargraves an encouraging reply. Reluctantly, Thomson delayed doing so. The delay saved Hargraves from humiliation and guaranteed him his place in history.

Before Thomson's letter requesting further evidence was delivered, Hargraves had heard from his partners, Lister and Tom: the young men had used their California cradle at Yorkie's Corner at the junction of Lewis Ponds and Summer Hill Creeks and washed out gold dust worth more than twenty dollars and a nugget weighing two ounces. When Tom's father, a Methodist local preacher, pointed to the first book of Kings, Chapter 22, Verse 48: "Hiram brought gold from Ophir", they called the place "Ophir".

Hargraves lost no time. He reported the discovery of Ophir to Deas Thomson and to the unenthusiastic editor of the *Sydney Morning Herald*. On 5 May 1851, the *Herald* announced halfway down a column devoted to "Domestic Intelligence" under a single-column heading: "Gold Discovery". The details were meagre but gave full credit to Hargraves "a resident of Brisbane Water, who returned from California a few months since." Hargraves went straight to Ophir and "called the attention of many people along the road to the discovery." He arrived on 6 May and found his publicity campaign unwelcome. Lister and Tom wanted to keep the discovery secret so that they could benefit from what they rightly believed to be a rich location. Hargraves, on the other hand, wanted as much publicity as he could obtain. Californian experience had taught him that gold-digging was a gamble entailing a good deal of hard work. He preferred a rich government reward and a gold-braided job as Gold Commissioner. He obtained both.

There is no space here to detail the complicated maneuvers that followed. The upshot was that Hargraves obtained £10,000 reward from the New South Wales Government, £5,000 (not all paid) from Victoria, and a salary of twenty shillings a day plus forage as a Gold Commissioner. After much argument, Johnnie Lister and William Tom received £1,000 each. "They merely laboured under my instructions," Hargarves claimed loftily. James Tom, Williams brother, pursued a vendetta against Hargraves for the next forty years and provoked two official inquiries. The first found in favor of Hargraves. The second accorded Johnnie Lister and William Tom the honor they deserved: discoverers of the first payable goldfield in Australia. Meanwhile, Hargraves's publicity had sparked off the first Australian gold rush. Sydney went through all the tribulations of early San Francisco before "Happy

Jim" Esmond discovered gold at Clunes and diverted the tide from Sydney and Ophir to Melbourne and Ballarat.

Gold from the Turon, which proved a more lucrative field than the original Summer Hill Creek, reached Sydney just before the first influx of eager gold-seekers arrived by sea from Melbourne. News of the Blue Mountains discoveries had thrown Port Phillip into turmoil. Legal formalities were under way for the new state of Victoria, which was proclaimed on 1 July 1851. People were not slow in suggesting that the new state would linger as a backward pastoral annex to a vigorous and expanding gold-rich neighbor. The rush from Melbourne threatened the small Port Phillip settlement with depopulation. Hundreds crowded the regular packet steamer and commandeered every available berth on small coasting craft. In an attempt to stem the exodus, leading citizens set up a Gold Discovery Committee which offered a reward of two hundred guineas for the first authentic report of a workable goldfield in Victoria. This is what "Happy Jim" Esmond had been waiting for. He finished his job erecting a building on Hodgkinson's station in the Pyrenees not far from Melbourne and formed a prospecting party with three fellow-workers, Pugh, Burns and Kelly, to make a systematic search, Californian style.

On 1 July, Esmond struck a promising patch of alluvial at Deep Creek on the northern side of a hill opposite Donald Cameron's station at Clunes. With a rich packet of specimens, including gold-streaked quartz, Esmond's party headed for Geelong to announce the discovery. At Geelong, Esmond went to Alfred Clarke, editor of the *Geelong Advertiser*, with his story. William Patterson, a local jeweller, tested the samples in Clarke's presence. Convinced, the newspaperman wrote an excited story headed "Gold in the Pyrenees". The announcement began:

> The long-sought treasure is at length found! Victoria is a gold country and from Geelong goes forth the glad tidings of the discovery. . . . We have been backward in publishing rumours of mineralogical discoveries; but satisfied now with the indubitable testimony before us, we announce that the existence of a gold field in the Pyrenees is a Great Fact fraught with the greatest importance and a preface to a glorious run of prosperity to Victoria and the Western District in particular.

Alfred Clarke did not exaggerate. Clunes, scene of the first Victorian rush, was never a rich field but it was the key that unlocked the richest alluvial goldfield in the world. Thanks to gold, California's population grew from 93,000 to 380,000 in ten years. The estimated population of Victoria in 1851 was 97,489. By 1861, it had grown to 541,800. The rush to be rich which marked San Francisco's growth from hamlet to city was even more marked in Melbourne. Melbourne expanded from a village of less than 5,000 in the

1840s to a town of 40,000—larger than San Francisco—by the early 1850s. The influx to the goldfields was even greater and exceeded the rush to California.

William Kelly, an English gold-digger experienced in both Australia and California, wrote in his reminiscences that he regarded the growth of San Francisco as "a miracle—the event of a lifetime—not to be again equalled in an age." That was before he saw Melbourne. "I lived to see this northern queen city (San Francisco) eclipsed by the superior radiance of a southern metropolis . . . Melbourne, young as she is, is withoud dought, the over-topping wonder of the world." Henry Kingsley, the English novelist, called Melbourne "a great city, which, in its amazing rapidity of growth, utterly surpasses all human experience. . . . I never watched the slow downfull of a great commercial city; but I have seen what to him who thinks aright is an equally grand subject of contemplation—the rapid rise of one."

With California and New South Wales in mind, Victoria's Lieutenant-Governor, Charles Joseph La Trobe, signed a Proclamation on 15 August 1851, asserting the Crown's primary right to the new treasure trove and threatening prosecution of any digger found working without first procuring the necessary license. Three days later, the *Government Gazette* published detailed regulations setting out the conditions under which the government would grant approved persons licenses to dig for gold. The primary condition was that they were not "improperly absent from hired service." La Trobe's attempt to contain the rush proved abortive but the license system remained and provided a constant irritant which led in the end to Australia's one "little rebellion"—the Eureka Stockade—three years later.

The new El Dorado, constantly expanded by new finds, attracted all sorts of men from all sorts of places. Some packed Bibles in their swags and felt a twinge of conscience if they picked up nuggets on a Sunday. Others, hardened criminals from Van Diemen's Land or back from California, were prepared to cut capers with the devil provided there was a prospect of easy money. Most were reasonably law-abiding, normally respectable citizens, chasing a pot of gold at the foot of their own particular rainbow.

One thing the gold-diggers had in common: a democratic spirit that saw money as the great equalizer. The goldfields in Australia, like the goldfields in California, proved to be no place for "us" and the "others". Almost to a man, gold-seekers were Lang's men rather than Wentworth's; anticonvict, anti-squatter and pro-freedom and independence. The gold rushes ended forever the squatter's dream of a resumed Virginia-like existence with convict serfs as labor. In London, the *Times* crystallized the absurdity of sending convicts to Australia:

Lord Grey evidently thinks that crime is in danger of becoming extinct and devises premiums for its encouragement. A little larceny is a dangerous thing. Dive deep into your neighbour's pocket, if you wish to visit El Dorado. Small crimes are henceforth to be punished, large ones to be rewarded . . . Be it known to all murderers, highwaymen, burglars and receivers of stolen goods, that New South Wales, the land of Ophir, the treasure-house of the earth, is the precise spot selected by the British Government . . . for the transportation of convicted felons. It is in gold chains that they are to expiate their offences.

FitzRoy, La Trobe, Wentworth and the squatters assumed that some men are by nature more suited to riches than others. They might have been right, as later examples of conspicuous consumption indicated. Nevertheless, there were soon 30,000 diggers on the Turon and at Ballarat and Bendigo to say them nay. In Sydney, in the year of the first payable gold discoveries, Earl Grey's new constitution, with a lowered franchise, gave more colonists than ever before a chance to register protest against their betters. In the 1851 elections, Dr. Lang, who had been at the bottom of the Port Phillip poll in 1843, headed the Sydney poll with William Charles Wentworth, the squatter's champion, at the bottom and John Lamb, an antisquatter Sydney businessman, in between. In a jubilant address from the hustings, Lang declared that if more than a thousand Scotchmen had not migrated to the goldfields Wentworth would have been rejected altogether.

7 *Dramatic Interludes*

The British barque *Black Squall*, which reached San Francisco from Hobart on 5 August 1851, after an eighty-four-day run, brought the first news of the Australian goldfields to California. This was nearly a month before Sir Charles FitzRoy's despatch to Earl Grey reached London with reports of Hargrave's discovery. Two days after *Black Squall's* arrival the *Johnstone* from Sydney confirmed the report, adding exciting details. Nine days later, when the *Edgar* arrived with the wives and children of successful Australian diggers who had decided to stay in California, two American ships, the *Dorset* and the *Walter Claxton*, had already sailed for Sydney with the first contingent of Californians and two more were loading for the voyage.

The *Alta California* played down the news from Australia. The editor suggested that most of those who had gone or planned to go were returning to where they had come from. He commented that many good citizens had come to California from Australia and he hoped that only the bad ones would go back. This was less than two months after the hanging of John Jenkins and a fortnight before the hanging of Whittaker and MacKenzie. The *Alta California* did not refer to the Committee of Vigilance but forecast that, with the development of goldfields in Australia, the Pacific Ocean was destined to be the great area of democracy in the future.

By the end of 1851, Californians were arriving in Sydney and Melbourne by the hundred. About nine per cent of the first 100,000 gold-seekers to reach Victoria were from the United States but there is no means of knowing how many were American-born. All were labeled Californians and were suspect because Australian concepts of "Yankee democracy" were as misconceived as American concepts of Australian crime. In California, Americans had tended to regard all Australians as ex-convicts. In Victoria, Australians regarded Americans as pistol-toting advocates of lynch law and mobocracy.

Newly-arrived Americans found the colonies in social and political turmoil. "There is a spirit abroad which must be carefully watched and promptly brought under control if this Colony is not to parallel California in crime and disorder," La Trobe wrote to Earl Grey at the end of 1851. In the beginning, serious crime was uncommon on the goldfields. "Men go to work leaving a bit of calico between thousands of pounds in their boxes and a robber, that is, if there is a robber," declared Lawrence Potts, who had worked with Hargraves and Davison in California and became one of the leaders against the universally condemned license-tax. "We are living in better order here than they are in Melbourne with all their blue coats, pistols and carbines included."

La Trobe's concern and Melbourne's lack of law and order were easy to understand. Melbourne was not only the gate of entry to the goldfields but the resort of hundreds of ex-convicts who had flooded across Bass Strait from Van Diemen's Land in search of easy money. The police, never a particularly fine body of men, had almost all resigned and gone to the goldfields. Desperate attempts to replace them brought into the force a riffraff of ex-convicts who saw better pickings as servants of the law than as its proclaimed enemies. Their officers were mostly young dandies conspicuously lacking not only the common touch but commonsense. The combination was destined to spark off an explosive situation when La Trobe and his successor, Sir Charles Hotham, tried to enforce universal collection of the license-tax from unlucky as well as lucky diggers.

By the time the first Americans reached Mount Alexander, where most of the Victorian diggers were now concentrated, Lawrence Pott's optimism was no longer valid. Bushrangers (Australian for "road agents") and other desperadoes were now thick on the goldfields and along all the tracks leading to and from the diggings. Australians quickly learned the practice of Yankee justice although they called it "the rights of Englishmen" and although actual lynchings were few, tar and feathers and "a ride out of town on a rail" became commonplace. Californians were alleged to be ringleaders in what the Gold Commissioner at Bendigo called "inciting the people to set up Judge Lynch." Actually, those who made the most display were usually returned Californians. In contrast real Americans, according to C. Rudston Read, an ex-British naval officer turned Gold Commissioner, were mostly hard-working and law-abiding.

Welcome or unwelcome—and most were welcome—Americans certainly fulfilled the forecast of James H. Williams, the American Consul in Sydney, when he assured Daniel Webster "our countrymen will eagerly seize upon this new field of profitable adventure." To encourage growing American business with Australia the State Department in mid-1852 appointed J. A. Henriques, a leading Melbourne merchant, as United States Consul in Victoria. Henriques, a member of an Anglo-American firm, was soon replaced by James A. Tarleton, who arrived from the United States by the *Golden Age* in February 1854. Business was by then extremely brisk. As early as November 1850, Dr. Lang reported seeing twenty American vessels in Newcastle harbor loading coal for San Francisco. Australian coal was more popular than Australian lumber. After the Great Fire devastated San Francisco in June 1851, speculators rushed Australian timber to California for rebuilding purposes. American carpenters found it unworkable compared with Oregon pine; the nails buckled when they tried to hammer them home. Consequently, the Bay was soon awash with unsalable timber, skippers preferring to dump it overboard rather than carry it back to Australia. In 1853, an American took the seeds of fourteen species of eucalypt back to California. Before the century was out there were well-established eucalyptus plantations in California, Arizona, New Mexico and Florida and Americans were as familiar with gum trees at Australians.

Whatever they might have thought about American diggers, governments in New South Wales and Victoria did everything possible to encourage trade. American ships were given equal rights with British ships in Australian ports and preferential duties were abolished in both gold states. The stimulus brought to Australia in earlier years by American traders and whalers was now repeated, especially in Melbourne, where import figures rose from £60,363 in 1852 to more than £1,660,000 in 1853. Although trading was less active afterwards, it continued stable, with American companies well established in both Melbourne and Sydney. Australians showed particular appreciation for American stoves, sewing machines, hickory-handled axes, canned vegetables, India-rubber clothing, prefabricated houses, Oregon lumber, "New York buggy-wagons" and New England ice, the import of which had slumped until renewed by American demand.

Early in 1853, an American who called himself "Professor" Sands erected a big tent just off Market Square in Melbourne and announced that he practiced "the art of hair-cutting and shaving on scientific principles." He set up four American shaving chairs and a row of spotlessly clean basins with hot and cold water for shampooing the luxuriant hair and beards of diggers come to town with money to spend. Shelves against the canvas walls displayed a wide range of American toilet products and "Yankee fixings" of various sorts. The Professor was a slight man, approaching to tallness, with a thin face and a restless eye. He seldom handled the scissors himself being satisfied as he told William Kelly, English writer and amateur gold-digger, "doin' the talkin' and tradin'. . . ."

There was no lack of customers. "Melbourne streets presented some curious scenes and strange social phenomena," reported George Wathen, a much-traveled Englishman who wrote a book about his Australian adventures. "After the first successful campaign on the goldfields and under the flush and excitement of sudden and easily acquired wealth, the diggers returned to Melbourne to 'knock down' their money. . . . On arriving, they would often place their gold or its produce in cash, in the hands of the publican in whose

Yankee Bigger. —

The Yankee digger was distinctive

*News from home. American visitors to the
Australian goldfields read home news*

house they put up, and they drank and revelled for days in a sty of sensual delight. . . ." A rash of marriage-brokers, shooting-galleries, bowling alleys, billiard saloons, livery stables, barbers' shops and hotels sprang up to meet the demand. "I have heard boastings at the diggings as to the shortness of time in which to 'knock' down a thousand or two pounds," wrote C. Rudston Read.

Later and less fortunate diggers, who could not afford such wild sprees, were more concerned in resisting what they considered unfair taxation under license fees which extracted the same amount from the unfortunate as from the fortunate. Diggers met in mass meetings and protested vigorously against payment for the right to work and demanded a tax on wealth not on labor. *"Union in strength"*, declared one poster stuck on gum trees throughout the diggings. "Ye are Britons! Will you submit to oppression or injustice? Meet—agitate—be unanimous—and if there is justice in the land, they will, they *must* abolish the imposition." There were appeals to French revolutionary precedent, tributes to American democracy, declarations of republicanism and one or two tents flew red flags. These manifestations were the extremes. Most diggers, although they attended mass meetings and voted against "taxation without representation", were decent, law-abiding men, anxious only to secure their rights. More and more diggers poured in from all parts of the world and fewer and fewer were faced with difficulty in finding the quickest way to disperse "a thousand or two pounds"—if they ever had that much to spend.

"Folks are coming in from the States in a reg'lar torrent," the Professor told Kelly one day. "Mighty tall strings—merchants from New York as well as diggers from California. The Californians don't like the legal ideas here, nowhow. The shuttin'-up at eleven of nights and at rantin' time on Sunday, goes against the grain considerable. One top sawyer who came slick down here to wake up us in the mixin' of gin-slings, cock-tails and brandy-smashers, got a warnin' for keepin' a man from spittin' with dry rot after 12 o'clock of a Saturday night, though he said he never shut his bar durin' his hull three years time in 'Frisco."

Professor Sands was referring to Samuel Moss, an American who ran Melbourne's plushest American rendezvous, the *Criterion Hotel* in Collins Street. The long bar and marble counters, grand mirrors, imposing decanters, spittoons, and "rows of undeniable down-easters" who dispensed the drinks, were a revelation to home-keeping Australians. Even those who knew or remembered England, thought that red plush furniture, gilt-emblazoned wall mirrors, decolleté ladies and bartenders in snow-white shirts were among the privileges of the upper classes. At the *Criterion* they were available to anyone with money to spend, an American example Australians were quick to follow.

The most notable of Professor Sands' "mighty tall strings" to arrive in Melbourne during 1853 was George Francis Train, a future independent candidate for the presidency of the United States, then a brash young man of twenty-four with a fortune to make. Train belonged to the famous Boston family which founded the Train shipping line to South America and the Baltic. He began his commercial career as shipping clerk to his uncle, Enoch Train, the New England merchant who launched the fast packet and clipper ships, built by Donald McKay of Newburyport, which revolutionized maritime history. George Train, according to his own story, was responsible for ordering MacKay's celebrated clipper *Flying Cloud*, which in 1853 made the trip from New York to San Francisco in eighty-nine days, nearly as quickly as a fast ship could travel from Sydney to California.

Enoch Train sent his nephew to Melbourne with Captain Caldwell, one of the firm's oldest ship captains, to found a subsidiary company to be known as Caldwell, Train & Company. New England manufacturers in those days were highly diversified and Boston the center of an important export trade to California, Australia and South Africa. Caldwell, Train & Company handled what Samuel Eliot Morison, in his *Maritime History of Massachusetts* (Boston, 1941) calls "the entire apparatus of civilized life, from cradles and teething-rings to coffins and tombstones . . . Ploughs and printing-presses, picks and shovels, absinthe and rum, house-frames and grindstones, clocks and diction-aries, melodeons and cabinet organs, fancy biscuits and canned salmon, oysters and lobsters. . . ." There was plenty of competition from England, whose shipping companies bought American and Canadian clippers for the Australian trade.

In Melbourne, George Train wasted no time in demonstrating his belief in Jacksonian democracy—the democracy which asserted the right of every man to make money how, when and where he could. Soon Caldwell, Train & Company was one of the liveliest and most profitable businesses in Victoria. At Port Melbourne, Train set up a store, prefabricated in Boston, for storing his imports of shovels, axes, hoes, canned goods, flour, kerosene and buggies. In town, on Flinders Street, he erected what he claimed to be the biggest structure in the colony—a huge office and store hung with iron shutters brought from England. On some lines the firm made as much as 200 percent profit and Train was soon making a hundred thousand dollars a year. To lay the dust in front of his establishment, he encouraged the importation of "a real old Boston watercart" whose driver skipped the shops of proprietors who refused to pay for the comfort of their customers.

"You will be surprised to see how fast this place is becoming *American-ized*," Train wrote home. "Go where you will from Sandridge to Bendigo, from the Ovens to Ballarat, you can but see some indication of the indomitable energy of our people . . . The true American defies competition and laughs sneeringly at impossibilities. He don't believe in the word . . . Melbourne, though situated so far out of the way, cannot fail to be a great city. All we require is a little energy and a good deal of money to make the wheel turn rapidly. The 'old chums' will not budge from office and take as little pride about putting things in shape as we should in fencing Timbuctoo. We must introduce a sprinkling of Yankeeism here and show the residents the meaning of despatch."

Train's "Yankeeism" included a fire company, with two Boston-made engines, a commercial exchange at Moss's *Criterion Hotel*, the regular use of iced drinks and an Australian beginning to what was destined to become the great American bereavement industry. When a Philadelphian died in Melbourne, Train reported: "A printed notice was sent to all the friends, gloves and long crape badges were provided for all present, and in an adjoining room a table was profusely spread with cakes and wine! The hearse was decorated with white plumes, illustrative of youth, and the church service was chill as the atmosphere and *no ladies* attended the funeral." One enterprising Yankee skipper, looking for a quick-selling return cargo, stacked coffins full of potatoes. "I'll land the potatoes safely and make an almighty dollar or two on the coffins," he explained.

George Train was full of Yankee notions for public as well as private benefit. The costly and inefficient lightering system at Port Melbourne aroused his ire. He suggested a pier with a telegraph to the Heads and a railway to the city proper. Having prodded local enterprise to go ahead with the railway he prompted Americans to contract to build a pier and encouraged Samuel McGowan, a pupil of Samuel Morse, to push ahead with a project to provide a telegraphic linkage between Melbourne and Williamstown, near the Heads.

Samuel Morse had introduced the electric telegraph into the United States in 1844 and McGowan had worked with a number of American telegraph companies before migrating to Australia early in 1853. He intended to form a private company to link Melbourne with the goldfields and with Sydney and Adelaide. The Victorian State Government preferred a publicly-owned service and called tenders for the construction of an experimental line between Melbourne and Williamstown. McGowan's tender was successful and in March 1852 the first telegraph line south of the equator began operation. The Victorian Government appointed McGowan Superintendent of an Electric Telegraph Department and by 1857 Melbourne was linked by telegraph to all main country centers and interstate to Sydney and Adelaide. McGowan remained head of the service until he died in 1887.

Train's greatest service to Australia was the promotion of Cobb & Co. coaches. Freeman Cobb arrived from Boston in July 1853, with some high-slung, leather-sprung, Concord coaches admirably adapted for Australian conditions where passengers wanted to travel long distances at high speed over rough roads. Train claimed that he loaned Cobb the money to start Cobb & Co., a company which dominated outback Australian road travel for the next fifty years. Cobb & Co. began business in January 1854, and continued to

Cobb and Co. was still going strong in Australia in the 1880s

run coaches in outback Australia until 1924. The original operators were all young Americans who had learned the business working with one or other of the two leading American express or carrying companies, Wells Fargo and the Adams Express Company.

Several American companies established branches in Melbourne and Sydney, including Hussey, Bond and Flak, provision general merchants of San Francisco. Americans conducted two of Ballarat's biggest shops and itinerant peddlars with Yankee notions regularly toured the goldfields, as did American auctioneers, American music hall artists and one or two American troublemakers, including an ex-Texas Ranger calling himself "Captain" Brown, who had a genius for public agitation and private profit. William Kelly, the friend of Professor Sands, included Brown among the Americans who had "served volunteering apprenticeships in Texas, Mexico and Central America, not from ordinary incentives of military honour and glory, but from the more material considerations of pillage and plunder. . . ." According to Kelly, a biased observer, these ex-mercenaries formed the backbone of the famous Californian Revolver Brigade at the Eureka Stockade confrontation in December 1854.

"Captain" Brown set up as antigovernment agitator and got himself elected to the Bendigo AntiGold License Committee. He soon became notorious for standover tactics in raising Committee funds from goldfields' storekeepers. On the complaint of a Bendigo storekeeper, who alleged that Brown had threatened to burn him out unless he handed over a substantial sum of money, the camp authorities arrested the Irish-American. When Brown boasted to the authorities that the diggers would storm the camp to rescue their most popular leader—Brown himself—the magistrate ordered his removal under guard to Melbourne where he passed out of Australian history forever.

In Melbourne, the *Criterion*'s many attractions included "a pretty ornate little vaudeville theatre, capable of containing an audience of 500." Here, manager Sam Moss presented such expensive items as Lola Montez and "Rainer's Celebrated Troop of Ethiopian Entertainers". The music halls attached to rival hotels had to content themselves with the ballads and songs of such popular British entertainers as Charles R. Thatcher, "the Colonial Minstrel", and his imitators. A popular skit, not admitted to the *Criterion*, was entitled "The Flash American Bar Man" and took a rise out of such Irish-Americans as Captain Brown.

"The Flash American Bar Man" was usually presented as a red-shirted Californian brandishing a pistol and singing the praises of democracy and lynch-law, accompanied with threats to put a bullet through the brain of anyone who crossed him. As the performer reached a burlesque crescendo his American clothes dropped away to disclose a close-cropped Irishman in knee-breeches waving a shillelah and cursing the Queen in a rich bog-trotter brogue. The cheers which usually greeted this buffoonery suggested that many Australian diggers shared the Establishment's view that Americans and Irish together were responsible for what the Reverend Mr. Mereweather, one of Melbourne's Episcopalian clergymen, called "the French Revolution without the guillotine": a subversion of all respect for religion, talent and education and the replacement of an aristocracy of worth with an aristocracy of muscle.

On 10 August 1852, William Peters, British Consul in Philadelphia, wrote a confidential despatch to the Foreign Secretary in London quoting American newspaper reports that the American exodus to the Australian goldfields favored the growth of republicanism in Australia. The reports said that ardent republicans had formed an Order of the Lone Star for the purpose of "extending the area of Freedom . . . Liberty and Republicanism" throughout the world. Sir John Pakington, who had succeeded Earl Grey at the Colonial Office, sent copies of Mr. Peters's report to Governors FitzRoy and La Trobe for information and comment.

FitzRoy sensibly and truly replied that the American Press exaggerated the extent of republican feeling in New South Wales. He suggested that this was because they took Dr. John Dunmore Lang more seriously than circumstances warranted. In the Governor's opinion, Dr. Lang's views, widely reported in the British Press, did not reflect either respectable or popular feeling. The "lower classes" were too prosperous to take an active interest in politics. The politically-conscious, on the other hand, were likely to treat offers of American aid towards the establishment of a republic with the contempt they had shown towards Dr. Lang's Australian League founded for that purpose. FitzRoy's assurance that the colonial public showed little interest in Lang's republicanism was borne out by the fact that his book on the subject sold only two hundred copies.

La Trobe was equally skeptical about the immediate impact of American sentiments. For the present the influx of Americans was too small to create an immediate republican threat to monarchial principles. However, he added, "if I write with hesitation as to the future, it is because I see in advance much that may loosen the bonds of attachment to the parent state." He felt there was more to fear from the activities of the colonial Press than from American influence.

American Press interest in Dr. Lang's views and the articles that aroused British Consul Peters's suspicions in Philadelphia, owed more to the rise of the Know-Nothing Party in America than to any real interest in the political state of the Australian colonies. The Party based its appeal on virulent feeling against the unprecedented influx of foreign and Catholic immigrants during the 1840s and 1850s.

In 1852, when Mr. Peters wrote his warning to the British Government, the Know-Nothing Party was front-page news in America. It owed its name to one of its many publications, *The Mystery*, which proclaimed that it was "published nowhere, sold everywhere" and was edited "by Nobody and Know-Nothing." In the aftermath of Jacksonian democracy, the Know-Nothings provided a refuge for white Middle West and Northern democrats and xenophobes suspicious of the Whig party's unabashed materialism and averse to the Southern Democrats' capture of Jacksonian slogans. The Know-Nothings considered themselves to stand for traditional American values and their nativism not only sparked off a flurry of antiCatholic and anti-immigrant riots but encouraged the formation of gimcrack fraternal organizations with grandiloquent titles and phoney rituals—the Order of United Americans, the Order of the Star-Spangled Banner and Mr. Peters's Order of the Lone Star.

Dr. Lang reveled in all such buffoonery but as Australia's first citizens had been English convicts and Irish rebels, not Puritan dissenters, he looked to Scottish immigrants and British gold-seekers, not the native-born, for national revival and an Australian Declaration of Independence. "You are the Apostle of the Independence of Australia, and this will be the foundation of your future fame," the gold-diggers of Sofala on the Turon Goldfields declared in a Complimentary Address to the fiery clergyman in October 1851.

At Sofala, early in 1853, miners drilled, burned effigies of William Charles Wentworth and pledged themselves to resist by force the New South Wales Goldfields Management Act which legalized a monthly license of thirty shillings for Australian diggers and sixty shillings for Americans and other aliens. FitzRoy sent troops to the Turon to maintain discipline but turned a blind eye to the local Gold Commissioner's no more than token attempts to enforce the law. The Commissioner had no difficulty in dispersing the crowd of 15,000 demonstrators by promising that the Act's provisions would be reviewed.

The issue between Lang, the Jacksonian democrat, and Wentworth, the British Whig, came to a head not on the Turon goldfields or at the Eureka Stockade but in the Legislative Councils of New South Wales and Victoria when elected members debated the draft constitutions authorized by Earl Grey's Constitution Act of 1852. Responsible government in Australia, when it came, was based on British constitutional precedents and owed little or nothing to American prompting or example. Australians, native-born and immigrant alike, opted for the British parliamentary and legal systems plus membership of the British Empire and the subsequent British Commonwealth of Nations—except that federation, an American-type federation, eventually became essential. Nevertheless, the debates in colonial legislatures drew on American arguments, both on the right and the left, to support what both Lang and Wentworth claimed to be British principles.

In June 1853, the Legislative Council of New South Wales appointed a Select Committee under the chairmanship of William Charles Wentworth to draw up a new constitution under the terms laid down in the Australian Colonies Government Act of 1852. "Mr. Wentworth's imbecile and nose-led committee," as Henry Parkes's *Empire* described it, prepared a Report and a Draft Constitution which, among other things, proposed a hereditary Upper House and a Colonial General Assembly to make laws in relation to inter-colonial questions. Sydney businessmen, who might have been expected to welcome intercolonial control over tariffs, coastal shipping and similar matters, were too furious with Wentworth's proposals for the establishment of a "bunyip aristocracy" in a nominated Upper House to pay proper attention to more practical questions. In any case, it was clear from Wentworth's own defense of the Report and Draft Constitution that the Committee's proposed Intercolonial Assembly bore no relation to federal union as it existed in the United States.

Defending his views when the Legislative Council considered the Draft Constitution, Wentworth drew on Washington, De Tocqueville and John C. Calhoun, whose *Disquisition on Government* had appeared in 1850, to attack the theory of majority rule and equal suffrage and to support the introduction of a colonial titled order into the constitution of the State. He brought all his big guns to bear on the "mere democracy" of the United States and declaimed eloquently against the corruption, demoralization and grasping at spoils he alleged to be characteristic of Jacksonian democracy. He declared that the American Constitution contained the germs of despotism, particularly presi-dential despotism, far more threatening to individual liberties than the monarchial system he approved. He carried his attack on American institutions to the point of opposing federation of the Australian colonies if this were to be achieved, as Dr. Lang proposed, on the American model.

"The opinions of the people of this colony and of this house are not in favour of American institutions," Wentworth declared and went on to warn the British Government not to take Lang's pro-American sentiments seriously. "He describes them (the people of Australia) as demanding a great federation of all the colonies of Australia, of New South Wales, Victoria, Tasmania and South Australia; each state to have a separate local government. (Shouts of laughter.) Absurd as is this notable scheme, treated as it would be by the utter derision of the people, the writer has had the audacity to describe it as peremptorially demanded by the colonists; the penalty of their being refused it being, their cutting the painter (derisive laughter)."

The Reverend John West, Congregationalist leader of the Australasian Anti-Transportation League and editor of the *Sydney Morning Herald*, reflected contemporary colonial opinion more accurately than either backward-looking Wentworth or forward-looking John Dunmore Lang. As against Lang and the republicans, he considered the glamor and good example provided by Queen Victoria and her Consort worth all the cost and prerogatives of royalty. On the other hand, he agreed that manhood suffrage was not only inevitable but desirable and that in Australia any attempt to found qualification for office on property must eventually break down. He did not doubt that "reputable and intelligent citizens" were sufficient in number to keep the public domain from falling to "low adventurers". As might be expected he added, the prevailing spirit of the colonies was democratic but it was the democracy of the middle classes not the mob.

As things turned out, the Australian colonies did not have to accept Wentworth's hereditary principle for their Upper House nor did they have to fight for their independence. When the various Draft Constitutions reached London, Cabinet handed them to the Law Officers of the Crown, who approved, with minor amendments, and the remark that they amounted to "little less than a legislative Declaration of Independence" and a step towards "what we are all looking forward to—the eventual parting company on good terms." In fact, although the new constitutions conferred responsibility on colonial legislatures, and made much colonial rhetoric sound empty and strained, they did not provide democratic government. Nominated Upper Houses gave the propertied classes firm control over Lower Houses elected on a greatly extended franchise which soon, at different times and in different ways, fulfilled John West's forecast that manhood suffrage was inevitable in a potentially egalitarian society like that of Australia. The political struggle henceforth was not between England and Australian colonies but between factions within the colonies themselves and these most often ended in compromise rather than naked confrontation.

On 23 June 1854, Sir Charles Hotham reached Melbourne, charged with straightening out Victoria's chaotic finances and disciplining democratical diggers who increasingly resisted paying the hated license-tax. The spare, tight-lipped sailor, who would have preferred command of a battleship to the governorship of a colony, was surprised at his enthusiastic reception. Southern colonists were tired of La Trobe's rather schoolmasterish morality and expected better things of a man who for thirty of his thirty-six years in the navy had been a fighting sailor rather than a diplomat. As it happened, diplomacy was not Sir Charles's forte. "New Chum Charlie", as the diggers called him, was soon launched on a disciplinary course that ended in fiasco and bloodshed.

The new regime began well. The mayor and corporation welcomed the Governor amidst salvoes of artillery salutes, and Melbournians packed the streets to greet Sir Charles as he stood on a decorated platform under a triumphal arch which read: "Victoria Welcomes Victoria's Choice." He replied with a few well-chosen banalities. "Mine will be a government of an honest heart and of a head that will turn neither to the right nor the left, and will regard no object but its duty," he said, conscious that his duty was to collect the license-tax and balance the budget. A naval aide, who noted the contrast between the unawed, easy-going colonial crowd and the stiff naval martinet sent to govern them, murmured an aside, "If he tries to ride these people like he rode us there'll be a shindy."

The shindy did not take long to develop. "I am told that contracts are concluded in the loosest manner and at the most extravagant rates," he reported to the Colonial Office on 22 July, after combing through the colonial accounts with an honest sailor's eye, "nor are matters on the Goldfields much better. Out of a population of 77,122 male adults only 43,789 pay the licence fee, whilst a frightful staff exists on paper for the collection." He had already put the Chief Gold Commissioner, William Henry Wright, on the Vice-Regal mat. "The irregularity which exists in the collection of the licence fee must be rectified," he insisted. "The men responsible for the deficiencies must be dismissed. . . ." With a wry smile, Chief Commissioner Wright suggested that the Governor should go to the goldfields and see for himself.

In August, Sir Charles toured the goldfields to see digger democracy at first hand. The diggers made the mistake of putting on a good show for him. They listened to his speeches without cat-calls or interruption. They played Sir Walter Raleigh to Lady Hotham, lifting her over mud-holes and clearing a path wherever she and Sir Charles ventured. They took the Vice-Regal couple to the best holes and showed them the biggest nuggets. Nobody made it clear that the good old days of rich strikes and buckets of champagne were over. Most miners were working hard for wages and less. The era of quartz mining had begun. Deep shafts, hard crushing and cooperative or company operation were becoming the order of the day. Basically, diggers objected to paying a fee for the right to work. They argued that the tax should be on the results of effort not on effort itself, which often went unrewarded. Sir Charles, however, heard over again the stories of the early alluvial bonanzas and how old so-and-so used to light cigars with five-pound notes.

"I gave them to understand that they must pay for liberty and order," Hotham reported to London on his return to Melbourne. To enable them to do it he ordered twice-weekly "digger hunts" to enforce payment of license fees. Chief Gold Commissioner Wright and Captain McMahon, Acting Chief of Police, warned the Governor that he was courting trouble. New Chum Charlie contended that the mass of the diggers were loyal and would not object to paying just dues for good government. He did not realize that the diggers had no confidence in Gold Commissioners drawn from among the unemployed gentry and ruffian policemen already known as "pigs".

Over the next few months the goldfields were the scene of raids, riots, charges and countercharges. Hotham, confident that the new constitution would offer the miners a legitimate forum for their complaints, had little patience with what he considered irresponsible democratic agitators and miners anxious to shuffle out of paying what he considered the trifling sum of £1 a month license fee. Government officials, including the Chief Commissioner of Goldfields, the Chief Commissioner of Police and the Chief Commissioner at Ballarat, Robert Rede, all advised the Governor against precipitate action in view of the agitated state of the diggers. After much dilly-dallying, Hotham decided to appoint a Royal Commission to determine the best method of raising revenue on the goldfields. This was on 17 November, too late to allay unrest among the diggers. At the same time he sent troops to Ballarat to maintain order. Meanwhile, the diggers had organized a Reform League.

On 27 November, Hotham agreed to receive John Basson Humffray, a Welsh Chartist who had helped organize the Ballarat Reform League, and two other delegates who carried a petition demanding the release of three diggers accused of complicity in a riot. The police had also charged an American named Carey but following representation from the American Consul, James M. Tarleton, Hotham had ordered his release. However, the Governor reacted angrily to the word "demand" in the diggers' petition and reminded the delegates that he and everyone else in the colony was subject to the rule of law. "You are absolutely taking the law into your own hands," he insisted. "You are setting aside the most important principle of the British Constitution." At this point, Humffray reminded His Excellency that, in perfect consistency with his office, he might, by act of grace, release the diggers as he had already released the American Carey.

"The Americans adopted a truly constitutional course in a case where they thought themselves aggrieved," Hotham retorted. "They signed a petition and presented it in due form through their consul. Have the Ballarat diggers taken the same constitutional course? No—I must take my stand on the word 'demand'. I am sorry for it but you leave me no alternative. . . . You know that a Commission has been appointed to inquire into the state of the gold-fields. When the Commission sits it will be for you to come forward and state fairly and frankly what you require. Tell the diggers from me and tell them carefully, that this Commission will inquire into everything and everybody—high and low, rich and poor. You have only to come forward and state your grievances and, in whatever relates to me, they shall be redressed. I can say no more than that."

Next day, 28 November, when Humffray and his two companions were posting back with the Governor's message, the Americans on Ballarat gave a gala dinner to welcome their Consul, James M. Tarleton to the diggings. Mr. Otway, a leading American among the six hundred on the field, was in

H F COX DEL.

LITH. OF WM. ENDICOTT & Cº. N. YORK.

POST OFFICE, SAN FRANCISCO, CALIFORNIA.

A FAITHFUL REPRESENTATION OF THE CROWDS DAILY APPLYING AT THAT OFFICE FOR LETTERS AND NEWSPAPERS.

ON STONE BY S.T. GILL

PRINTED BY PENMAN & GALBRAITH

VIEWS IN ADELAIDE Nº 1.

HINDLEY STREET
FROM KING WILLIAM ST.

Published by Penman & Galbraith Adelaide

the chair and Mr. Tarleton sat under the crossed flags of America's Stars and Stripes and Britain's Union Jack beside Mr. Resident Commissioner Robert Rede, Police Magistrate Henry Hackett and other leading citizens. The room buzzed with mutual assurances of Anglo-American cooperation in much the same vein as had become commonplace at the Fourth of July dinners which were by then a regular feature of Melbourne's social life. Approximately thirty-five per cent of the estimated eight or nine thousand Americans in the colonies were businessmen. They often indulged in "spread-eagleism" and talk of manifest destiny but, according to L. G. Churchward, an Australian authority on Americans in Australia, "by this they meant the expansion of American commerce and not the extension of American republicanism."

At the Ballarat dinner on 28 November, Mr. Otway had just risen to propose the first toast—the loyal toast—when a dusty police trooper arrived with an urgent whispered message for Mr. Commissioner Rede. Mr. Rede, who sat across from Mr. Tarleton on Mr. Otway's right, passed on the news: diggers had attacked the column of troops Sir Charles Hotham had sent to reinforce the goldfields' police. A drummer boy had been shot and an American driver, under contract to the government, badly mauled. Mr. Rede and Mr. Hackett left at once, followed by several other guests. Mr. Otway brought the excited gathering to an attentive hush. "Gentlemen," he said, "our British guests have been unexpectedly called away, I must demonstrate the loyalty of my fellow countrymen to the lawful ruler of their chosen country . . . Gentlemen, the Queen, God bless her!"

In the awkward pause that followed Sam Irwin, Ballarat correspondent of the pro-digger *Geelong Advertiser*, stood up. "Fellow-diggers," he said, "while I and my fellow-colonists claim to be and are loyal to our sovereign lady the Queen, God bless her, we do not, and will not, pay our respects to her menservants, her maidservants, her oxen, or her asses." In the burst of cheering that greeted this sally, Irwin slipped away to find out what the trouble was along the Geelong Road. There was trouble enough. A mob of diggers had waited among rocks at the entrance to Eureka Gully not far from Bakery Hill. When the main column had passed, they charged the wagon train under cover of a ragged volley that wounded several soldiers and a drummer boy. Overturning wagons and manhandling drivers, the diggers searched for the cannon rumor said the military intended to use to intimidate miners. There were no cannon.

Captain H. C. Wise, in command of the reinforcements, sensibly kept the main column moving until he reached the shelter of the Government Camp. When Commissioner Rede arrived he sent the captain with a troop of mounted police to restore order. The police soon broke up the crowd found looting the overturned wagons and brought the drummer boy and Young, the injured American, back to camp.

Next day, Wednesday, 29 November, diggers held a mass meeting on Bakery Hill, under the chairmanship of Timothy Hayes, to hear the report of Humffray and his fellow Ballarat Reform League delegates who had arrived back after their interview with Hotham in Melbourne. That morning the crowd were for Humffray and a voice called for three hearty cheers for New Chum Charlie. When these had died down a young Irish engineer named Peter Lalor stepped forward to move "that a meeting of members of the Reform League be called for Sunday next, at two o'clock, to elect a central committee. . . . into the way some officials abuse their powers."

Things were set for constitutionalism and commonsense when Frederick Vern, an excitable German, rushed forward and delivered a passionate and largely incoherent speech which ended, "That this meeting being convinced that the obnoxious licence fee is an unjustifiable tax on free labour, pledges itself to abolish the same by at once burning all their licences. . . ." Despite efforts by the Catholic priest, Father Downing, and other moderates, diggers yelled approval when Vern gave the lead by burning his license although by this time many had drifted away, unwilling to commit themselves to the hot-headed action demanded. In the Government Camp when news of the license-burning reached Mr. Commissioner Rede, he decided that the time had come to make examples of men who defied the law. December licenses were due next day, 30 November. Mr. Rede decided to send out police to collect them.

Throughout the diggings the warning cry "Joe! Joe! Joe!" swept from claim to claim as marching foot police and mounted troopers began their hopeless task. Before long, pistols cracked among the mullock heaps and showers of stones and clods of earth thudded among the police. Mr. Rede decided to call in the military. A marching column of redcoats moved towards the diggings where Mr. Rede read the Riot Act, calling upon the diggers to disperse and return to their lawful avocations. When nobody paid heed Rede authorized the soldiers to fire a warning volley over the heads of the crowding diggers. As the men began to disperse, police darted forward and made several arrests.

"I was working in a shaft at the Eureka, 140 feet deep," Lalor said afterwards. "Mr. Hayes was at the windlass and the diggers were employed as usual. Suddenly the news spread that the diggers were being fired on at the Gravel Pits. 'To arms!' was the cry and all that could muster arms moved forwards in great confusion towards the Gravel Pits. When we reached Barker and Hunts store on Specimen Hill we saw that the military had taken up a position behind some logs on Bakery Hill. We did not interfere with them. The 'Southern Cross' was procured and hoisted on the flagstaff belonging to Barker and Hunt; but it was immediately hauled down and we moved to the holes on the Gravel Pits Flat. . . . As soon as we commenced moving towards the holes, the bugles of the military sounded a retreat, and the detachment withdrew to the Camp."

Humffray, Hayes and other leaders of the Ballarat Reform League saw that all hope of moderate measures was over. They withdrew from the armed hotheads.

Without opposition from Vern, who boasted his military experience, the self-appointed delegates who marched to Bakery Hill appointed Peter Lalor their commander. Less than a thousand men remained by this time. Solemnly they filed past Lalor, who stood rifle in hand under the Southern Cross flag, and intoned, "We swear by the Southern Cross to stand truly by each other and to fight to defend our rights and liberties!" The stage was now set for the tragedy that followed. Vern and a few volunteers began to drag stones and logs to form a barricade. According to W. B. Withers, first official historian of Eureka, the Americans on Bakery Hill that night drew up a Victorian "Declaration of Independence" in company with James McGill, who had formed a Californian Revolver Brigade, Frederick Vern, Raffaello Carboni and other militants. Carboni denied that he had any hand in such a Declaration and McGill, when challenged later by Carboni, denied that there had ever been such a document.

James McGill, a mysterious individual who may or may not have been a member of the Order of the Lone Star, was an Irish-American who claimed to have attended a military academy in the United States. According to his wife, in a letter written long after the events reported, McGill was sent to Australia to carry out "serious duties". She was never clear who sent him or what these duties were except that they were supposed to include protecting the American Consul. An unreliable chronicler, George Francis Train asserted that McGill's purpose was to set up a Republic of Victoria on the lines of Sam Houston's Republic of Texas or Fremont's Bear Flag Californian Republic. If this were true his Independent Californian Rangers at Ballarat were not over anxious to become involved with Peter Lalor and those who took the oath under the Southern Cross.

"Thus far the Americans had not taken an active part in the affair," wrote American Charles Ferguson in his account of Eureka, "but the time had now come when we were compelled to act or stand neutral. Others . . . began to accuse us of cowardice. Therefore, a meeting of Americans was called and held at the Adelphi theatre, to determine as to the duties and obligations of the occasion. Many were enthusiastic and desired to enlist in the Digger Army. As for myself, I could not see the necessity or the propriety of rushing into a revolt against government authority until we considered what it was going to amount to. . . . We regarded ourselves as foreigners, and had no right to be foremost in an open attack against the government. This meeting caused much hard feeling against the Americans, the diggers contending that it was everybody's affair. . . . We told them that if they went on they would have our sympathy, and if they made a stand they would not find us wanting. . . ."

According to Ferguson, a sly-grog operator and theatrical entrepreneur rather than a digger, Lalor interviewed the Americans and asked if they would "hold themselves in readiness, for he had no doubt when the time came and we were wanted, we would respond with alacrity." McGill then formed his California Rangers with "the distinct understanding that we were independent of the others, and not the least under their control." Word came that the military were expecting cannon from Melbourne. McGill thereupon took three hundred of the best armed men on Saturday, 2 December, left the Eureka Stockade to intercept the convoy from Melbourne. During Saturday, many of Lalor's followers left the Stockade, either to requisition food, powder and shot from Ballarat storekeepers or to carouse in the township with admiring or doubtful diggers who had no intention of themselves becoming involved.

Other accounts of McGill's departure from the Stockade differs from Ferguson's. About four o'clock in the afternoon an American doctor named Charles J. Kenworthy arrived on Bakery Hill with a letter from Humffray addressed "To the Commander-in-Chief of the Armed Diggers, Eureka." The letter described Kenworthy as an American volunteer anxious to offer his humanitarian services to the diggers. It seems more likely that he was a go-between for the American Consul and that he urged McGill to withdraw his Rangers and not become involved. Soon after Kenworthy and McGill talked, McGill led two-thirds of his Rangers out of the Stockade. They marched north not east, from which direction the cannon were expected. Explaining this later, McGill contended that he was told there was a cannon the diggers could use on a station property near Creswick. Whichever story is correct there was only a handful of Americans in the Stockade when Captain Wise, of the Fortieth Foot, led his small force of redcoats and police up Bakery Hill at 4.00 A.M. on Sunday, 3 December 1854.

"They came down on us just as the light of day was breaking," wrote Ferguson. "We were formed in line and the first order received was 'California Rangers to the front!' The Fortieth regiment was advancing but had not as yet discharged a shot. We could see plainly the officer and hear his orders, when one of our men, Captain Burnette, stepped a little in front, elevated his rifle, took aim and fired. The officer fell. Captain Wise was his name. This was the first shot fired in the Ballarat war. It was said by many that the soldiers fired the first shot but that is not true. . . . No sooner did that officer fall than the soldiers were ordered to fire on us, which they did, and then charged. The fire had a terrible effect but we returned it with like effect, as deadly as theirs."

All was soon over. Sergeant Harris took command of the 182 redcoats when Captain Wise fell mortally wounded. The mounted police, ninety-four

*Eureka Stockade, the largest of Australia's little
rebellions*

in number, crashed through the flimsy barricades on the right and left flanks while the soldiers stormed over them in a frontal attack. Lalor went down in the first volley with a broken arm. Diggers—Ferguson says he and an American named Hall were among them—dragged the rebel leader clear of the Stockade and hid him behind piled slabs on the Eureka Lead. A few soldiers and twenty-two diggers were killed and twelve diggers wounded. Among the dead and wounded diggers, twenty were from Ireland, four from England or Scotland, two from Germany, two from Canada, one from New South Wales and the origins of five were unknown. Two Americans, Charles Ferguson and John Josephs, a negro, were among fourteen rebels charged with treason. No jury could be found to convict them and they were all released except Henry Seekamp, vitriolic editor of the *Ballarat Times*, who served three months' imprisonment.

George Train claimed that McGill, whom he called the "head of the insurrection" escaped from Ballarat disguised as a woman. Several days later he appeared at Train's Melbourne office demanding all the Colt revolvers held in stock. "We have elected you President of our Republic," McGill is supposed to have said. "Damn your republic," Train reports himself replying. "I am not here to encourage revolutions but to carry on my business." Nevertheless, Train smuggled McGill aboard one of the American ships in harbor, where he posed as a ship's officer. Hotham, always reluctant to proceed against Americans, agreed not to prosecute McGill if he agreed to leave the colony. According to Carboni, who was among those discharged from custody, McGill was back in Ballarat a year later, when he dismissed the supposed "Declaration of Independence" as "a gratuitous falsehood" which must have originated from overindulgence in "Toorak small beer."

In May 1855, the Melbourne *Age*, which had gathered up the *Argus*'s mantle of radicalism, essayed a trial balloon in favor of "a flag of our own." When there was no favorable response the *Age* backed down, declaring that its republicanism involved no disloyalty to Her Majesty the Queen. Always ready to oblige, Dr. John Dunmore Lang drafted a "Declaration of Independence" on behalf of the "Sovereign People of Victoria" but there were no takers. Most of the 20,000 diggers on the Ballarat field appeared to agree with Hotham and Humffray that the men at Eureka died for something they already had. The new constitution had opened the way for responsible government and the promised Royal Commission, which reported in March 1855, recommended the substitution of a gold export duty in place of a monthly license-tax. In place of the monthly license, diggers were required to take out a Miners' Right, on payment of £1 a year. This gave them legal possession of the claims and the right to vote.

At the first Legislative Council elections after Eureka, Lalor and Humffray were unopposed for Ballarat. Lalor, who lost an arm, kept under cover until the excitement had died down and was never prosecuted. He lived to become Speaker of the Legislative Assembly under the new constitution while Humffray eventually became Minister for Mines. In Victoria, as in New South Wales, the stage was set for liberal bourgeois government on the British rather than on the American model. "If we are to have a revolution," grumbled the editor of the *Argus*, Edward Wilson, during the antilicense agitation, "let it be an English revolution." When, at an early imbroglio in Bendigo, the American flag was hoisted above the Union Jack, Wilson commented, "They may rest assured that if any flag is to be hoisted in Bendigo in preference to the British, it should not be the American; they would have a flag of their own."

8 *The Gilded Age*

A little before sunset on Wednesday, 25 January 1865, the Confederate cruiser *Shenandoah*, a fully rigged steam sloop of 1,200 tons register, flying at the gaff the Confederate ensign, dropped anchor a short distance from Melbourne's Sandridge Pier. Her captain, James I. Waddell, a Carolina-born ex-lieutenant of the United States Navy, was short of coal and stores and his steam-driven lifting screw had suffered damage. He was also short-handed and had a number of Yankee prisoners, including two women. In his first communication to the Governor, Sir Charles Darling, he reported that he wanted to rid his ship of prisoners. He did not mention that he needed to recruit volunteers for his undermanned raider for he must have known that this was forbidden in Britain or British colonies where, nevertheless, the Southern cause was popular.

When Yankee-immigrant Samuel McGovern's electric telegraph clicked the news from Williamstown to Melbourne that *Shenandoah* was on the way into Hobson's Bay hundreds of eager sight-seers streamed along the shoreline. The exploits of the Confederate raiders *Alabama*, sunk outside Cherbourg the previous year, and *Shenandoah*, which inherited *Alabama*'s glamor, were well known in the colonies, for Melbourne and Sydney newspapers reported Civil War battles and exploits in full. In Australia, as in England, respectable opinion favored the South although the working classes and radicals tended to champion Lincoln and the antislavery North. In Melbourne, the *Argus* was enthusiastic for the South, the *Age* cheered on the North and the *Herald* tiptoed the neutral line which represented official British policy.

First Lieutenant John Gimball posted straight out to Government House, Toorak, with a letter from Captain Waddell seeking permission to coal his ship, take aboard stores, dispose of prisoners and put *Shenandoah* on slips for repairs. The *Argus* learned that the Confederate vessel carried eleven prisoners, Captain Nicholls, master of a sunken Yankee ship, his wife, and a stewardess, besides eight men who had declined to serve a Confederate ship as many captured Yankee sailors did. Captain Waddell solved the prisoner problem

146

quickly. He reported next day that the men had "escaped" by rowing quietly ashore and that the ladies had crossed to the *Jeanne Payne*, an American ship lying in the bay where, as the *Argus* reporter wrote, ". . . it is said that their fervently expressed wishes were not for the welfare of their captors."

Next day the Governor, Sir Charles Darling, summoned a full Cabinet meeting for eleven o'clock to consider Captain Waddell's requests. "There was a full attendance," the *Argus* reported, "and so anxious were the Government to preserve the neutrality of the port that, though instructions received from England are explicit and full, more than two hours were spent in deliberation before a decision was arrived at. . . . The regulations name forty-eight hours as the limit of a [belligerent] vessel's stay but this term can be extended to allow her to repair bona fide damages. The Ministers, therefore, felt at liberty to accede to Captain Waddell's request but they required him to report the repairs his ship needed, that their own officers might judge the time that ought to be allowed him. Captain Waddell was noted, also, that he could not be permitted to leave port within twenty-four hours of the departure of any American vessel."

The people of Melbourne took *Shenandoah* and her officers and crew to their hearts. The exclusive Melbourne Club entertained Captain Waddell and his officers; crowds enthusiastically greeted the Confederate uniform whenever it appeared in the streets; there were picnics and outings for officers and men alike. During the first weekend, 28 and 29 January, *Shenandoah*, reported the *Argus*, was "besieged with boats containing visitors anxious to gratify their curiosity by a personal inspection." Special trains took passengers from Melbourne to Sandridge, and craft of all kinds, from steamers to rowing boats, took excursionists from Sandridge to the *Shenandoah's* anchorage. During the weekend more than seven thousand booked for Sandridge at Melbourne railway station and, again according to the *Argus*, "the visitors showed their Southern sympathies by cheering the vessel heartily as they took their departure from her."

Meanwhile, the United States Consul, William Blanchard, had not been idle. He called on the Victorian Attorney-General, George Higinbotham, whose grandfather had been American Consul in Dublin, protesting against the *Shenandoah's* presence. He had been instructed that the vessel was not a belligerent but a pirate. Captain Waddell had bought the ship *Sea King* in England, fitted her with guns, painted out her old name and rechristened her *Shenandoah*. As *Sea King* or *Shenandoah* she had never been in a Confederate or an American port and had no claim to be a properly constituted ship of war. Victoria should therefore prove its neutrality by arresting the *Shenandoah* as a pirate. Mr. Blanchard was particularly incensed at colonial newspapers likening Captain Waddell's deeds to those of Drake and Raleigh on the Spanish Main. He pointed out that far from attempting to break the Northern blockade and risk battle with U.S. ships of war, Captain Waddell confined his attentions to unarmed merchantmen and whalers.

In the Victorian Legislative Assembly on 31 January, Graham Berry, proprietor of the suburban *Collingwood Observer* and an opposition member of parliament, agreed with Mr. Blanchard. "There was a general feeling in the public mind," he contended, "that the Government should declare what course they would take and what they would do." For his part, he maintained that as the *Shenandoah* had sailed originally from an English port, she ought, under the Queen's proclamation, to be confiscated. "The question was important," he asserted, "as it might ultimately affect the relations of the Mother Country with a friendly nation, against whom this piratical vessel conducted its enterprises." By this, Berry meant that the South's desire was to embroil Britain in war with the North. Britain, for her part, had passed no opinion on the legality of the Confederate Government but recognized its right as a beligerent to enter and leave European ports.

From the discussion that followed Mr. Berry's intervention it was clear that the Victorian Government wished to keep out of America's Civil War. The Consul now came forward with evidence that Captain Waddell had been recruiting crew in Melbourne, contraray to the Foreign Enlistments' Act. The information came from Walter J. Madden, who had deserted the *Shenandoah* and sought sanctuary at the United States Consulate. Madden said that a man named Charley and others were aboard the *Shenandoah* that afternoon. Mr. Blanchard hastened to Mr. Higinbotham, the Attorney-General, who reluctantly agreed to have a warrant sworn by a magistrate authorizing the police to search the vessel. Armed with a search warrant Police Superintendent Lyttleton and two constables, plus Walter J. Madden, went down to the *Shenandoah*, now on the slips under repair.

First Lieutenant John Gimball received them on the dock. Captain Waddell was ashore and he suggested that Lyttleton and his men came back later, when the Captain was aboard to receive them. Next day, when the Superintendent and his men arrived, Captain Waddell was waiting. As commander of a ship-of-war he refused to recognize the legitimacy of the Superintendent's warrant. The police party would board his ship at their peril. If reinforcements were brought up he was prepared to "fight his ship". This was not because he had anything to hide but in defense of his right, as a belligerent, to resist foreign interference with his legitimate rights. To gild the bitter pill he added, on his Southern honor, "We have no one aboard who should not be there." Apparently satisfied, Lyttleton and his men withdrew. After dark the same day, an over-alert patrolman arrested Charley and three other Melbourne men leaving the *Shenandoah* for a night on the town. Captain Waddell explained that the men were stowaways and that he had put them ashore as such. Nevertheless, the authorities charged four men under the Foreign Enlistments' Act.

Faced with irrefutable evidence from the four men arrested leaving *Shenandoah*, the Government prevented Captain Waddell from launching his ship from the slips when repairs were complete. A large party of police surrounded the dock to see that no Australian helped in the process of launching. Captain Waddell, in letters to the Governor, claimed that the authorities, by denying him dock labor, had "seized" his ship. He indicated darkly that under such circumstances a warship was entitled to fight its way out. The inference was that, given sufficient provocation, he was prepared to use his four smooth-bore 68-pounders and two rifled 32-pounders to shoot-up Melbourne. In a leading article, on 16 February, the *Argus* begged him to "distinguish between the actions of the government in this case and the sentiments of the community at large." Two hundred of the community at large had met the previous night in the *Criterion* hotel to discuss the crisis.

After a good deal of wild talk, which showed an almost complete lack of knowledge about the real issues between North and South, the *Criterion* meeting came to the by no means unanimous decision "that the course adopted by the Government in seizing the *Shenandoah* was ill-devised and likely to be subversive of our friendly relations with neighbouring neutral states." Meanwhile, wilder spirits among pro-Northern Americans in Melbourne were prepared to treat the *Shenandoah* as a belligerent if Captain Waddell insisted on his right to resist a civil search warrant: they concocted a plot to blow the *Shenandoah* out of the water. Thus, the police cordon which prevented Australian labor helping move Captain Waddell's ship also balked American gunpowder-plotters from blowing up the vessel.

Finally, without again testing Captain Waddell's Southern honor, the authorities assumed there were no more British subjects illegally aboard *Shenandoah* and allowed the captain dock labor to clear his ship. On 17 February, *Shenandoah* was ready. Unassuaged by the *Argus*'s assurances that he had not abused the hospitality of the port, Captain Waddell intimated that the treatment he had received had not only been an insult to him personally but to his Government, to which he intended to make a full report. Only too anxious to rid themselves of his presence the Government shut its collective ears to reports that at least seventy Melbourne men were waiting at Williamstown to join *Shenandoah* as Confederate recruits.

Not so Mr. Blanchard, the United States Consul. He hurried to the Crown Solicitor, Mr. H. F. Gurner, and demanded that the port authorities seize and search *Shenandoah*. Mr. Gurner was about to leave his office, anxious to get home to dinner. He received Mr. Blanchard coolly and told him it was not Crown Law business. He advised the Consul to see a magistrate if he insisted on another search warrant. Desperate, Mr. Blanchard went to the Attorney-General, Mr. Higinbotham, who was evasive. He advised the Consul to approach Police Magistrate E. P. S. Sturt. Mr. Sturt recommended Mr. Blanchard to approach the Water Police, to see if they would help. He issued no warrant to authorize the police. Mr. Blanchard gave up and went home to write an angry despatch to Washington, a despatch which, in due course, achieved effective results. Mr. Gurner's dinner, Mr. Higinbotham's evasion and Mr. Sturt's advice eventually cost the British Government £807,375 ($US3,875,000)!

Writing from London on 22 November, to a friend in Melbourne, a member of the *Shenandoah*'s crew described the exploits Charley and his friends had missed. On leaving Melbourne, Captain Waddell made his way to the North Pacific where he wrought havoc among the Massachusetts whalers operating the fisheries there. He sank thirty-seven vessels in all and was said to be responsible for the price of whale oil rising from $140 to $240 a ton on the world market. According to the *Australian News*, which published the crewman's letter, Captain Waddell by that time "had reason to believe that the war was over and that he had no longer a commission from any existing Government." According to the sailor correspondent, however, the *Shenandoah* did not learn "the sad news of our defeat" until 2 August, off San Francisco, when she gave chase, by mistake, to the British barque *Barracouta*. "The next day the crew were all disarmed, and the guns struck below, and we made the best of our way to England."

This, however, was not the last Melbourne heard of *Shenandoah*. Prompted, no doubt, by Mr. Blanchard's despatches, the United States Government made a claim against Great Britain for damages to the extent of $US19,077,798, of which sum $US6,303,039 was on account of *Shenandoah*. The British Government agreed to submit the claims to arbitration. The five arbitrators, who sat at Geneva in 1872, were Lord Chief Justice Cockburn, Great Britain; Charles Francis Adams, the United States of America; Viscount d'Itajuba, an Italian diplomatist; Count Schlopis, a Brazilian; and Jacques Staempfli, a Swiss. The tribunal decided, by three votes to two, that Great Britain was responsible for the negligence of Victoria, a British colony, in allowing *Shenandoah* to put to sea, and should be called upon to pay compensation for the belligerent acts Captain Waddell committed after leaving Melbourne.

Like America, Australia had a gilded age—the rush to be rich, Australian historian Georffrey Serle called it—the period after the gold rush and Civil War when dreams of that better country, whose riches are more durable than silver and gold, sought by Pilgrim Fathers and colonial radicals alike, were swamped by more immediate and more practical considerations. For the ordinary man, these were, of necessity, how to feed and clothe and bring up his family; for the energetic and ambitious, how to achieve wealth and social approval; for the ruthless few, to attain unbridled power over man and nature. The old, easy, spacious days were gone for ever. Economic pressures and managerial responsibilities, plus the urge to get rich, put up barbed wire fences between man and man, group and group, as well as between property and property.

The spreading pastoral kingdoms out west, beyond the boundaries, came up against the arid alkaline facts of nature, on the one hand, and faced, on the other, the challenge of homesteaders and selectors who demanded a share of common earth. Mines and manufacturers provided increasing percentages of the national wealth and farms developed into wide-acred factories for the production of hogs, corn and wheat. Because distance and environmental conditions were against it, Australia had nothing to compare with the rapid pace of America's industrial and technological revolution, although when European and American inventions were adapted to serve Australia's primary-producing economy they speedily contributed to industrial growth.

In Australia, once homesteaders had broken the squatters' grasp on the land, they discovered that the country was unsuited to the idyllic contented yeoman type of settlement that Catholic philosophers, English Romantics and John Dunmore Lang had taught them to admire. The Selection Acts of the 1860s, based in part on America's Homestead Act of 1862, were followed by fraud, squalor, disillusionment and various degrees of moral and material wretchedness. Like American homesteaders, Australian selectors had to learn to live with the land rather than live off the land, as so many of them had hoped to do. It meant harder, more continuous work than on the goldfields and called for greater business acumen than running a suburban shop. Farms, rather than becoming rural retreats from urban pressures, had to turn into mechanized productive units before they provided anything more than a scratch livelihood for a man and his family.

American technology and methods helped the process of adaptation but Australian farmers were soon devising agricultural implements and machinery for themselves. Ring-barking, hickory-handled axes, four-wheeled buggies, methods of irrigation, clanking windmill pumps and barbed wire came from America; Australian farmers developed their own types of harvesters, stump-jump plows and marketing systems. They were also prominent in developing wheat strains to meet the twin challenge of rust and dry conditions.

Australia borrowed methods of irrigation and dried fruit culture from California, though as early as 1851 an inventive Australian journalist, James Harrison, contrived the world's first effective mechanical refrigerator, opening the way for the later development of frozen meat export to Britain. John Ridley of South Australia, invented a locomotive thresher in 1843, never having heard of the McCormick reaper developed in Virginia ten years earlier. Ridley did not patent his reaper and refused all suggestions of reward. In 1844, Hugh Victor McKay, a young Victorian farmer born in a slab hut with a bark roof, invented a harvester which was an improvement on Ridley's in that it combined winnowing with stripping. McKay founded the Sunshine

Harvester Works and devised many more agricultural implements adapted to Australian conditions. While Ridley, McKay and others developed better and cheaper means of harvesting, access to markets still remained an Australian problem. Clipper ships and steam ships provided half the answer, railways the other half, plus marketing schemes to offset a decline in world prices compared with earlier boom times.

Developments in mining, agriculture, irrigation and marketing techniques enabled Australia to break away from an exclusively pastoral society. By the end of the nineteenth century, when levels of welfare to be achieved by exploiting the land showed signs of diminishing, no major change in political and social structure was necessary to achieve the beginnings of an industrial society. In this, Australian development can be most usefully compared with the development of America's Middle and Far West after the Civil War. The essential difference was between "the great Australian emptiness" and the rich grazing and farming lands of the American interior. The Great Lakes and the Mississippi river system, with Chicago as a hub, provided a marketing and transportation complex quite lacking in Australia, and which could only be devised under highly unfavorable environmental conditions.

A comparison between railways in America and Australia brings out the difference between the two continents. The Civil War turned out to be the first "railway war", with Atlanta, where four railroads crossed, a place of immense strategic importance, as everyone who has read or seen *Gone With The Wind* knows. After the war, railroads crisscrossed the United States in every direction while gangs of Irish, Southern whites, blacks and Chinese drove transcontinental tracks across plains and over mountains at the phenomenal average rate of a mile a day. Australian tracks, by comparison, edged tentatively out from coastal towns through miles of country which promised no freight. To provide for scattered settlements state governments had to take over pioneer companies which, compared with the American giants, never showed a profit.

Giant locomotives speeding across the continent became symbols of American progress, "the pulse of the continent." In Australia, until well into the twentieth century, steam trains were a leisurely we'll-get-there-sometime mode of transport, with crews and passengers on the best of comradely terms, more fit for comic book humor than symbolic expression. Certainly, no Australian poet ever felt moved to emulate Walt Whitman's "To a Locomotive in Winter", beginning:

> Thy black cylindrical body, golden
>   and silvery steel,
> Thy ponderous side bars, parallel
>   and connecting rods, gyrating, shuttling
> at thy sides. . . .

The Civil War and the railway era ruined Mississippi river traffic. Mark Twain revisited his boyhood haunts in the 1870s. He found most of the paddle-steamers tied up and old men in riverside towns mumbling gummily about a past that had gone for ever. Twenty years later, traveling by train from Sydney to Melbourne he noted "tiny cabins, built sometimes of wood, sometimes of gray-blue corrugated iron . . . the doorways and fences . . . clogged with children—rugged little simply-clad chaps that looked as if they had been imported from the banks of the Mississippi without breaking bulk." Nobody, apparently, told him about the River Murray Steam Navigation Company and its American and Australian river-pilots who aimed to revolutionize the river-trade as Cobb and Co. had revolutionized coaching.

Although shallow and uncertain compared with the Mississippi system Australia's Murray River and its main tributaries, the Darling and Murrumbidgee, provided 4,000 miles of navigable inland water throughout the wool-growing southeastern sector of New South Wales and Victoria. Small steam boats, not comparable in size with the Mississippi giants Mark Twain knew, could enter the Murray near Adelaide in South Australia and travel more than 2,000 miles to western New South Wales. In 1853, forty-four years after Robert Fulton demonstrated the practicality of steam-boat traffic, the first paddle steamer went up the Murray River from South Australia. Using riverside timber for fuel, steamers proved cheaper carriers than bullock teams. However, in ordinary seasons, the Murray channel, meandering in great curves through a flat countryside, was only navigable from June to December. The Darling River was even more treacherous. Sometimes winter rains did not come at all and riverboats were left stranded on baked mudbanks for twelve months or more waiting for a river that did not appear.

In 1859, the Australian firm of Murray and Jackson set up a store and river port at Wentworth, near the junction of the Murray and Darling, terminal point of Sturt's journey down the Darling in 1829. There were still several thousand Americans in Victoria and some of them, remembering the Mississippi, were attracted to the new venture. Murray and Jackson began business with the three steamers, all stern-wheelers, *Lady Daly*, *Lady Darling* and *Settler*. *Lady Daly* flew the Stars and Stripes in honor of her American pilot, Captain Peleg Jackson, and supercargo, A. L. Blake. In 1863, a third American, Augustus Baker Peirce, destined to become the most colorful of the Murray River pilots, joined the company at Wentworth.

A New Englander, then in his early twenties, Peirce had deserted ship at Melbourne to try his luck on the goldfields. Disappointed, he had tried acting, coach-driving, photography and journalism before arriving at Wentworth in hopes of becoming a Murray River pilot. Blake, supercargo on the *Lady Daly*, told him that there was no hope of a steamer job for an inexperienced man but urged him to apply for the necessary work of charting the 1,360 miles

Steamers on the Murray at Echuca, Western
New South Wales

Right: *Mississippi paddlewheelers*

the steamers were traveling between Goolwa, near the mouth of the Murray in South Australia, and Albury, on the border between New South Wales and Victoria.

Murray and Jackson gave Gus Peirce the job and he set off in a rowing boat with a companion to handle the oars and do the cooking while he sat in the bows and made his chart. Whenever he noted a snag he went ashore and blazed a tree as a warning sign to steamer pilots. Gus, whose theatrical experiences had introduced him to Lola Montez and other goldfields' notables, soon became a well-known figure at every riverside pub. During the off-season he took up quarters on the *Lady Daly* at Goolwa, copying his chart on long narrow strips of tracing-cloth which were wound in sections on rollers fitted into the glass-topped chart-box in the wheelhouse of the steamer. The pilot unwound the chart as he chugged slowly along, avoiding snags and sandbars and recognizing his position from the landmarks sketched in beside the course shown on the chart.

According to Ian Mudie's *River Boats* (Adelaide, 1961) Captain Gus soon became a legend. "That inimitable Yank who should surely have been a millionaire except that he was always broke," was how one of his old river associates described him. By then Wentworth was a thriving river port handling four hundred steamers and small craft a year. Captain Gus benefited in no way financially from this. Indeed, he was often reduced to paying his drink bill by using his considerable skill as artist and draughtsman to paint murals of steamers on the walls of riverside hotels. The Steampacket Hotel at Echuca—one of more than fifty pubs in this once important river port—had a series famous up-and-down the river. All have disappeared though several specimens of Captain Gus's work are now housed in the Adelaide Art Gallery.

As in America, railways eventually replaced river steamers, which were too slow and unreliable. For wool-growers, anxious to catch ships for speedy transport to overseas markets, time was worth money. Furthermore, the Murray River system did not serve inland territory that railways and roads could not reach. The country through which the long rivers meandered was almost all wool country. Once the wool traffic was lost the countryside could not provide enough minerals or other low-value commodities for which cheap transport was more important than speed. River traffic was greatest in the last decade of the nineteenth century. After that roads and railways ended the Murray River transport era, with its picturesque paddle steamers and colorful personalities, just as surely as a similar process of elimination took place in America.

Cheap land, steel-bladed plows, windmill pumps and barbed wire enabled Western ranchers and homesteaders to open up and protect rich new lands. Railways and Chicago's markets and factories were the catalysts that turned pioneering peasants and open range farmers into factory farmers. The great maw of Chicago sucked in perishable raw materials from farms and ranches and ejected them in an endless flow of durable marketable commodities. In the process Jefferson's dream of a nation of democratic, independent yeomen farmers went by the board. The novelist A. B. Guthrie put living flesh on the bare bones of historical fact when he described the process: "First lawlessness, then loose law and order, then churches and schools and social sanctions and, finally, a town not a camp. The preacher and schoolmaster are harbingers, and homesteaders . . . hasten the change. . . . People . . . seeking homesites . . . bringing plows and grains and garden stuff and hope and the seed of their loins."

The process did not stop there. The American homesteader and his wife finally won the West and laid firm foundations for a new utilitarian civilization. Then came a vast influx of European immigrants who swamped the original homespun pioneering values of the firstcomers. Some were natural pioneers who, in Vernon L. Parrington's phrase, saw "the golden light of promise flooding the wind-swept plains." Others hungered for community with their fellows in villages, towns and cities and provided labor for spreading railways and growing industrial towns. Rural villages quickly became industrial cities: human warrens under palls of smoke where financial panics and cruel economic slumps were the facts of life and relations between capital and labor grew bitter and violent.

Australia went through much the same process except that economic takeoff found an initial springboard in the exploitation of minerals, and industrial cities almost all grew on the edge of a continent, urbanized from the beginning, where the links were coastal rather than continental. There were no Great Lakes and no Chicago. Ballarat, Bendigo, and other camps that grew into towns on the old alluvial goldfields, first became mining municipalities with company-owned deep mines and hired miners, then settled down to placid country town existence. As the guide books put it, they served "productive pastoral and agricultural districts growing wool, cereals, fruit and vegetables" and manufacturing such light commodities as bricks, tiles, cement, furniture, beer, foodstuffs, tinware and light machinery.

Australia, like America, became a country for the common man but the common man continued to come mostly from the British Isles. Australian immigration, despite Dr. Lang's doubts about the Irish, offered no threat to established British values. Australians were different because an antipodean environment had modified the original British stock not because newcomers had swamped it. Australia's burgeoning population had nothing of America's feverish growth. Newcomers provided a market for light industry but Australia still lived off the sheep's back and depended for its prosperity on overseas markets for primary products. Australia grew to maturity as an outpost of British liberal capitalism rather than as the independent nation of republican sentiment as forecast by Dr. Lang.

Australia offered ample opportunities for the ambitious, locally-born and immigrant alike. Compared with Great Britain there were no rigid class distinctions, no redundant poor, no hereditary wealthy, no insurmountable social or economic barriers to prevent the shrewd and hard-working from getting on. Yet it was not a country, like America, from which a newsboy like Thomas Edison could illuminate the world, where an iron-founder like Andrew Carnegie could preach the *Gospel of Wealth* as a new revelation, or where a smart young bookkeeper like John Davison Rockefeller could become the world's first billionaire by practicing the Puritan virtues of industry and abstinence. It was, however, a country which attempted to provide equal opportunities for all-comers without realizing that equality of opportunity was not essentially egalitarian, as reformers hoped and politicians preached. Rather it substituted economic for social class distinctions and made the assertion "Jack's as good as his master" a compensatory defiance rather than a social fact.

Both Australia and America were increasingly urbanized but both had sufficient "outback" or "wild west" to nurture the myth that bushranging and banditry were forms of social protest rather than crimes of violence against society as a whole. The James brothers and Billy the Kid had their Australian equivalents in Frank Gardiner, who finished up a respectable saloon-keeper in San Francisco, Ben Hall, who was shot dead in a gun fight, and Ned Kelly, the doyen of them all, who was hanged after creating an imperishable legend. "Game as Ned Kelly" is still a meaningful phrase in Australia although the bushranger died on the scaffold in November 1880. In the post gold-rush era selectors and small farmers had a real respect for the Kelly gang and other native-born bushrangers, who came from the same social class, a respect largely denied to pre-gold rush ex-convict robbers who, with a few exceptions, were more brutally criminal.

It may be true, as E. J. Hobsbawn suggests in *Bandits* (London, 1969) that later urban generations tend to idealize bushrangers and bandits as symbols "of ancient lost virtue, a spiritual Indian territory for which, like Huckleberry Finn, man can imagine himself 'lighting out' when the constraints of civilization become too much for him." This should not be allowed to swamp the fact, as Hobsbawn stresses and as President Theodore Roosevelt put it, "there is something very curious in the reproduction [on new continents] of essentially the conditions of ballad-growth which obtained in medieval England; including . . . sympathy for the outlaw, Jesse James [and Ned Kelly] taking the place of Robin Hood." Certainly, in Australia, there is a whole crude contemporaneous ballad literature celebrating Wild Colonial Boys who, in their post-gold rush manifestations, sprang from the small squatter and selector class that warned, helped and admired them.

George Boxall, English author of *The Story of the Australian Bushrangers*

(London, 1899), though holding the curious belief that Australians and New Zealanders had attained "the most advanced stage in Anglo-Saxon evolution", did not contribute to the myth that Australian bushrangers robbed the rich to help the poor. "I have no desire to raise any doubts as to the generosity and benevolence of Robin Hood," he wrote, "but I can find no evidence of any such beneficence on the part of any of the Australian bushrangers," who were by circumstance compelled "to share . . . ill-gotten gains with those who supplied . . . food and information. . . ." Boxall reminds us that "the Judas who betrayed" is as much part of the legend as the friends and mistresses who collaborated with outlaws or refused to help sheriffs and police. Boxall concluded that Gardiner, Ben Hall, the Kellys and others owed their popularity to the fact that they were raised in poor localities where morality was low and where the convict tradition of hatred for the representatives of law and order lingered long after it had died down among immigrants in growing towns and cities.

Billy the Kid was an underprivileged youth, abandoned at fourteen, who picked up Spanish in the saloons and back alleys of New Mexico and achieved identity as a professional gunman in a murderous feud between rival commercial factions. Sheriff Pat Garrett shot the Kid through the heart on 14 July 1881, eight months after Ned Kelly "died game" on the scaffold at Melbourne's Pentridge jail. A contemporary balladist concluded that Kelly's death proved "crime doesn't pay" but added:

> Yet when I look round at some people I know
>   And the prices of things that we buy,
> I just think to myself, well perhaps, after all,
>   Old Ned wasn't such a bad guy.

"Old" Ned was twenty-six when his mother, serving a three-year sentence in the same jail, admonished him: "Mind you die like a Kelly, Ned!" Legend has it that when the police captured Kelly, after his epic gunfight in plowshare armor at Glenrowan, they found in his pocket a declaration for a Republic of Northeastern Victoria. Some who cherish the myth that Kelly robbed the rich to help the poor sacrilegiously compare his final summons to his accomplices with "Christ summoning His disciples." Others see him as a successor to the diggers who died at Eureka. John Manifold, a modern balladist, ends his poem, "The Death of Ned Kelly":

> And so they took Ned Kelly and hanged him in the jail,
> For he fought single-handed although in iron mail.
> And no man single-handed can hope to break the bars;
> It's a thousand like Ned Kelly who'll hoist the Flag of Stars.

Billy the Kid, who died at twenty-one, enjoyed almost equal deification. Immediately after his death his index finger, "the one which has snapped many

*Ned Kelly, bushranger, died defiant and gave
the language the phrase "game as Ned Kelly"*

Right: *Billy the Kid did not live to see the
gallows*

a man's life into eternity", reported the *Daily Optic*, was preserved in alcohol and exhibited in the newspaper's office. "If the rush continues," the editor commented, "we shall purchase a small tent and open a side show to which complimentary tickets will be issued to our personal friends." Billy's personal friends, "the Spanish-speaking people of New Mexico", execrated Garrett, "the Judas who betrayed him", and continued to regard Billy as a folk-hero who "was good to Mexicans", an American Robin Hood who stole from the white people and gave to the Mexicans. In neither case do the facts support the legend.

The new America and the new Australia were able to meet and compare notes at the immense exposition held at Philadelphia in 1876, centennial year of the birth of the United States. The gilded occasion, which cost the then enormous sum of $US10 million, was intended to heal Civil War wounds as well as to present the new country's industry and culture for the admiration of the world. "Shall the bitterness and animosity engendered by the war remain forever?" demanded the Centennial Commission. Was it not time for all to wish that "the errors of the past be hidden in high and holy aspirations for the future of our restored nationality?" If this is what the Centennial Exposition meant to many Americans it meant something quite different to the Europeans, Japanese, Egyptians, Russians, Turks and Australians who crowded to admire the wonders of American technology exhibited in the huge buildings filling seventy-five acres of Philadelphia parklands set aside for the great occasion.

The Centennial planners, for all the nostalgic folksiness of New England exhibits in buildings modeled on "the style of houses common to Colonial times", had taken the nation's measure: after the Main Hall, where stands in colored marble with silver mountings dispensed popcorn and soda water, the Machinery Hall took pride of place, with the Agricultural Hall third. The twin vertical cylinders of George Henry Corliss's colossal steam-engine, which provided power for the whole exhibition, stood over the Machinery Hall like the pylons of a massive Egyptian gateway. Beyond it spread row after row of exhibits that demonstrated America's advances in the fields of invention, applied science and technology. The London Crystal Palace Exhibition of 1851 had given striking proof of America's technological advances, the Civil War had demonstrated the predominance of machine power, the Centennial Exhibition gave notice that the United States was now on the way to becoming a world power.

Tucked away almost unnoticed in an obscure corner of the Education Building an amazing new device attracted little attention. Most of those who lingered regarded it as not more than an intriguing novelty: the telephone, just patented by Alexander Graham Bell. Spectators were more interested in sewing machines, an American invention valued by the whole world, which occupied half-a-mile of exhibition space. Penny-farthing bicycles aroused a great deal of comment although those who sought easy transport for suburbanites who could not afford a carriage and pair had to wait another ten years before a British inventor produced a bicycle fit for mass use. There was general appreciation for the process of nickel plating, a technique in which American craftsmen surpassed all other.

Great Britain and her colonies, including Australia, made the second biggest showing at the Centennial Exposition, sending more than three thousand exhibits. Australia, although rejecting American republicanism for English monarchy, showed eager curiosity in American technology. Gold-diggers had learned to appreciate the excellence of American axes, shovels, firearms, stagecoaches and buggies. Townsmen and settlers were now anxious to discover the extent of American progress in the arts of urban and rural living.

Americans welcomed the prospect of new custom from Australia where environmental conditions were in many respects so like the cattlemen's kingdom of New Mexico and the arid Southwest. "The Australian colonies are less known in our country than they should be," declared the *New York Herald*, welcoming the Australian exhibits, "while our commercial relations with them are by no means what they could be made, and what we trust they will become. A people of genuine Anglo-Saxon vigour and intelligence is rapidly growing up in this distant land, possessed of qualities which should make commercial intercourse between them and us easy and possible. We are sincerely pleased that the Exhibition is to be the occasion of the people becoming more intimately acquainted with the people of the United States." Although Australian exhibits were mostly pastoral, agricultural and mining, Victoria, proud of infant industries nurtured by tariff protection, sent an exhibit consisting almost entirely of manufactured goods. The degree of manufacturing development led some commentators to suppose that Australia was already self-supporting in many articles, particularly clothing.

By 1876, Australia had passed out of its exclusively pastoral age and was entering an industrial era. Large numbers of Australians were still engaged in mining and land speculation but an increasing percentage of the workforce was involved in manufacturing. The major industries were textiles and clothing, metals and machinery, building materials and food, brewing and tobacco. Smallness of scale, high labor costs and competition from imports prevented anything like the spectacular rise of American industry. Nevertheless, more and more enterprising entrepreneurs took advantage of a growing consumer market, capital imports, skilled immigrant labor, government contracts and a pool of child and female labor. Nor was industrial development confined to the capital cities. Country towns in the wheat and wool-growing areas developed industries to process local products: flourmills, wool-scours, tanneries, dairy factories and meat-freezing works. Local blacksmiths, in many instances, expanded their forges to make agricultural implements.

Most surprising of all to American observers was the extent of Australia's comparative heavy industry. During the 1850s William Kelly in the United States and Henry Bessemer in England, working independently, discovered methods of treating pig iron in blast furnaces. An Englishman, Robert Mushet, improved on the Bessemer converter and from these developments the Bessemer process of making steel was evolved. Adopting and adapting the new process, American companies soon brought the use of steel within the reach of everyone. Light-weight steel hoops were even used for ladies' crinolines enabling women from poor families to dress in the height of fashion formerly reserved for women able to afford expensive dressmakers. Australia had to wait until the 1880s for cheap locally-manufactured steel but several hot blast furnaces and rolling mills were operating by the 1870s. If they did not all survive they paved the way for more successful operations later.

By the 1870s Melbourne and Adelaide foundries using local and imported pig iron were producing agricultural and mining implements and machinery for use all over Australia. Hugh Lennon, a Melbourne blacksmith who in less than twenty years became one of Australia's largest producers of farm machinery, claimed that Victoria led the world in the manufacture of agricultural implements. There was such a demand for plows that his output of 600 a year fell short of requirements but he could not obtain enough skilled labor to expand further. Ned Kelly used Lennon's moldboard steel plowshares for his armor, a wonderful advertising boost for the firm's product. Martin and Company, engineers of Gawler, South Australia, had already begun a steady expansion which by the 1880s enabled the firm to build fifty-two locomotives for the South Australian railways. By this time, the Danks Foundry in Melbourne, which specialized in taps, steam and safety valves and pumping machinery, had opened a branch factory in England and observers were hailing Melbourne as the Birmingham of the Pacific.

If all this activity was not fully reflected in the Philadelphia Centennial Exhibition of 1876 it was amply displayed in the Melbourne exposition of 1880 and the Melbourne Centennial Exhibition of 1888. American watches, machine tools, school furniture and agricultural implements were displayed at the first. In 1888, American typewriters, sewing machines, carriages, lawn mowers, lamps and musical instruments attracted wide attention. It was an age of exhibitions. Melbourne had already staged five but Joseph Reed's new Exhibition Hall, the southern capital's most spectacular building, demanded something special and Graham Berry, now Premier, determined to match Reed's flamboyant declaration of faith in a city of whose citizens a poet exclaimed:

The Philadelphia Centennial Exhibition. New
South Wales was a proud exhibitor

*Exhibition Building, Melbourne. The Victorian
Government set out to eclipse Philadelphia*

> Hers is a people ever in extremes,
> Or in a nightmare, or in golden dreams.

English architect Joseph Reed arrived in Melbourne during the gold rush but found his fortune in providing extravagant buildings for an extravagant age rather than in digging for gold. His career typified Australia's gilded age. He landed in 1852 with hardly a penny in his pocket and made a rapid fortune which he lost during the economic debacle of the 1890s. In between he left an indelible mark on Melbourne. He designed the Town Hall, the Public Library, Ormond College, the Trades Hall, churches, banks and many of the baroque mansions in which successful gold-seekers, pastoralists and speculators enjoyed their rich rewards before the inevitable crash. In the mid-1870s, he won a competition for a building to house what the promoters called the "first International Exhibition in the Southern Hemisphere", evidently with the Philadelphia Centennial in mind.

Reed won $600 and the commission to build the Hall ready for use by 1880. The result still occupies several acres on a hill northeast of the city and its great dome, standing astride the cross of the plan, was said to be not only the biggest but the most beautiful dome in the world, St. Peter's, St. Paul's and Philadelphia notwithstanding. The building's overpowering size and exact proportions compel admiration even today, when architectural grandiloquence is out of fashion. The late Robin Boyd, most trenchant critic of "the great Australian ugliness", did not hesitate to declare that "despite all the building's tawdry features [cherubs, flying angels and pensive draped figures], it still has a grandeur and magnificence of scale which cannot be experienced in any other Australian building of this century." Reed's Exhibition Hall matched Graham Berry's ambition to introduce Australia to the world and the world to Australia although it is typical of the spirit of the time that, for Graham Berry, Victoria was Australia and Melbourne the only fit portal for the continent.

The Exhibition was the culmination of Australia's gilded age. "During the years 1887-88 the speculative fever had manifested itself in every stratum of society," wrote Henry C. Turner in *A History of the Colony of Victoria* (2 vols., London, 1904). "The talk of the streets, the clubs, the trains, the luncheon-rooms and the dinner tables centred round the rise or fall of stocks, the chances of subdivisional sales, or the wonderful luck that had followed the operations of divers well-known leaders in the arena of competitive finance. On 20 January 1888, the day's operations on the Melbourne Stock Exchange exceeded £2,000,000 sterling, the great bulk of the transactions being in Broken Hill Mining Companies' shares. Gray-haired men, who had been known on 'Change for a whole generation as honourable and prosperous merchants, saw their junior clerks leaving them with the reputation of having made competencies in a few months by assuming risks at which their employers would have stood aghast."

Sir Henry Loch, according to *Table Talk* "the most popular Governor who has ever represented Her Majesty in this colony", invited four thousand guests to the Jubilee Ball in mid-1877 and thereafter every day was a carnival day to celebrate the approaching Centennial. By rights, Sydney, capital of the founding state, should have had the honor of holding the Centennial Exhibition but New South Wales lacked an Exhibition Hall and left it too late to build anything to match John Reed's masterpiece. Accordingly, the Premier of Victoria, Duncan Gillies, tactfully suggested to the New South Wales Government that Victoria should mount an Exhibition late in 1888, after Sydney's celegrations were over. New South Wales grudgingly acquiesced whereupon Victoria proceeded to mount a "World Fair" to celebrate Australia's centenary and to display "the results of the industrial progress of the colonies since their foundation. . . ." Victoria invited every government in the civilized world to take part and most of them accepted.

Determined to put on a show that would rival if not eclipse the Philadelphia Centennial, the Victorian Government spared no expense. Melbourne's most honored citizen, Chief Justice George Higinbotham, was asked to head the planning commission. When he protested at what he considered unbridled extravagance Premier Gillies replaced him with an accommodating politician. The government initially budgeted £25,000 but the eventual cost was more than £250,000 which, at that time in that place, was universally acknowledged as an extravagant total. A thousand sailors from visiting foreign warships—including American—marched in the opening procession and ten thousand spectators crowded into the Exhibition Hall for the opening ceremony. Over the next six months more than two million passed through the turnstiles. From Sydney, the *Bulletin* mocked at southern self-importance and more sober newspapers considered the whole affair a costly blunder. "Costly it was certainly, but a blunder—no," commented Australian novelist Ada Cambridge. "I should think that no money ever spent gave so much direct enjoyment to so many people."

The United States occupied 6,000 square feet of exhibition space. Appropriately enough, cash-registers and typewriters occupied a prominent place. Thomas Edison's phonograph attracted widespread wonder, but the finest display was in the machinery section. Besides praising the agricultural machinery, high-speed automatic cut-off engines, pumps, printing machines, lathes, wood-working machines and a wide range of tools and labor-saving devices, the adjudicating jury made special ecstatic mention of "a complete electric lighting plant in full work, which kept up a constant illumination every evening by means of arc and incandescent lamps, both plain and colored" plus "electric trams which . . . ran across the northern end of the annexes." Gold medal awards went to the McCormick harvester, the National cash register, the Singer sewing machine, the Houston electric tramway motor and dynamo, and many other developing innovations including steam laundry washers and a silver medal for a carpet sweeper.

By 1888 "Marvellous Melbourne" had benefited greatly from American innovations. Most visitors agreed that the city, with its grid-plan, style of architecture and bristling telegraph and telephone poles, had an American look. Nor were comparisons with parts of London, Paris and New York mere hyperbole. By the 1880s Melbourne was not only the most bustling Australian metropolis, with a population of more than half-a-million, it ranked as thirtieth among the world's cities, seventh in the British Empire and was already larger than Birmingham, Boston and most European capitals. American Francis Broadman Clapp, from Massachusetts, had introduced Melbourne to the most modern form of developed urban transport—cable trams. Another American, Elisha Graves Otis, provided the means for another urban amenity, the automatic lift, though he did not visit Australia.

Francis B. Clapp, who arrived in 1853, not only formed his own transportation companies but founded an Australian family which made the name "Clapp" synonymous with efficient transportation throughout Australia. He began his Australian career by taking over Cobb & Co.'s Melbourne-Ballarat line in December 1857. By 1859, he was the largest mail contractor in Victoria. Late in the 1860s he sold his Western Districts coaching business and, after a trip to Europe and America, formed the Melbourne Omnibus Company with William McCulloch and Henry Hoyt.

The company imported omnibuses from America and stabled 600 horses in the metropolitan area to service regular routes at a price that undercut the hansom cabs that were then the most popular form of urban transport. In 1883, the Victorian Government passed a Tramway and Omnibus Act which authorized municipalities to construct tramways. The Tramways Trust built the rails that linked Melbourne with the city's growing suburbs and Clapp's company leased the rails and ran the horse-drawn tramway services that provided cheap suburban transport. In 1884, Clapp convinced a Victorian Parliamentary Select Committee that cable trams, then operating in the United States, were suitable to Melbourne's transport needs.

Clapp's Melbourne Omnibus Company and the Melbourne Centennial Exhibition of 1888 were both harbingers of things to come. Early in 1888, Clapp's employees struck against the company's American-style management. When bus drivers attempted to form a union, Clapp dismissed them and refused to deal with trade unions in any shape or form except the benefit-society union the company itself formed and financed. A series of confrontations followed during which 200 men lost their jobs. The company rewarded loyal employees with a bonus equal to a week's wages. When boomtime ended, similar struggles led to growing bitterness between employers and employed, capital and labor. Meanwhile, the benefits of electricity, so much admired at Melbourne's Centennial Exhibition, began to make themselves felt throughout Australia. Before the end of the century, electric light had become commonplace throughout the continent while in most cities and big towns electric tramways became the most popular form of urban transport.

The Exhibition left a rather different legacy in Lefebevre's celebrated nude *Chloe*, one of the most popular exhibits. Young and Jackson, two diggers who had struck it rich, bought the painting for the bar of their new hotel on the southwest corner of Swanston and Flinders Streets, opposite Melbourne railway station, the world's busiest corner according to the more extravagant Melbourne-lovers. *Chloe*, a serious work of art which won the Grand Medal of Honor at the Paris Salon in 1876, was intended for the Victorian National Gallery once the 1880 Exhibition had ended. Soon after the donor, Sir Thomas Fitzgerald, had presented the picture to the Gallery, a Committee on the State of Religion and the Sabbath reported to the Presbyterian Church Assembly that "the recent introduction of a certain French picture into the Gallery" was "likely to suggest impure ideas."

Chloe, known to thousands of American GIs who frequented Young and Jackson's during World War II, immediately became the center of a heated controversy. She had her champions, even among the clergy. When Dr. Rentoul declared that "representations of the nude in colour were improper" one Assembly delegate reminded him that elders and ministers of the church did not hesitate to visit art galleries in Europe where nudes were rampant. The press took the matter up. Correspondents demanded the removal of the "indecent picture of a naked woman" and asked whether the Gallery trustees would like to see a nude picture of a sister or daughter hanging on public view. Fred McCubbin, John Longstaff and six other well-known Australian artists defended the work as "pure and elevating in sentiment and masterly in execution." Finally, the original donor demanded his picture back and *Chloe* ended up in Young and Jackson's bar.

If France contributed to Australia's art consciousness, following the Melbourne Exhibition of 1880, America was destined to stimulate antipodean theatre-goers and temperance-workers as well as factory farmers and industrial managers. During the gold rushes Australian playgoers had demanded the best and George Coppin with other colonial entrepreneurs did all they could to provide Shakespeare as well as such entertainers as Lola Montez and Batters the Tinker. English-born Coppin professed to despise the star system but following a visit to America in 1864-66 he was responsible with others for bringing to Australia Edwin Booth, brother of Abraham Lincoln's assassin, Laura Keene, who was on stage in *Our American Cousin* when the President was shot, and a number of other well-known American actors and actresses.

He himself introduced *Coppin in California*, a program of low comedy. In 1873, Coppin engaged a young, newly-married American couple, Mr. and Mrs. James Cassius Williamson, recommended by a San Franciscan agent as "young, handsome, sober", with the additional advantage that they "sing *and* dance good."

J. C. Williamson and his wife, who played under her maiden name of Maggie Moore, arrived in 1874 with a popular American melodrama, *Struck Oil*, and were a huge success. In 1875, they took the play to London, via India and Egypt, where it ran for a hundred nights at the *Adelphi*. After a two years' run with the same play in America, the Williamsons returned to Australia in 1879 with several Gilbert and Sullivan operas for spectacular presentation during the 1880 Exhibition. Due to American influence, a lighter more spectacular type of entertainment became popular in Australia, so much so that, according to D. E. Bandmann, an American actor, the new managers systematically demoralized public taste in their desire to attract audiences.

In 1882, J. C. Williamson joined with two Englishmen, George Musgrove and Arthur Garner, to form the famous "Triumvirate" which brought to Australia many famous European and American stars including Sarah Bernhardt, J. L. Toole, Nellie Farren, the Gaiety Girls, Dion Boucicault, Robert and Florence Brough and many others. In 1886, the Triumvirate demolished the old Princess Theatre, which had served Melbourne playgoers for thirty years, and on the site erected the new Princess Theatre "a structure unrivalled, so far, in the history of Australia." A contemporary chronicler, describing "this temple of the drama in Spring-street" declared "nothing that wealth and lavish enterprise can effect" had been spared "from the splendour of the marble staircase that forms its entrance to the picturesque dome that crowns a noble effort of architectural design" and "the mechanism that permits the roof to roll away and suffers the spectators on a hot summer night to look up into the delicious coolness of the star-besprinkled sky. . . ."

Maggie Moore continued to be the most continuously popular actress on the Australian stage. So deep was the affection she aroused in the general public that she was awarded the greatest honor Australians can bestow on its goddesses—a racehorse was named after her! Divorced from J. C. Williamson in 1899, she toured England and America from 1903 to 1908 but returned to the Australian stage where she continued to win laurels until she retired in 1925, at the age of seventy-four. She returned to America to live with a sister and died in 1926 after being knocked down by a San Francisco cable tram.

The 1880s were notable for American influence in other avenues than the theatre. On 9 February 1883, Livingston Hopkins, destined to become one of Australia's best-known caricaturists, arrived in Sydney from New York. A grave, courtly man, born at Bellefontaine, Ohio, on 7 July 1846, he migrated to Australia at the invitation of William Henry Traill who, with Jules

Francois Archibald and James Edmond, made the Sydney *Bulletin* the ebullient, irreverent champion of Australian nativism and acted as nursemaid for the growth of a still influential school of Australian literature and black-and-white art. The *Bulletin*'s Red Page, conducted by Australia's first considerable critic, Alfred George Stephens, who joined the magazine in the 1890s, gave, as he said, "a measuring rod to beat those indulging in antics around the parish pump." Although the magazine never lost its original pawky sense of humor and narrow nationalism it grew into a magazine comparable with the most influential English and American literary publications. It established a national style and provided a still admired Australian prototype. According to A. A. Phillips, a contemporary Australian critic, *Bulletin* writers wrote "of the people, for the people, and from the people. In that task almost their only predecessors later than Bunyan were Burns and Mark Twain—and neither had the full courage of his convictions."

On the art side, and the *Bulletin* was notably a pictorial as well as a literary weapon against complacency, snobbery and conventional thinking, Livingston Hopkins worked with a notable team which, at various times, included Phil May, Will Dyson, "Low", and Norman Lindsay. The *Bulletin* made its first appearance on 31 January 1880, and had no staff artist until Traill appointed Hopkins in 1883. Before coming to Australia, the American artist had been a young soldier in the Civil War, author of an illustrated *Comic History of the United States*, illustrator of de luxe editions of *Knickerbocker's History of New York*, *Don Quixote* and *Gulliver's Travels*, and had settled in New York as a contributor to *Scribner's*, *Harper's* and other publications. Originally engaged for three years, Livingston Hopkins, universally known as "Hop" of the *Bulletin*, remained for thirty years and like the *Bulletin* itself became an Australian institution. He died in 1927.

During the 1880s, Silas Lyon Moffett, an American book canvasser, gave a great fillip to Australian black-and-white art by launching the *Picturesque Atlas of Australia*. Intended as a "boost Australia" subscription publication the project grew far beyond its original commercialism. Moffett, described as a strange mixture of booster and visionary, developed an enthusiasm for Australia similar to that shown later by Mark Twain. He decided to produce a lavishly illustrated work of historical authenticity, asked specialists to write separate chapters on discovery, settlement and development and engaged a talented team of Australian and American black-and-white artists to draw 800 illustrations. The art editor, F. B. Schell, and two of his regular staff, W. T. Smedley and W. C. Fitler, were Americans. They supervised the work of such subsequently famous Australian artists as Julian Ashton, Tom Roberts, Frank Mahony, William MacLeod and W. C. Piguenit. Horace Baker, an American who headed the staff of engravers, produced from the artists' drawing the best examples of wood-engraving ever done in Australia.

9 *Commonwealth and Empire*

On 7 November 1900, Orlando H. Baker, American Consul in Sydney, wrote in a large scrawling hand to Secretary of State David J. Hill in Washington, informing him that a new Pacific nation was about to be born—the Commonwealth of Australia. "Elaborate and magnificent preparations are being made, not by Australians alone but by the representatives here of other Governments," Mr. Baker said. "In an interview with Sir William Lyne, Prime Minister of New South Wales, he expressed a wish that the United States would join in the celebrations. Accordingly, I ask a liberal allowance to properly decorate the U.S. Consulate buildings and to fit out whatever display we may as resident American citizens, be required to furnish in the procession, fireworks, etc."

A request had also been made to President McKinley to send a small body of troops to "represent the great American federation at the inauguration of the Australian Commonwealth." In the upshot no American soldiers or sailors joined the impressive procession of Imperial troops that marched on 1 January 1901, when the Commonwealth of Australia, "the newest nation on earth" was, according to the *Sydney Morning Herald* "imbued with the breath of constitutional life."

In Sydney's Centennial Park sixty thousand people had gathered in the hot midsummer sunshine for the ceremony. The Queen's Proclamation constituting the Commonwealth was read and then Lord Hopetoun rose and stood with bared head while Mr. Blackmore read the Letters Patent appointing him the first Governor-General. When the new Governor-General had sworn to "well and truly serve the Queen" and "to watch over the interests of the people", the Royal Standard was broken above his head, massed bands played "God Save the Queen" as practiced hands slapped rifle butts in the ordered movements of the Royal Salute and cannon shot spread the news through suburbs and city.

The celebrations had been an Imperial occasion from the moment on 15 December 1900, when John Adrian Louis, seventh Earl of Hopetoun, soon to be first Marquis of Linlithgow, steamed into Sydney Harbor aboard H.M.S. *Royal Arthur* between two rows of beflagged merchant ships and escorted by warships of Britain's Australian Naval Squadron. Ill, and unacquainted with the convolutions of colonial politics, His Lordship made the initial mistake of calling on the Premier of New South Wales, Sir William Lyne, a noted anti-Federalist, to form the first Commonwealth Government. Lyne, who had distinguished himself in British eyes by sending the first New South Wales contingent to the South African War, received curt replies when he dangled portfolios before the eyes of leading Federalists. His Lordship then turned to "Toby" Barton, a stout, able, popular lawyer, with an impeccable Federalist record, who had coined the notable phrase: "For the first time in history, we have a nation for a continent, and a continent for a nation."

On Christmas Day 1900, Barton was able to advise Hopetoun that he had formed the first Commonwealth Government. He completed the task in twenty-four hours, a still unbeaten record in Australian politics. Scottish-born colonial poet J. Brunton Stephens struck the appropriate Imperial note in his poem "Fulfilment", published on the front page of the *Sydney Morning Herald* on 1 January, which ended:

> O Lady, in whose sovereign name
> The crowning word of Union came
>   That sheds upon thine honoured age
>   The glory of a rising light,
> Across our record's earliest page,
>   It's earliest word, thy name we write—
> Symbol, Embodiment and Guarantee
> Of all that makes us and maintains us free—
> Woman and Queen, God's grace abide with thee!

Reporting the inauguration the *Herald* was dimly aware that it celebrated the century of the common man as well as the birth of a new nation. The crowds gathered on yellow grass in the wide open spaces of Centennial Park represented something new and strange in Imperial experience. Magna Carta, the American Declaration of Independence, the Union of Canada, had been wrested by force or the threat of force from hidebound authority. The Australian Constitution, on the other hand, had been proclaimed in "a broad-bound common park of the people . . . under the eyes of more than a hundred thousand men, women and children, citizens of the budding nation . . . men and women whose thoughts were unfettered for happiness in the contemplation of a nation dawning of its own volition—riding free on a foundation of freedom, not adopting a constitution under any form or semblance of coercion or compulsion or actual threatening danger."

There was something particularly appropriate, the *Herald* declared, that the

Australian Proclamation of Liberty should have been made in the open air of a park dedicated to the people by the people's Premier, Sir Henry Parkes, the "Father of Federation". He was, alas, no longer alive to see come to fruition his long-cherished dream of a new sun-kissed British dominion under "a goodly fabric of free government", as he himself had worded it in the Tenterfield Oration of 1889. His speech had been in effect, Australia's Declaration of Independence, a declaration not of defiance to the British Empire, whose Queen they honored and whose principles of freedom the Constitution enshrined, but freedom from narrow views and the chicanery of politicians who lacked the broad vision of statesmanship. Liberty, the *Herald* asserted, was the bridge between peoples of British stock throughout the world including, by implication, Americans as well as Australians, Canadians, South Africans and New Zealanders.

The *Herald* overestimated the number of people who crowded Centennial Park to hear the Proclamation read. Nor did the newspaper give due weight to the narrow-minded selfishness that had almost prevented its consummation and was to continue to fret the edges of Parkes's "goodly fabric". At conference after conference political intrigue and personal jockeying for advantage had threatened again and again to rend the fabric which Parkes, Alfred Deakin, Edmund Barton and others were trying to stitch into the seamless robe of nationhood. "Looking backwards," wrote Deakin, the gifted Victorian statesman and a member of Barton's first cabinet, "the future will be tempted to say that Australian Union was Australia's destiny from the first and nothing could have prevented its consummation. . . . If this be true, it is certainly not true of its present accomplishment, whatever might have resulted in later times . . . with other men and other means."

The Commonwealth Constitution, drafted on 12 March 1898, "after an all-night sitting and under conditions of great nervous irritability", as Deakin candidly admitted, was necessarily an American rather than a British document. It was a federal not a unitary constitution and like the American Constitution, it had to be a written constitution and not left a vague Burkean construction of precedent and custom, as was the British Constitution. The six former colonies became States of the Union and the States remained sovereign in all matters not specifically delegated to the Federal Government. The Commonwealth thus assumed control of the postal service, defense, customs and excise and foreign relations, and obtained power (not in the United States Constitution) with respect to conciliation and arbitration for the prevention and settlement of industrial disputes. The British system of cabinet government was retained as against the American presidential system.

To those who cherish it, the Commonwealth Constitution remains a charter of freedom which safeguards State rights and enables the people to retain local control over matters such as police, education, health, roads, local government, and the administration of justice. To those who regard it as a relic of the horse-and-buggy age it is a strait-jacket on progress, a conservative influence which takes little or no account of the fundamental changes which make the twentieth century not a prolongation of the nineteenth but a new historical dimension with advantages and problems peculiarly its own. The argument, on both sides, is exaggerated. In Australia, as in the United States, new ends succeed eventually in finding new means so that, in effect, if not in theory, both the United States of America and the Commonwealth of Australia have become seaworthy ships of state with enhanced federal powers despite the shifting ballast of State rights.

To many who watched the celebrations on 1 January 1901, as well as most of those who played leading parts, Britain was still "Home" and Britannia justly ruled the waves. In 1901, Britain's Imperial role had almost universal approval from most Britons and many Americans. American Anglophiles included Captain Alfred Theyer Mahan, U.S.N., the quiet, studious president of the United States Naval War College and widely-read author of a seminal book, *The Influence of Sea Power on History* (1890). Mahan was friend and confidant of President William McKinley's recently-appointed Assistant Secretary of the Navy, Theodore Roosevelt. He was also persona grata to Britain's patrician Establishment. In 1893, as the reluctant Commodore of a United States Naval Squadron visiting England, Mahan was guest of honor at a State Dinner given by Queen Victoria at Osborne. The Prince of Wales asked him to dine. He talked with the Prime Minister, Lord Salisbury, until midnight at a private dinner. He became the first foreigner ever entertained at dinner by the Royal Yacht Club and was the first man to receive honorary degrees from the Universities of Oxford and Cambridge on the same day.

Mahan was not only compulsive reading for British and American naval officers. During Cowes Week, Kaiser Wilhelm II of Germany invited the quiet American aboard his steam yacht, *Hohenzollern*, with fateful results for many of those who watched the Queen's Jubilee in England and the Commonwealth inaugural ceremonies in Australia. Wilhelm II devoured rather than read Mahan's book and ordered a translation to be placed in the library of every German warship. All German naval officers were ordered to study it. The Kaiser already dreamed of a Germany strong enough and militant enough to provide a focus for a powerful European counterbalance to the British Empire, the United States of America and Czarist Russia. He now conceived the idea that Germany must rival Britain as a global naval power. Similarly in Japan, every Japanese naval captain received a translation of Mahan as part of his equipment. Mahan noted with some concern that more of his voluminous writings were translated into Japanese than into any other language. His main work was available in French, Italian, Russian and Spanish as well as in German and Japanese.

American practice soon trod hard on the heels of theory. Theodore Roosevelt and Senator Henry Cabot Lodge became advocates of a great American navy. Mahan himself believed that in winning the West his countrymen had been diverted from their natural heritage, the sea. "Whether they will or no," he declared, "Americans must now begin to look outward." Roosevelt and Lodge saw a Pacific Fleet as the natural consequence of the manifest destiny which had carried the American people westward across the continent from the Atlantic. In 1898-9, the United States defeated Spain in a war the Spaniards did not want. During 115 days' action, the U.S. Navy annexed Cuba, Hawaii and Manila and left an American army fighting Filipinos who saw no virtue in replacing Spain with the United States as their colonial masters. As Roosevelt saw it, Americanizing the world was now America's destiny. He and Cabot Lodge were eager to share the White Man's Burden with Britain. They overlooked the fact that non-whites were as capable as whites in drawing conclusions from Mahan and from other, less comforting, seminal books published in Europe and America during the 1890s and early 1900s.

Ever since the 1850s, when Commodore Matthew Perry, of the United States Navy, had forced open two Japanese ports to Western trade, the Japanese had been able to observe which way the world was going. During the Meiji Era Japan eagerly followed Western-style plans of modernization and social reform. Within twenty years the country changed from an inward-looking conservative feudal society to a progressive, industrialized, outward-looking modern state. By 1894, Japan felt strong enough to adapt Mahan's precepts to national policy and attacked and defeated China in a war over territorial rights in Korea. By the Treaty of Shimonoseki, Japan gained Formosa and virtual suzerainty in Korea. In 1900 she joined with the United States, Britain, Australia, Germany and other European nations in an expeditionary force which put down China's antiforeign Boxers and extracted heavy indemnities from China. In 1904-5, Japan defeated Russia in a war over Korea and became the first Asian state in modern times to defeat a European power.

Despite these developments, actual or potential, it was natural in 1901 that Australia's Governor-General and the Commonwealth's first Prime Minister should continue to think of the southern continent as a perimeter of Europe, rather than as part of a developing Pacific axis. In 1869, Ferdinand de Lesseps completed the Suez Canal and transformed trade between Europe and Asia, although Australia's heavy freights of wool and minerals continued to be carried in fast, comparatively cheap sailing ships. Meanwhile, mails and Imperial despatches sped by train across Europe to Marseilles and were transferred to steamships using the Suez route. In 1875, when Disraeli borrowed £4,000,000 from the Rothschilds to buy the Egyptian Khedive's 177,000 shares in the Canal, Australians whole-heartedly approved. The Suez rapidly became an essential link of Empire, in defense of which in the years to come thousands of Australians were to die. Not until World War II, when Japan struck at Pearl Harbor, did an Australian Government dismiss thoughts of Suez and turn its eyes homeward to the Pacific where America's destiny had long lain.

The failure of the United States to send a contingent of troops for the Commonwealth inauguration was probably due to President McKinley's and Theodore Roosevelt's absorption in the 1901 presidential campaign, already under way. McKinley and Roosevelt, now Vice-President, represented Imperial sentiment, expressed in its most extreme and unctuous form by Senator Albert Beveridge on 8 January 1900, when he said, apropos a bill for the construction of the Nicaragua Canal: "We will not renounce our part in the mission of our race, trustees under God, of the civilization of the world." He added that God had been preparing the English-speaking and Teutonic peoples for this mission for a thousand years. Against this sort of popular rhetoric, antiImperialists somewhat reluctantly placed their faith in equally-rhetorical William Jennings Bryan, the silver-tongued Populist champion of·the West and South against the money-power of the East. In the Philippines, where national Aguinaldo was leading a popular rebellion against the United States, guerrillas went into action shouting "Aguinaldo-Bryan". This gained few votes for the Democrats.

At home, Roosevelt was the only man on the Republican side capable of matching Bryan in popular appeal. He campaigned on a policy of "a full dinner-pail" for the working man and denied that expansion in any way threatened American institutions or went against American tradition. The question, he insisted, was not "whether we shall expand—for we have already expanded—but whether we shall contract." Cabot Lodge backed Roosevelt's argument, exclaiming, "Manila and its magnificent bay is the prize and pearl of the East; . . . it will keep us open to markets in China . . . Shall we hesitate, and make, in coward fashion, what Dante calls the 'great refusal'?" McKinley and Roosevelt were reelected with fifty-two percent of the votes cast and with a greater margin over Bryan than in the Presidential elections five years before. Six months later an anarchist fanatic assassinated President McKinley and Theodore Roosevelt became President of the United States of America. As in England, so in America, imperialism had greater popular appeal than anti-imperialism.

In 1901, when Edmund Barton, clubman, classicist and highly successful barrister, took direction of the new Commonwealth of Australia, the British Empire stood proudly at its splendid zenith. Since the defeat of Napoleon in 1815, the nineteenth century had been a British century. "The culture of the day, the thoughts and aims of men, are English thoughts and aims," Emerson wrote in 1856. "A nation considerable for a thousand years . . . it has . . . obtained the ascendant and stamped the knowledge, activity and power of mankind with its impress. Those who resist it do not feel it or obey it the less. The Russian in his snows is aiming to be English. The Turk and the Chinese also are making awkward efforts to be English. The practical commonsense of modern society, the utilitarian direction which labor, laws, opinion, religion take, is the natural genius of the British mind. The influence of France is a constituent of modern civility, but not enough opposed to the English for the most wholesome effect. The American is only the continuation of the English genius into new conditions, more or less propitious."

The extravagance was no less true in 1901 than in 1856. There seemed no reason to suppose that in the twentieth century the British Empire should not continue to meet what Emerson laid down as the "one test of national genius universally accepted": success. The children in Australia who learned from their schoolbooks that they belonged to an empire on which the sun never set were as ready as the schoolchildren of England to regard the phrase, in Colin Cross's words, "as a prophetic rather than a geographic statement." The process had begun in 1583 when Sir Humphrey Gilbert took possession of Newfoundland and reached its climax in what James Morris called the "muddled grandeur" celebrated at Queen Victoria's Jubilee in 1897, when the Empire comprised some 372 million people inhabiting 11 million square miles of territory. There seemed no serious rivals for the British cultural and economic suzerainty of the world that Emerson had proclaimed forty years earlier.

There were some though not many among those who contemplated or shared Queen Victoria's Jubilee, and the later inaugurations of the Commonwealth of Australia, who realized that the growing points of the twentieth century were quite other than the full-fruited branches of a spreading Empire, and that rising French, German and Italian imperialists envied or feared Anglo-Saxon domination. The green shoots of a new epoch were everywhere plain to see but few grasped the full significance of what prescient English journalist, W. T. Stead, saw as the "Americanization of the world." In America itself, the brothers Henry and Brooks Adams sensed what was happening although they knew that Americanization represented no more than the spearpoint of processes deriving from English and European laboratories and research centers as well as from American workshops and factories.

Beneath the outward pomp and circumstance of Imperial occasions a second industrial and social revolution was in the making. The first industrial and social revolution at the end of eighteenth century precipitated Britain into world leadership, the culmination of the Renaissance vigor that had carried European civilization from the Mediterranean to the Atlantic and from the Atlantic to a European perimeter which girdled the globe. The second industrial and social revolution, although seeded in the first, was different in impact and tempo. As Geoffrey Barraclough points out in *An Introduction to Contemporary History* (London, 1964), it brought about fundamental changes "at practically every level of living and in practically every quarter of the globe." It precipitated radical changes in man's way of looking at himself and his fellows, saw the rise of mass democracy, mounted a powerful challenge to the liberal humanism which Victorian Englishmen took for granted as the apogee of civilization, shifted the global axis from Europe and the Atlantic to Asia and the Pacific. Above all, the new science and technology shook man's confidence in himself and his future. Progress from lower to higher, from worse to better, no longer seemed so certain nor so comforting. The old bourgeois society, based on classical scholarship, religious observance, free trade and strict public and private probity, was inwardly crumbling. The new society, eager to put electric power, the combustion engine and a proliferation of labor-saving machines at the service of all men, was struggling to break the bonds of the old and solve problems, as J. Ortega y Gasset put it, without any active collaboration with the past. A rising generation would agree with Henry Ford that "history is bunk."

The urgent thrust of the new century came to Australia across the Pacific as well as through the Suez Canal. This was not because the new interpretation of America's manifest destiny took as much account of Australasia as of China and Japan, Hawaii and the Philippines. Once steel had replaced whalebone in women's corsets and gas and kerosene took the place of whale oil as the cheapest and most popular forms of illumination (followed by electric light) the American whaling industry declined and with it direct American interest in Australia. However, for the rest of the century, H. H. Hall and W. H. Webb managed to maintain regular shipping links between Sydney and San Francisco. From the Australian point of view the importance of these links was not so much trade as the fact that mails to Europe across the Pacific and the United States, arrived two weeks earlier than by sea. By this means, too, American technical publications were regularly received in Australia. Consequently, American trade to Australasia continued slowly but steadily so that Australia benefited from American technology in the shape of a swelling volume of steel and electrical products, communications equipment, machinery, household gadgets, factory and mining machinery, office equipment and automobiles.

Although many technological innovations and most scientific discoveries originated in Europe, it was American managerial enterprise that brought them into mass use or practical application. The "robber barons" of the gilded age who drew on the flooding millions of immigrants as a seemingly inexhaustible sea of cheap labor, also paved the way for the consumer society that followed.

The oil monopoly, the steel trust, the railroad combines, and thousands of lesser but equally ruthless exploiters of the old world's redundant poor and the new world's abundant raw materials had, by the beginning of the twentieth century, thrust the United States into world leadership in technology and applied science. This is what English journalist W. T. Stead and American historian-philosopher Henry Adams meant by "Americanization", the "degradation of democratic dogma", the disappearance of the frontier, the fading of the American dream. Americanization meant something quite different to Australian farmers, housewives and businessmen and to "new" Americans. For Australians, Americanization meant improved methods of mining, transportation and lighting, more efficient farm machinery, labor-saving household gadgets, sewing machines, the Model T Ford and Hollywood's dream-world of romance and vicarious adventure.

Nor did new Americans share the disillusion suffered by American writers, publicists and labor leaders such as Edward Bellamy, Henry George, Laurence Gronlund, Jack London, Theodore Dreiser, Samuel Compers, Eugene Debs and others. For most immigrants, America meant freedom from the knout and the constant fear of famine, a good suit, collar and tie and hard hat for Sunday wear, above all, free education for sons and daughters. For these advantages they did not regret exchanging Europe's pogrom-ridden ghettos, foetid back alleys and miserable peasant hovels for a seventy-hour-week in American workshops and factories. The degradation of democratic dogma, so far as most immigrants were concerned, resolved itself into familiar, back-slapping, first-name-using Tammany Hall politicians prepared to trade practical services—finding a job for a bright boy, wangling a team-place for a precincts baseball champion, making a flush toilet work, producing a bottle of whisky or wine when a new baby was born—in return for votes.

By doing little things for little people Tweed Ring in New York, Matt Quay and Boise Penrose in Pennsylvania, and lesser but equally notorious "honest grafters" in Memphis, Jersey City, Kansas City and elsewhere, gained control of municipal government and milked city revenues for their own and their party's aggrandizement. While Henry Adams traveled Australasia, the Orient and Europe, seeking a religious or aesthetic principle of unity to replace the multiplicities of technological and democratic America, "muckrakers" Lincoln Steffens, Mark Sullivan, Ray Stannard Baker, Finley Peter Dunne and Frank Norris, backed by Theodore Roosevelt, campaigned against crime, corruption and combines with such effect that they succeeded, as far as it was humanly possible, in bringing petty grafters, as well as those scarified by Theodore Roosevelt as "malefactors of great wealth", within the law. By the first decade of the twentieth century reform was more respectable and more vote-winning than honest graft. Meanwhile, the first generation of new Americans had become full-blooded Americans no longer needing Tammany Hall crutches and capable of producing such American national heroes as Joe DiMaggio, Knute Rockne and Irving Berlin.

Henry Adams in 1891 and Mark Twain in 1895 mistook Australia's cordial easy-going ways and open-minded receptiveness to technology for Americanization. "The Australians did not seem to me to differ noticeably from Americans, either in dress, carriage, ways, pronunciations, inflections, or general appearance," reported Mark Twain. Some Englishmen and Australians were saying the same thing. In 1886, journalist Frank Cowan, in what Australian writer Sidney J. Baker calls "a Walt Whitmanish saga of our merits and demerits" wrote of Australia as "the Yankeeland beneath the Southern Cross" and a succession of observers since deplored or hailed the Americanization of Australia. These observers attributed more significance to similarities than they actually possessed for, as Sidney Baker puts it, "To be *like* the United States is not to *be* the United States."

The differences were due to environmental and economic circumstances, particularly immigration. The inflow of immigrants into Australia during the late nineteenth and early twentieth centuries was not only significantly less than the inflow into America but it was basically British and entailed no radical adjustment to new conditions and no Tammany Hall. Thus, Australia's Labor Party and labor movement were fundamentally different from America's equivalent developments. British law, British precedent, the British ideal of top-hatted, frock-coated personal and public probity lingered, if not always lived up to.

"Critics who think that a discussion is settled by the mere use of catch-words have charged Labor members with being subject to the control of a 'machine'," wrote Scottish-born Australian Labor leader and politician William Guthrie Spence in 1909, five years after the election of the first Federal Labor Ministry in Australia. "By this they infer that the leagues and unions directing the Labor Movement are akin to the 'machine' run by American Bosses. He must be a stupid man indeed who can see any analogy between the two. Bossism is simply the Boss and his friends controlling a limited organization for their own ends. The Labor Movement has no Bosses, and no personal ends to gain. In the past a few men have come into it to try to make a stepping stone by which to attain political position but one has only to look at its rules to see that there is but little if any chance for that sort of person to do so now. The Australian Trades Union and Political Labor Movement has been absolutely without a suspicion of anything of the kind known as 'graft' in America. Such an evil as bribery is unknown . . . selfish schemers are soon seen through and get short shift."

W. G. Spence may have confused American political "Bosses" with American industrial bosses and gilded the probity and idealism of Australian Labor leaders and politicians but what he said was substantially true. The growth of the Australian trade union movement paralleled the pattern of

British rather than American development. By the beginning of the twentieth century Australian union organization and political influence were ahead of rather than behind British or American example. There were better and more influential theoreticians in America and Britain but practical reformers and unionists all over the world looked to Australia as an exemplar in such democratic processes as the "Australian ballot", forerunner of most modern methods of secret voting, introduced in Australia more than thirty years before it was adopted in the United States; the eight-hour day; factory legislation; industrial conciliation and arbitration; the minimum wage and similar indications of the now widespread belief that the State should assume responsibility for the material well-being of its citizens as well as for law and order, war and peace. American reformers and students took a keen interest in Australian developments and, besides a spate of magazine articles, this interest found expression in such books as John H. Whigmore's *The Australian Ballot* (1889), Henry D. Lloyd's *Newest England* (1903), Victor S. Clark's *The Labour Movement in Australia* (1906) and P. S. Collier's *Minimum Wage Legislation in Australasia* (1915).

"The practical objectives of the labour party are not so much socialist as social-democratic," wrote American academic Victor S. Clark in 1906. "They look towards collectivism, but recognize wages, profits, and the conditions of capitalist production as matters to be accepted in present legislation. . . . Australian labour leaders know little or nothing of Marxian theories. Few of them know even by title the principal text-books of Continental Socialism. The writings of Henry George and Edward Bellamy did something to popularize collectivist doctrines. . . . More recently one or two English socialists have visited Australia and Mr. Tom Mann has been employed as a salaried organiser by the Melbourne Trades Hall. But the policy of the Labour party is shaped by home conditions. There is little social idealism among the rank and file of the working classes."

Professor Clark accurately diagnosed that Australian unionists and Labor politicians, like their American counterparts, were mostly seeking immediate concrete results and that it was "merely an accident" that the policy thus determined tended towards socialism. This does not mean that ideas and ideals did nothing to temper the essential pragmatism of Australian trade unionism and politics. Edward Bellamy's utopian *Looking Backwards* (1888) was widely read and had considerable influence on Australia's first important socialist thinker, William Lane, editor of the Queensland *Worker*, which serialized the American book. W. G. Spence dismissed Bellamy as "very pretty" but according to a writer in the *Centennial Magazine* (September, 1890), "Bellamy has not appealed to the Australian reader in vain: tens of thousands of men and women in all walks of life have fallen under the fascination of this splendid dream."

In 1893, disgusted with Australian concentration on day-to-day issues in the here-and-now, Lane took a shipload of idealists and misfits to found a "New Australia" in Paraguay. His departure and subsequent disillusionment increased Australian disdain for utopianism but socialist ideas continued to influence Australian thinking. American Laurence Gronlund's *Co-operative Commonwealth* (1884)—"a more practical philosopher than Bellamy" said the *Centennial Magazine*—was particularly popular. "You cannot buy a copy of his book in Melbourne or Sydney today," the *Centennial* reported. "The booksellers have sold 'clean out' . . . Gronlund's Socialism is no Utopia. He just takes human nature as it is and existing institutions as they are, and traces the tendency of industrial evolution to its logical conclusion."

Enthusiasts issued cheap editions of Bellamy, Gronlund and Henry George's *Progress and Poverty* (1879) at eightpence each and these sold by the hundred thousand. After 1900, works by American writers Jack London and Daniel De Leon, and English translations of Marx and Engels published by the Kerr Press, Chicago, circulated widely in Australia alongside such British writers as William Morris, George Bernard Shaw, Sydney Webb and others. These books and such organizations as the Knights of Labor, the Single Tax League, the Australian Socialist League and other short-lived ideological organizations were indications of the climate of opinion at a time of deep economic cleavages. However, the turmoil of the nineties produced strongly-knit trade unionism and a constitutionally-minded Labor Party rather than any fundamental change in society.

American single-taxer Henry George, who made a triumphal progress through Australia in 1890, had the most lasting influence on Australian economic and political thought. George argued that "poverty in the midst of plenty" was due to private ownership of land and "unearned increment" of rent. His remedy was a single tax on land so arranged that it would make it unprofitable for anyone to own land who did not use it to full capacity in the community interest. This doctrine had particular appeal to Australian radicals who resented the squatters' early monopolization of land and to would-be farmers interested in land reform.

The reformer-to-be first visited Australia in 1856 as a fifteen-year-old ship's boy aboard the American ship *Hindoo*, out of New York, with a load of lumber for Australia. Back in America as a penniless journalist, George eloped in 1861 with Annie Fox, born in Sydney, who had been brought by her grandparents to San Francisco after her parents separated. The marriage helped determine George to accept an invitation to make a lecture tour of Australia and New Zealand.

The Australian tour was a success from the moment a Sydney reception committee presented Annie George with a red-and-gold shoulder ribbon emblazoned "Welcome, Australia's Daughter" until the Mayor of Sydney gave the couple a civic farewell three months later. Between these two social occasions Henry George toured New South Wales, Victoria, South Australia and Queensland, delivering lectures which were received with enthusiasm greater than anything he had experienced before. He was fêted and banqueted, and the constant round of speeches and official dinners proved later to have been too great a drain on his strength; he spoke every evening and sometimes twice a day during his entire stay in Australia." In December, after returning to America via India, Italy, Switzerland, France and Great Britain, he was stricken with aphasia. He recovered from the attack, which was accompanied by a slight brain hemorrhage, yet his physical condition remained impaired until his death seven years later at the age of fifty-eight.

Summing up the influence of Henry George on Australian social thinking and practice, Australian economic historian T. A. Coghlan, in his *Labour and Industry in Australia* (London, 1918), says that "while land taxation became a leading principle with all classes supporting the labour movement, the doctrine of the Single Tax was never officially adopted in any colony." He explains this by pointing out that George was a free-trader while the Australian Labor Party demanded high customs duties no matter what other taxation was imposed. "Outside the circle of official trade unionism," Coghlan continues, "considerable enthusiasm was displayed for Henry George by persons moved to indignation by his eloquent pictures of the wrongs and disabilities of the poorer classes, and by his demand for social reform. . . . On the question of social reform his words were received throughout a very wide circle, and by the working classes generally, with a respect that almost amounted to veneration. Discontent was rife amongst all classes of workers and though such result was far from being sought by him, Henry George's visit to Australia served to fan the smouldering ashes of social revolt. . . ."

The growth of the labor movement and social democracy in America, Australia and Great Britain was part of what Ortega y Gasset somewhat grandiloquently called "the rise of the masses" while Marx and Engels called it "the class war". The phenomenon was accompanied by the growth of big business in America and Britain and the appearance in Australia of what were later called "multinationals". America's success in the development of such new products as electrical goods, machine tools, communications equipment, automobiles, and methods of mass production, underlined the fact that Britain's erstwhile industrial leadership was over.

Supported by rising tariffs and stimulated by growing markets for new products, not only America but Germany and other European countries penetrated traditional British markets and were often even able to defeat more conservative-minded British manufacturers on their home ground and throughout the Empire. Frock-coated, top-hatted probity proved no match for brisk salesmanship and mass-produced new lines.

British businessmen did not succumb, as was sometimes feared by contemporary critics, to "Made in Germany" and "American Invaders". Industrial entrepreneurs such as W. H. Lever built up huge manufacturing complexes to profit from the remarkable increase in mass purchasing power which accompanied the growth of a pragmatic trade unionism more concerned with higher wages and shorter hours than with Marxian or Georgian theory or utopian socialist speculation. On the distribution side, Thomas Lipton and other chain-store pioneers spread multiple shops in every town and suburb throughout the country. Nevertheless, Britain's huge export of capital to the Empire and elsewhere starved home industry and banked down the reequipment of old industries and the establishment of new.

Money tied up in the production of heavy textiles, coal and railway equipment for nonexpanding markets was not available to provide either middle or working-class homes with the labor-saving devices, smart fashionable clothes, leisure-time gadgets and entertainment which, in America, demonstrated more and more that if some of the rich were getting richer not all the poor were getting poorer. Americanization may not have marked an end to ideology, as some later optimists contended, yet it soon made much of the speculation that had agitated the nineties seem as curiously old-fashioned as Lord Hopetoun's plumed hat and Mr. Edmund Barton's frock-coat must have seemed to the following generation, brought up on Charlie Chaplin, William S. Hart, Mary Pickford, Rudolph Valentino, Douglas Fairbanks and the Gish sisters.

Motion pictures had an international beginning. Three Frenchmen, Mark Roget, Louis Baguerre and Dr. E. J. Marey, provided the theoretic and practical basis for later developments. In England, William Friese-Greene, according to some historians, single-handedly solved all the problems of photographing and projecting motion picture film. Nevertheless, it was an American, George Eastman, who in 1888 developed the cheap, flexible, unbreakable celluloid film essential to popular photography as well as to commercial cinema. A year later two Americans, Thomas Edison and William Dickson, produced moving pictures in the Kinetoscope, a one-at-a-time, penny-in-the-slot peepshow which was publicly demonstrated in New York on 14 April 1894. Certainly it was prophetic of future trends that it was an American showman, Carl Hertz, who first showed motion pictures to a mass audience in Australia, in 1896.

The cinema was destined to become the world's most extensive medium of entertainment and, before the advent of radio and television, the most effective agency for disseminating ideas. People in Sydney, Melbourne, Hobart, Adelaide, Brisbane and Perth, not to mention Alice Springs and Kalgoorlie,

Australian gold diggings, a record of the gold rush by an unknown artist

The mines of Placerville. The American diggings were not so very different

were soon more familiar with New York, Chicago and Los Angeles and with a legendary Wild West, than with London or Birmingham, and the Public School spirit which was supposed to govern the Empire. By 1900, with the introduction of electric projection, film-makers had seen the story-telling (and propaganda) possibilities of the new medium. Within a few years Australia, Britain, Denmark, France, Germany, Spain, Russia and the United States were producing a regular stream of one-reel adventure stories, dramas, comedies and other features to feed a continuous demand.

Australia was early in the field on both the production and distribution sides of the new industry. The Salvation Army in Australia produced one of the world's first feature films, *Soldiers of the Cross* (1900), well ahead of the British-made *Attack on a China Mission* (1901) and Edwin S. Porter's *The Life of an American Fireman* (1902). The Tait brothers' sensationally popular *The Kelly Gang* (1906) compared more than favorably with Porter's *Great Train Robbery* (1903) and ran for 100 minutes compared with Porter's eleven minutes. These films set the pattern for the next seven or eight years during which Britain and France emerged as leaders of the film industry. By 1914 the United States was making a bid for the leadership Hollywood gained during the first World War and held until television replaced the cinema as the world's most universal form of popular instruction and entertainment. Hollywood's early popularity was due to more technically advanced and sophisticated production than the Australian industry could then match. By this time, during the 1920s, American interests had captured Australian distribution outlets and blocked any possibility of Australian film-making competing on an equal footing.

J. D. Williams, a Canadian who had read in an American newspaper that Australians were avid moviegoers, arrived in Sydney during 1909 to open an Australian equivalent of the "nickelodeon". Harris and Davis had opened the first American nickelodeon in Pittsburgh in 1905 and within three years there were between eight and ten thousand throughout the country. Williams's Colonial Theatre on George Street, Sydney, provided a continuous show (10.00 A.M. to 10.00 P.M.) for admission charges of threepence and sixpence. It was so successful that he opened another continuous show opposite. In 1912 the Greater J. D. Williams Amusement Company (formed in 1910) financed "a vast and splendid auditorium" in Sydney, named the Crystal Palace. Besides a cinema this establishment contained Winter Gardens, Electric Studios, and Halls of Athletic Exercises. To mark the opening Williams distributed great quantities of American icecream and popcorn.

Williams was by then in business in Melbourne and during the next few years he did more to organize cinema management and film distribution in the American manner than anyone else. In 1913 he formed Union Theatres Ltd. which combined his Amusement Company with the Tait brothers and other local exhibitors. The chain started on 6 January 1913 with twenty-nine cinemas throughout the country and by 1920 Union Theatres claimed to have seventy-five percent of all Australian exhibitors on its lists and to be the biggest buyer of films in London and New York.

Like moving pictures, the automobile arrived early in Australia. Experiments with European-derived ideas began in America and Australia about the same time. In Australia Herbert Thomson and his cousin Edward Holmes built a steam car in their modest Armidale workshop in 1898. Although aware that similar developments were taking place in Europe and America they had no outside data to work on and Herbert Thomson was entirely responsible for the design of the Thomson Motor Phaeton. It proved a most efficient vehicle and ran for several years. Between 1898 and 1900, Thomson and Holmes drove their car more than two thousand miles, exhibiting it at a number of agricultural shows in New South Wales and Victoria. By 1900, the cousins had developed a kerosene-driven car which, in a test sponsored by the Vacuum Oil Company, they drove from Bathurst in New South Wales to Melbourne, a distance of 493 miles over bad roads and bridgeless creeks. They completed the trip in nine days at an average driving speed of 8.72 miles per hour.

The Tarrant Motor Company, of Melbourne, produced the most notable of early Australian-made automobiles. Their first vehicle, a two-cylinder chain-driven model, was a failure. Their second, completed in 1901, was efficient with two forward and one reverse gears. Mr. W. Chandler, of the Melbourne hardware firm of D. and W. Chandler, bought the vehicle for £275 and obtained years of service from it. The Tarrant Company made five more similar cars before switching to four-cylinder models which also gave good service.

Despite early entry into the automobile industry and a waiting market, Australia lacked the technological background and population to make cheap cars for the ordinary man the basis of a new mass industry. Early Australian cars, like early European cars, were individually constructed for a limited market. In America, petroleum technology had developed sufficiently to make possible an abundant supply of kerosene and gasoline. The machine-tool industry was geared to manufacture the lathes, screw-cutting machines, dies and presses on which mass production depended. The system of subcontracting and the manufacture of interchangeable parts had reached the stage when many enterprises were linked to automobile manufacture. All that was needed was a man or men capable of organizing already existing techniques into a new giant industry that could supply a continuous flow of reasonably cheap vehicles for general private and commercial use.

In Europe, and even in America until Henry Ford and General Motors developed simple standardized low-cost cars for people with an average income, the automobile was regarded as a rich man's toy. As late as 1900, the *Detroit News-Tribune*, in a typical newstory of the time, dismissed the ambition to own a horseless-carriage as "a dreadful malady" suffered by "gilded youth" endeavoring to cure ennui, "this black trouble which holds in its clutches that smart class of society freed from the necessity of earning their daily bread." For a price equivalent to the cost of a "labouring man's house and lot" the idle rich could include one of the new-fangled machines among the "works of art, tapestries, gorgeous furniture" they collected to kill time. More sober observers considered the automobile a passing craze likely to collapse as suddenly as the earlier cycling craze had collapsed leaving many manufacturers bankrupt.

Meanwhile, Henry Ford, Ransom E. Olds, Henry Leyland and others were endeavoring to produce cheap, simple models to take the place of the complicated and expensive European motorcars which supplied the rich man's market satirized by the *Detroit News-Tribune*. Ransom E. Olds subcontracted for engines, transmissions, radiators, bodies, wheels, tires, springs, cushions, lamps and other accessories, and assembled the parts, producing a car selling at £650 and so simple that any local mechanic could repair it. To begin with, Olds placed an order for 2,000 engines with Henry Leyland who built to Olds's specifications but was able to obtain greater horsepower by closer machining. When Olds refused the massive 10.25 horsepower engines eventually developed, Leyland helped organize the Cadillac Company in 1902. John and Horace Dodge, who ran a twelve-man machine shop in Detroit, took up Olds's contract for transmissions and by 1901 were employing 150 men making transmissions for Henry Ford as well as for Olds.

Henry Ford proved the most persistent of the manufacturers who experimented with cheap automobiles. "Other manufacturers as prosperity came their way thought that the whole world grew more prosperous with them," reported one of the earliest (1914) marketing studies in the automobile industry; "they built automobiles for themselves instead of the public." Ford saw that America's (and Australia's) farmers, land agents, traveling salesmen, doctors, parsons and others who had to make long journeys regularly in all sorts of weather, provided a ready-made market for a cheap, easily-driven and easy-to-repair road vehicle. He set out to capture this market and succeeded with his Model T which became a universal utility as well as a universal joke. Other manufacturers soon followed suit and Ford, although he made several fortunes did not hold premier place because, from its birth in 1908 until its death in 1927, he permitted no fundamental change in his cherished Model T. History, which Henry Ford dismissed as bunk, caught up with the Model T Ford and passed it. Nevertheless, it was the right machine in the right place at the right time.

Ford's biggest rival, especially on the Australian market, proved to be

*The Tarrant car was the first automobile manu-
factured in Australia*

The T-model Ford stood up to Australia's roads
better than most

General Motors Corporation, formed in 1908, the year in which Henry Ford declared he was about to launch a car that would sell by the million. Following the incorporation of General Motors, W. C. Durant, Buick, Oldsmobile, Oakland and Cadillac joined the new organization, destined to become one of the largest single industries in the world. General Motors incorporated into its growing empire a host of affiliate companies that manufactured steering gears, spark plugs and many other accessories and parts.

From the beginning, American manufacturers entered the export market. The first Oldsmobile was recorded in Australia in 1901, a Ford in 1906. By 1912, both Ford and General Motors were exporting wholly assembled cars into Australia for a growing market. While Henry Ford concentrated on one model, General Motors experimented with several, made in different factories under different names. Finally, in 1913, General Motors turned out the low-priced Chevrolet, the first serious challenge to the Model T Ford. In 1917, both Ford and General Motors began using an increasing proportion of Australian manufactured body parts. In 1925, the Ford Motor Company of Australia Pty. Ltd. began assembling Model T Fords at Geelong, Victoria. In 1926, General Motors established a sales subsidiary, General Motors (Australia) Pty. Ltd.

Australians also played an important part in the early development of flying machines and aviation, another aspect of the general revolution in transportation and communication which made the opening decades of the twentieth century the beginning of a new epoch in the history of mankind. As with moving pictures and automobiles, men all over the world were working on the problem of producing a usable heavier-than-air machine. In most instances, experimenters in Europe and America did not know what the others were doing. Consequently, it is hardly surprising that the work of Lawrence Hargraves, who worked out types of rotary engines and wingspans widely used in early aviation, went largely unnoticed. On 12 November 1894, at Bald Hill, Stanwell Park, south of Sydney, kites designed and constructed by Hargraves lifted him sixteen feet into the air. "A safe means of making an ascent with a flying machine . . . is now at the service of any experimenter who wishes to use it," Hargraves asserted in one of a series of papers he read to the Royal Society of New South Wales.

In February 1895, a London publication, *Engineering*, reprinted part of one of Hargraves's papers. A L. Rotch, of the metereological observatory at Harvard University, read the article and constructed box-kites according to Hargraves's specifications. Modifications of these were adopted by the United States Weather Bureau and used for weather observation throughout the continent. In 1899, Hargraves visited England where he read papers and exhibited models at a meeting of the Aeronautical Society of Great Britain. He experimented successfully with model aero-engines as well as box-kite gliders.

Hargraves (who died in 1915) always regretted that Australian authorities did not emulate the United States and offer a substantial prize for the construction of a practical flying-machine. As early as 1898, when Samuel Pierpont Langley, secretary of the Smithsonian Institution, was experimenting with power-driven planes, Hargraves told the Royal Society of New South Wales, "It appears regretable that Australians should leave to Americans and others the tardy adoption of views circulated by this society." However, similar views were in wide circulation at the time and there is no evidence that Wilbur and Orville Wright, bicycle manufacturers from Dayton, Ohio, owed their success to Lawrence Hargraves when they made the first successful flight in a man-carrying, power-driven aeroplane at Kittyhawk, North Carolina, on 17 December 1903. Santos Dumont made the first officially-recorded flight in France in 1906, using a machine embodying Hargraves's box-kite principles. Meanwhile, the Wrights had improved their earliest model and by 1908 had emerged as leaders of a new infant industry.

In 1909, Australian flying enthusiasts inspired by Hargraves's successes, formed an Aerial League which persuaded the Federal Government to offer a prize of £5,000 for the first Australian-made aeroplane to fulfil conditions drawn-up by military authorities. Ignorant of the then possibilities, the military specified that to win the prize the machine must be capable of hovering, with the result that no entries were forthcoming. Military-backed experiments continued and in December 1909, George Taylor became the first man in Australia to rise in the air on a heavier-than-air motorless biplane with box-kite planes so designed that it could fly against the wind. In the same month, the first imported aeroplane reached Australia—a Wright brothers' machine.

By this time other Americans had entered the business both as manufacturers and flyers. Aero clubs were formed, exhibitions organized and barn-storming and stunting became a precariously established profession. In 1910, Galbraith Perry Rogers flew from New York to San Francisco in forty-nine days and sixty-eight hops, averaging a speed of 51.59 miles an hour with slightly more than eighty-two hours in the air. In 1911 Harriet Quimby, editor of *Leslie's Magazine*, became the first licensed woman pilot. A few weeks later Matilda Moisant teamed up with Miss Quimby in an exhibition team. In 1912, Ruth Law made a nonstop flight from Chicago to New York.

In Australia, two boys destined to become world-famous aviators began their careers before the 1914-18 war produced its crop of daring young fliers. Harry G. Hawker, a Melbourne blacksmith's son, joined the English Sopwith training school in 1912, at the age of twenty-two, and soon ranked with the greatest mechanics and test pilots of his era. In June 1913, he achieved a height record of 13,000 feet and again in June 1915, with 18,338 feet. In May 1919, he attempted to cross the Atlantic from Newfoundland but failed after flying more than 1,000 miles. Luckily, a merchant ship sighted his

*Orville and Wilbur Wright's flight soon had its
emulators in Australia*

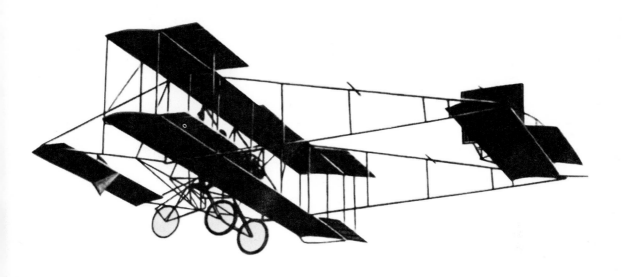

John Duigan's plane was the first to fly in
Australia

ditched plane and took him safely aboard. He became a British national hero, rewarded with an Air Force Cross (he was in the Royal Naval Service) and a *Daily Mail* award of £5,000. On 16 July 1921, he was killed at Hendon when his Nieuport Goshawk biplane caught fire during a practice flight.

Bert Hinkler, a Queensland youth who early in the century spent all his pocket money constructing gliders in which he made successful flights, worked his way to England when war began and started a practically faultless career as pilot and mechanic. Among other exploits he made the first solo flight from England to Australia using a tiny Avro-Avian with a wing span of twenty-six feet and an overall length of twenty-three feet. Hinkler won wide acclaim for a remarkable flight from New York to London via Jamaica, Brazil and Africa. He was killed in January 1933, when his plane crashed into the Tuscan Mountains, Italy, during an attempt to break the flying record to Australia, which then stood at eight days ten hours. Ross Macpherson Smith, who made aviation history in 1918 with his brother Keith by flying from England to Australia for the first time, learned his flying in the war. So did Charles Kingsford Smith, first man to fly the Pacific from the United States to Australia. These exploits belong to postwar history when for the first time aviation began to affect and ultimately to threaten the lives of ordinary men and women in all countries.

10   *Pacific Axis*

From the beginning the twentieth century has been an American century so far as most Australians are concerned. It began with the growing import of American farm and mining machinery, films and motor cars, household gadgets and novelties. In 1908 came the monumental success of a full-dress visit from the American fleet that involuntarily left more than two hundred New Australians behind. An American architect, Walter Burley Griffin, pupil of Frank Lloyd Wright, in 1911 won an international competition for the design of a new Federal capital, Canberra, which, with some variations, is now largely as he envisaged it. In 1913, a flamboyant Canadian-born, American-educated Minister for Home Affairs, King O'Malley, took part with the Governor-General, Lord Denman, and a Labor Prime Minister, Andrew Fisher, in the official inauguration of the new capital. In September 1918, Australian and American troops fought alongside each other in the main attack on the Hindenburg Line which ended World War I, battle experience to be shared again in New Guinea, Korea and Vietnam.

Decisive recognition of the new center of political gravity that had arisen in the Pacific came on 27 December 1941, when Australian Labor Prime Minister, John Curtin, appealed for American help in the struggle against Japan. "The Australian Government regards the Pacific struggle as primarily one in which the United States and Australia must have the fullest say in the direction of the democracies' fighting plan," Mr. Curtin said. "Without any inhibitions of any kind I make it quite clear that Australia looks to America free of any pangs as to our traditional links of kinship with the United Kingdom."

Five days earlier, on 22 December, the first of thousands of American troops and airmen had arrived in four ships, including the heavy cruiser *Pensacola*. Less than four months later, between 4 and 8 May 1942, American and Australian ships and planes, in the Coral Sea Battle, ended any danger of a direct Japanese attack on the Australian mainland. In 1908, the U.S. Navy had visited Australia by courtesy of the British Government. Before 1942,

America had faced the naval rivalry of Japan. Now, the United States had won command of Pacific seaways and the defeat of Japan was only a matter of time.

The seeds of the future were already planted in 1902 when the Anglo-Japanese Alliance roused apprehension in Australia and New Zealand. Australians and New Zealanders were anxious to establish British hegemony over the Pacific and throughout the second half of the ninteenth century kept needling the British Government to forestall other powers, particularly France and Germany, by preempting Pacific islands. Britain, despite the glories of Empire, was not in an expansive mood. The British Navy regarded itself as a universal nanny, always on hand in cases of natural disaster or human folly but without the slightest desire to engage in provocative muzzle-to-muzzle rivalry with Germany or any other Power. Certainly, Britain ruled the waves and needed the most powerful navy in the world to preserve the Pax Britannica that benefited everybody. There was some hypocrisy in this assumption of universal benevolence though not much. So far as the British Government was concerned, the New Imperialism that Kipling hymned and the multitude applauded during the Queen's Jubilee, was defensive. Backward-looking cynics might even call it a dying glow, although it was hardly that. A desire to keep things as they were, would be nearer the mark.

Until 1890, the U.S. Navy, in the words of President Cleveland's Secretary of the Navy, William C. Whitney, did not have the strength to fight or the speed to run away. Captain Mahan's persistence changed that. Reluctantly at first, Congress laid down four battleships, *Oregon*, *Indiana*, *Massachusetts* and *Iowa*. At their trials in 1895 and 1896, the *Indiana* and the *Iowa* impressed British observers as equal and better than anything in the British Navy, which in 1897 possessed 330 ships, including 53 ironclads, compared with America's 56 ships, Germany's 68 and Russia's 86.

From May to July 1899, twenty-six nations met at the Hague at Czar Nicholas II's suggestion, to extend the Geneva Convention of 1864 to naval warfare. Britain favored naval limitation, provided it maintained the status quo and left the British Navy supreme. The United States sent Andrew White, U.S. Ambassador in Berlin, and Captain Mahan. Mahan made it clear that America was not interested in naval limitation especially in view of the developing importance of the "open door" in China which he said would require a considerable increase in American naval power.

The first Hague Peace Conference failed to limit naval expansion but, to assuage the Czar and appease their own consciences, the delegates authorized the establishment of a permanent Court of Arbitration. A second Hague Conference was held in 1907 with equally negative results so far as naval limitation was concerned. Originally called in 1904 at Theodore Roosevelt's suggestion, it had to be postponed because of the Russo-Japanese War.

Between the first and second Hague conferences, Britain fought and nearly lost a war against the Boers in South Africa; the United States organized Hawaii as a territory of the Union; an international expedition, including Australia, Britain, Germany, Japan and the United States, landed in China in support of the U.S. policy of an open door to Western trade; the United States established virtual hegemony over Cuba and the Philippines; the British annexed Ashanti on Africa's Gold Coast; Australia passed an Immigration Restriction Act and enfranchised women; the United States acquired the Panama Canal Zone; in Russia, Lenin and Trotsky emerged as leaders of the Bolshevists against the Menshevists in the Russian Social Democratic Party; Theodore Roosevelt became President of the United States; Japan defeated Russia and exercised a protectorate over Korea; Irish malcontents formed the Sinn Fein Party; Sun Yat Sen organized a union of Chinese secret societies to expel the Manchus; Germany provided for the construction of more battleships; the Liberals under Campbell-Bannerman won a landslide electoral victory in Britain; and Britain and Japan renewed their Alliance for another ten years.

The last item aroused loud indignation in Australia. Hitherto, the Chinese had constituted the "Yellow Peril" so far as Australia was concerned, and the Chinese were feared not as Imperialists but as migrants who threatened to undermine Australia's cherished standard of living and her racial purity. Throughout the gold era, when Chinese diggers came in by the thousands, there was growing animosity towards them which broke out in violent anti-Chinese riots at Lambing Flat, New South Wales, in 1861, Clunes, Victoria, in 1873 (when Chinese miners were used as strike-breakers) and in North Queensland in the late 1870s. The Sydney *Bulletin*'s radical Manifesto, published on 29 August 1891, denounced the Chinese, along with religious influence in politics, foreign titles and Imperial federation. Even Henry Lawson, Australia's most popular radical poet, agreed with the peculiar reasoning of the *Bulletin*, trade unionists and the Commonwealth's first Prime Minister Edmund Barton that the doctrine of the equality of man was never intended to include racial equality.

Once Japan began building a major navy Australians became apprehensive of something more than unrestricted immigration from Asia. The Japanese had shown no interest in the gold rushes and unlike the Chinese were known as a non-migratory people. Nevertheless, the new Commonwealth Government acutely embarrassed Great Britain when it included Japanese in the dragnet of undesirable immigrants excluded by its Restrictive Immigration Act of 1902. Britain had a military alliance with Japan and brought such strong pressure to bear that the Australian Government in 1904 concluded an agreement with Japan permitting the entry into Australia of Japanese businessmen and their families.

As only token advantage was taken of this concession Australians were not overconcerned about Japanese immigration, compared with Chinese, which had reached flood proportions before being restricted. When Japan defeated Russia in the Russo-Japanese War of 1904-5 things were different. Australian statesmen and newspapers openly condemned Britain's alliance with Japan and made it clear that American assurances of protection would not be unwelcome. From the beginning, the *Bulletin* was satirically indignant at what it called "the motherland's misalliance" with Japan. More restrained but equally apprehensive, the Brisbane *Courier* expressed conservative opinion when it said, "The marvellous uprush of the Japanese Power has created no small uneasiness in these colonies. . . . Were Japan to turn her naval arm against what lies in Australian waters, we should go down." The literary magazine *Lone Hand* echoed similar concern less politely:

Against the two white peoples with important establishments in the Pacific, the United States and Australia, are arrayed millions of brown men, ambitious and arrogant in Asia for more than four hundred years. Alfred Deakin, Prime Minister of Australia when the American Fleet visited the Commonwealth in 1908, was anything but a brash colonial politician. Well-educated, well-read and philosophically-minded he was the last man to echo popular prejudice or to sacrifice liberal principle for expediency and votes. Nevertheless, he, too, welcomed the American Fleet as part of "the *entente cordiale* spreading among all white races who realize the Yellow Peril to Caucasian civilization, creeds and politics."

With the foregoing overheated atmosphere in mind it is easier to appreciate the almost hysterical enthusiasm with which Australian Government, press and people welcomed the visit of Rear-Admiral Charles S. Sperry, U.S.N., with sixteen American battleships—the Great White Fleet—in August and September 1908. Sydney spent £50,000 on wood, plaster, cardboard and bunting. Pitt Street was renamed American Avenue for the week and the streets of what some Americans called a "subtropical Boston" were arched with flags and flowers while gold-painted eagles perched on every lamp-post. A huge papier mâché *Mayflower* hid the facade of the Customs House and a replica of the Statue of Liberty rose to a height of five stories in front of the *Daily Telegraph* building. The *Telegraph*, emulated slightly more conservatively by the *Herald*, devoted a main-page spread and twenty columns of newsprint to the occasion on 20 August, the day the fleet arrived, and rose to ever greater space and enthusiasm on each successive day of the Sydney visit.

According to the *Telegraph* one hundred thousand people crowded the shores and headlands of Sydney Harbor to see the Great White Fleet arrive, undeterred by stories from New Zealand about the riotous behavior and disreputable conduct of a great many of the men on shore at Auckland, where there had been club-swinging battles between shore patrols and sailors. The Sydney arrival was impressive. Watchers on the heads were baffled at first by sea haze. "Then, all at once, the mist faded," wrote a *Telegraph* reporter, "and the majestic battleships showed themselves for what they were—the most overwhelmingly powerful navy that ever floated in Australian waters. The effect was simply stupendous. . . ." The "Great White Ships", the reporter continued, represented not only "a cruise unique in naval history" but "the fighting arm of the Great Republic—a long, strong, hard-hitting arm, ready to strike terrible blows in defence of the white man's cause should it ever be assailed in this part of the world. . . ."

The flotilla, led by the U.S.S. *Connecticut* (16,000 tons), Admiral Sperry's flagship, included five 16,000-tonners, four 14,000-tonners and seven other ships in the battleship or cruiser class, representing the biggest and best in naval architecture and gunnery at that time. The U.S. Navy also kept abreast of other technological devices, including the use of telephone, wireless, and electric power.

By contrast, many of Britain's battleships looked better than they were. British naval officers still basked in the aura of Nelson and preserved a hierarchial order already under challenge on land. British sailors regarded engineers with amused contempt. "Their mammas," snarled impatient reforming Admiral Sir John Fisher, "were not asked to take tea with other mammas." In the mess, ship's officers with names like Smythe, Forsythe-Jones, Ponsonby and Stanhope patronized as "mechanics" and "greasers" engineer officers with names like Smith, Jones, Brown and Jenkins.

The commissioned sailors, who dipped into their own pockets to subsidize batmen and mess stewards, and kept Jack Tars busy scrubbing decks and polishing brasswork, completely disregarded the elementary fact that without mechanics and greasers Britain's great ships-of-the-line, their slightly out-of-date dowager bulk handsome in fresh paint, polished brass and gilded bolt-heads, could never have put to sea. The U.S. Navy, on the other hand, established machine shops and blacksmith shops on every ship and sought mechanics and tradesmen rather than sailors for seamen, putting up with the sloppy marching and shore patrol battles this sometimes entailed.

President Theodore Roosevelt, in an address at the Naval War College, Rhode Island, the month before, had made clear his concept of what the United States Navy should be. "I want a first-class fighting navy or no navy at all," he said, "because a first-class fighting navy is the most efficient guarantee of peace this nation can have. There are always a number of amiable, well-meaning people who believe in having a navy merely for coastal defense. A purely defensive navy would be almost useless. To advocate such a navy is like advocating a school prize for fighting in which one should do nothing but parry. I hope this nation will never have to hit. We should do everything we honorably can to avoid trouble but when we do go to war that war will only be excusable if the navy is prepared to hammer its opponent until he quits fighting. You cannot hammer an opponent if you wait for him to come to your coast to hammer you first. For the protection of our coasts we need fortifications so that the navy be left free to stretch out and destroy the enemy. That is its function."

As Admiral Sperry was well aware, stretching out to destroy an enemy did not entail taking British colonies under America's wing, or muttering suspiciously about the Yellow Peril, thus offending Britain's ally, Japan. He endeavored to be what the Melbourne *Argus* proclaimed him, "the perfect diplomat, another Lord Chesterfield." Certainly he pleased the Governor-General, Lord Northcote, and the State Governors of New South Wales and Victoria, by his reiterated references to Australia as "the brightest jewel in the Crown of that Empire to which we owe our traditions, political and military" and to the Royal Navy and its "glorious traditions" which enabled British people everywhere to rest secure "under the shadow of the Fleet . . . without undue and burdensome expenses. . . ." In his opinion he managed to keep the Australians happy without telling them what they wanted to hear: the American Navy's readiness to protect Australia from the Yellow Peril.

"You cannot imagine how careful I had to be," he wrote afterwards. Every utterance was "jealously watched and noted" by Japanese and British as well as Australian observers. He felt he was "sailing under false colors" for he knew that the "astounding demonstrations" and "hysterical heartiness" of the welcome could "only be due to popular sentiment looking for us to take sides against Asia." He kept edging away from Mr. Deakin's veiled invitations to speak out and took refuge either under Lord Northcote's urbane assumption that the Queen and her colonial Prime Ministers were one, or in mutual assurances of common ancestry, common heritages, common language, and common political institutions. Dutch-descended Executive Officer Coontz who sometimes listened to thirteen speeches in a day, found it all "an awful fizzle" but another commentator showed more understanding when he observed: "Blended with their song of joyous welcome was a cry of pathos and grim desperation. The Australians are telling something extremely important to Great Britain, and its echoes cannot be ignored in Downing Street."

British comment was mostly judicious. The *Daily Chronicle* declared that "this colonial fraternization is very gratifying in Britain, where the maintenance of the most friendly relations with the American people and Government is an object of universal desire and an axiom of our policy." The *Morning Post* hoped that the presence of the American Fleet would prompt the statesmen of the Commonwealth to support Mr. Deakin's desire for a stronger naval force in the Pacific and noted with satisfaction that "the Lords of the

Admiralty have latterly shown a disposition to meet the needs of the case. . . ." Only the *Daily Graphic* mentioned the Yellow Peril and suggested that "the phenomenal festivities" that had greeted the Americans indicated "how deeply the Englishman in the Pacific feels with the Yellow Peril problem, which is paramount there. . . ." The *Graphic* regretted President Roosevelt's contribution to international tensions and drew attention to its "grave significance to British statesmen." *The Times* feared that "a spectacular display has valuable uses in impressing the masses, who will remember the sight for years, and draw important political deductions therefrom."

The popular press in America exulted in the attention the Great White Fleet aroused and referred to the "green-eyed envy" Great Britain must feel at Australian suggestions that the United States should proclaim a new Monroe Doctrine for the Pacific. Some editorialists assured Australians that they would someday be part of a new American Empire. The New York *Sun* took a more republican view: "The only possibility is for us to admit them as states within our Federal Union." One New Zealand correspondent informed the *Sun* that it was sad to contemplate "the tragedy of the passing away of a once mighty power" as that of England. With that power now "fast-decaying" in the Pacific, the writer added, "I am no traitor in wishing for the Pacific supremacy of the Stars and Stripes." The New York *Times, Herald, Tribune* and other responsible newspapers carried stories expressing amazement at the glowing welcome Australians had given the American Fleet. The New York *Herald* correspondent, who accompanied the Fleet, declared that "the Australian friendship will not be forgotten. . . . Australians are truly kinsmen, and the word will stick."

The British *Navy League Journal* huffed and gruffed over the whole affair. "We watch the success of President Roosevelt's mammoth Hurrah Party with benevolence and amusement," it declared, "even though it consorts ill with the present engagements of the Empire." The British press concluded, however, that the United States would not disrupt, or wish to disrupt, "the present engagements of the Empire", that is, the Anglo-Japanese Treaty. Despite the New York *Sun*'s insistence that by "hands-across-the-sea" Australia now meant hands across the Pacific to the United States, most American newspapers were agreed that in the event of any ultimate quarrel between Britain and Japan regarding the integrity of Australia, America would not interfere either way. The real lesson to be drawn from the enthusiastic welcome given to the Americans in Australia was the need for more British ships in the Australian squadron to reassure Australians that Britain still ruled the waves.

In Melbourne, more than three hundred American sailors deserted, and over two hundred, aided by Australian girls and hidden in Australian homes, were never picked up. Including the men who deserted in Auckland and

Sydney, the Fleet lost almost the equivalent of the crew of a Fourth Division battleship. The Japanese press reported the matter with Oriental gravity: seven hundred American sailors had run away because they feared to fight the Japanese navy! One Jackie explained to the Sydney *Telegraph*: "They told me Auckland was the candy but this is the real striped stick. I thought I'd throw a triple somersault when I came through the Heads. The wise guys on the Bowery told me we were bumping up against kangaroos and blacks in Australia, and a few sporting whites, and here I am, and on the dead square level, I think I'm back on dear old Broadway."

When the tumult and the shouting died and the Captains and the Admiral had departed things were much as they had been before—except that Mr. Deakin eventually obtained his ships. The Commonwealth had inherited a handful of out-of-date, unmanned gunboats and torpedo boats from the States and had set up a Naval Board to organize a local squadron or flotilla as an integral part of the British Navy. Deakin had earmarked sufficient money to build several torpedo boats when Andrew Fisher succeeded him in November 1908. Fisher, the Leader of the Labor Party, who had joined enthusiastically in the welcome to the American Fleet, brought in a Defense Act on similar lines to Deakin's, using the money Deakin had set aside to build three torpedo boats. Meanwhile, Sydney enthusiasts initiated a movement for presenting a Dreadnought to the British Navy. The Premier of New Zealand, Sir Joseph Ward, with still greater enthusiasm, offered two.

Sydney citizens contributed £100,000 and then brought pressure to bear on the Premiers of New South Wales and Victoria to make up the money and offer a Dreadnought jointly if the Commonwealth declined to do so. Prime Minister Fisher, who preferred to build a local squadron as the nucleus of an Australian Navy, suggested an Imperial Conference on naval affairs and at the same time offered to place all Australian ships at the disposal of the Lords of the Admiralty whenever war seemed likely. In the event, the Conference evolved an entirely new system of defense for the Pacific, including a Pacific Fleet in three units, each led by a battlecruiser, based respectively on Australia, the East Indies and China. The East Indies and China units remained under direct Admiralty control, the Australian unit was paid for, controlled and eventually manned entirely by Australians.

The Royal Australian Navy was thus born, and in those days it was taken as axiomatic that if Britain were at war Australia was automatically at her side wherever required. When war eventually began Andrew Fisher, campaigning during a wartime general election held in September 1914, pledged Britain Australia's support "to her last man and her last shilling." Labor won the election and Fisher became Prime Minister until he handed over leadership in October 1915, to William Morris Hughes. A brilliant, fiery Welshman, Hughes did not permit his radical politics to inhibit in any way his pro-

Empire convictions or prevent him from becoming the beloved "Little Digger" of Australia's Imperial Force (A.I.F.).

Ironically, Japanese warships escorted the first Australian convoy overseas. It carried four infantry and two Light Horse brigades (including one of each from New Zealand) to the Middle East, nucleus of the Australian and New Zealand Army Corps (ANZAC) which won its battle honors on Gallipoli. Nor were the British Empire and Navy quite so fast-decaying as the New Zealand correspondent to the New York *Sun* had assumed. High noon, rather than twilight, occurred on 21 November 1918, when an American observer, Rear Admiral Hugh Rodman, saw the British Grand Fleet, the mightiest navy in world history, receive the surrender of the German Navy at the Firth of Forth, Scotland. A squadron of six American ships stood by while the British light cruiser H.M.S. *Cardiff*, in the gray dawn of a clear day, marshaled a German armada—fourteen capital ships and fifty-six smaller vessels—for the final humiliation. The scene reminded Admiral Rodman of his home on a farm in Kentucky where he had often seen a small child herding a mob of sullen bullocks.*

The British Commander-in-Chief, Admiral Sir David Beatty, drew up his fleet—thirty-six battleships, eight battlecruisers, thirty-six cruisers and more than one hundred destroyers—into two parallel lines. The German ships steamed slowly between them into the Firth to an agreed anchorage. Then Beatty signaled: "the German flag will be hauled down at sunset today, Thursday, and will not be hoisted again without permission." When Adolf Hitler's rejuvenated German navy went to war its menace lay in submarines rather than battleships. By then, Germany's ally, Japan, possessed a navy the size and threat Alfred Deakin and Andrew Fisher had feared forty years earlier.

Labor Prime Minister John Curtin's plea for American help on 27 December 1941 echoed in more urgent and more justified accents Deakin's anxieties of 1908. The decisive naval battles of the Pacific War came in the Coral Sea on 4 to 8 May 1942, and at Midway in the following June. They were battles fought mainly over the rim of the ocean between ships that saw each other, if they saw each other at all, as blips on a radar screen, and destroyed each other with planes launched from aircraft carriers. The days of battleships were over but aircraft carriers did not prove the fulcrum of a new balance of power. British and American scientists were devising that fulcrum in strictest secrecy outside the knowledge of all but a handful of worried men. In August 1945, Hiroshima and Nagasaki provided seared and shattered symbols of the new pattern that would shape a postwar world.

The Fall of the British Empire, by Colin Cross (London, 1965).

It would be a mistake to suppose that a continuous policy linked Australia's tumultuous welcome to America's Great White Fleet in 1908 with Mr. Curtin's plea for American aid in 1941. Though the course was charted which led to the signature in 1951 of the Pacific Security Agreement between Australia, New Zealand, and the United States (ANZUS), the countries concerned did a good deal of tacking, or simply lay becalmed, before arrival. In 1908, 1918, 1928, when Kingsford-Smith flew the Pacific for the first time, and in 1938, when Neville Chamberlain proclaimed "peace in our time", Great Britain still appeared the world's dominant power, an arbiter of the world, a global rather than a European power.

Between the wars Australia's policy, except for a brief, climacteric interlude under William Morris (Billy) Hughes, reverted, in practice if not in theory, to the traditional colonial concept of leaving Imperial matters to George—in the persons of His Britannic Majesty King George V's ministers at Whitehall. Even Hughes, champion as he was of Australia's independence, stressed the benefits of association with Britain. As late as 1921 he told the Australian people, "When the voice of Australia speaks as part of the British Empire, with its 500,000,000 people, its mighty Navy, its flag on every sea, its strong-holds on every-continent, its power and its glory shining and splendid, acknowledged by them all, then she speaks in trumpet tones that are heard and heeded throughout all the earth." In so far as Australia's traditional policy was logical and not lazy, it represented a desire to achieve diplomatic unity in what was now known as the British Commonwealth of Nations plus a reliance on British naval power based around the presumed impregnability of Singapore.

Ironically, the growth of the concept of Commonwealth rather than Empire and Australia's self-assertion at Versailles, in the person of Mr. Hughes, made Commonwealth diplomatic and military unity more and more precarious. Consequently, once Japan had exposed the hollow nature of the Singapore myth, Australia had no other alternative than to follow what, after all, had always been Mr. Churchill's advice. As early as March 1914, as First Lord of the Admiralty, he warned Australia and New Zealand not to count on the British Navy in the event of a world war. If the worst came to the worst, he said, "the only course of the five million of white men in the Pacific would be to seek the protection of the United States." Britain's chief preoccupation then, as later, was Europe and her own vulnerability as a European island dependent on Atlantic seaways.

Billy Hughes's policy was simple, logical and entirely self-centered. He wished Australia to be an independent nation in her own right but was well aware that Australia was not strong enough, economically or militarily, to stand alone in the Pacific. Faced with more than the possibility of a post-war expansive Japan he wanted buffer territories and powerful friends. With reluctant British acquiescence, Australia had administered Papua since 1907.

Her first military action in World War I had been to send an expeditionary force to occupy German New Guinea. Prime Minister Hughes now wanted international recognition for these *faits accomplis*. Britain still had an alliance with Japan although Hughes doubted whether Britain's counsels of moderation would be sufficient to restrain Japan's ambition. Consequently, he turned first to America.

Like Theodore Roosevelt, whom he admired, Hughes combined reforming zeal in internal affairs with a belligerent foreign policy. He did not suffer delusions or advocate expansion for expansion's sake. He simply took it for granted that the wartime American alliance represented civilized law and order versus vaunting militarism and that Anglo-American dominance in the Pacific was essential to Australian security. In a speech at the Union Club in New York on 31 May 1917, he suggested that the United States should establish a Monroe Doctrine in the South Pacific. The United States, Australia and New Zealand, he said, possessed common interests in the area and he would expect the United States to support Australia at the Peace Conference as on the battlefield. In particular, he sought American support for Australian control over New Guinea and resistance to Japan's desire for control over Pacific islands adjacent to Australia.

These arguments might have appealed to Theodore Roosevelt but President Wilson had different ideas. He was pledged to collective security and the League of Nations and wished to see an international order replace the Pax Britannica that had failed to prevent World War I. He was aware that the British Empire might have lost the war with Germany had it not been for the reluctant intervention of the United States. Liberal, scholarly, tight-lipped, President Wilson had no sympathy for provocative white-superiority nationalism, nor for Empire heroics, as represented in the person of Mr. Hughes.

As things turned out, the Treaty of Versailles and the Washington Conference on the Limitation of Armaments, 1921-22, temporarily solved Australia's problem. At Versailles, with British support, Australia secured a C-class mandate over the eastern half of New Guinea, a concession Mr. Hughes welcomed as "differing from full control as a ninety-nine years' lease differs from a fee simple." The Washington Conference, which short-circuited Australia by recognizing Great Britain as spokesman for the whole British Commonwealth, substituted a Four Power Treaty (United States, Britain, France and Japan) for the Anglo-Japanese Alliance that had worried the United States as well as Australia. A concession was made to the new state of affairs by allowing Australia and New Zealand to participate in the Four Power Treaty as associates of Great Britain.

Not without reason, Americans had some difficulty in understanding the new concept of British Commonwealth of Nations in place of the British Empire. Lord Rosebery, a Liberal Imperialist, had first used the term, viz a viz the British Empire, speaking in Adelaide Town Hall in January, 1884. "Does this fact of you being a nation," he asked his Australian audience, "imply separation from the Empire? God forbid! There is no need for any nation, however great, leaving the Empire because the Empire is a commonwealth of nations." From then on, the word "commonwealth" meaning "we're all in this together" rather than riches held in common, became the favorite word of Empire statesmen and publicists. The new Australian nation confused matters a little by calling itself a "Commonwealth", too. Nevertheless, the name stuck and did, in fact, for all its vagueness, indicate something new and strange in the political spectrum although, as it happened, the new and strange proved a mirage rather than a hard outline of the shape of things to come.

When in 1923 Hughes lost the Prime Ministership to Liberal Stanley Bruce, the new government found an appropriate means of reconciling Australian and British interests by arranging for R. G. Casey (now Lord Casey) to become Australia's liaison officer with the British Cabinet. This enabled Australia to keep fully informed on British policies and to present Australian opinions and interests in London at the highest level. The arrangement worked admirably because Australia saw no particular need to challenge British concepts of Australia's interests. Outsiders, meanwhile, confessed themselves politely baffled when they tried to grapple with the facts, economic and constitutional, that were supposed to provide solid framework for Rudyard Kipling's poetic view of the new relationship:

> A Nation spoke to a Nation,
> A Throne sent word to a Throne;
> "Daughter am I in my mother's house,
> But mistress in my own."

The extravagances of the Yellow Peril scare had died away even before World War I although more sober observers than Kaiser Wilhelm II and William Morris Hughes were not unaware that Europe's as well as the British Empire's predominance faced a threat from Asia. The threat, at that stage, was primarily demographic. Asia's population mounted inexorably while few if any Western countries, not even Hitler's Reich, could boast a replacement birth rate. Australia, New Zealand, the United States and Canada crossed their fingers and passed stringent immigration laws to stem what they feared would otherwise become an uncontrollable tidal wave of humanity from Asia. The fear was exaggerated but not greatly. In Queensland, before restrictive legislation was passed, Chinese had poured in by the thousands and on many goldfields outnumbered Australians and Europeans. A. M. Carr-Saunders, in his authoritative *World Population* (London, 1936) concluded that if there had been no American or Canadian restrictions the population of the western seaboard of North America would have been largely Asian by the mid-1930s.

Few people in Australia, New Zealand or North America paused to consider that immigration restriction was no more than a palliative and one that served only one of two or more interested parties. The United States and Australasia, both in their different ways content to shut their eyes to the world at it was, ignored the looming shadow of Asia's new needs and Russia's new philosophy. The United States, once the Senate had repudiated President Wilson's internationalism, withdrew into isolationism. Australia, free from Billy Hughes's abrasive diplomacy, believed that Great Britain still had most of the answers to Australia's international problems. Some members of the Labor Party were a little more restive, a little inclined towards American-style isolation, than Liberal and Country Party members, yet neither they nor anybody else had any clear idea of what an independent Australian policy should or could be.

The establishment of Communism in Russia and the success of nationalism in China aroused approval on the left and uneasiness on the right yet the implications of these changes provoked no serious debate. Nor did Japan's increasing claustrophobia prompt Australians to recall Mr. Churchill's 1914 warning or to extend any purposeful political feelers towards the United States. When the shock of reality did come, in September 1939, Robert Menzies, the Australian Prime Minister, told the Australian people in a broadcast to the nation: "It is my melancholy duty to inform you officially that, in consequence of a persistence by Germany in her invasion of Poland, Great Britain has declared war upon her and that *as a result* [author's italics] Australia is also at war." Everything seemed to be just as it was when Andrew Fisher unhesitatingly pledged Australia "to her last man and her last shilling" when the Kaiser's War began twenty-five years before. Events soon showed that the world had changed even if Mr. Menzies and his government had not noticed it.

Businessmen, navalmen, airmen, entertainers, athletes and technicians continued to build foundations for bridges destined to cross the Pacific. From America's point of view, investment and trade with Australia between the wars remained comparatively unimportant. Australia and New Zealand between them absorbed no more than one or two percent of America's total exports while the Southwest Pacific area as a whole supplied only about one percent of United States imports. From the beginning of the century until World War II, Australian imports from America were second to those from the United Kingdom. On the other hand, the United States usually ranked only fourth or sixth among countries buying goods from Australia. During the same period, Britain remained not only Australia's biggest customer but virtually her only source of developmental capital. In short, despite theoretical changes in constitutional relationships, until the 1940s, when Japan and the United States demonstrated that the global center of gravity had shifted from the Atlantic to the Pacific, Australia remained what she had always been—an outlying extension of British imperialism.

Nevertheless, whenever the export market for primary products boomed and Australia could afford United States imports, the stream of American goods—motorcars, gasoline and oils, tobacco, machinery, electrical appliances —reached mounting peaks, especially in 1922 and 1930. Despite the importance of American imports and technology to Australian social and economic development, Australia's between-the-wars economic policies continued to turn on a London-Canberra axis. The Australian Tariff Act of 1921 aimed at encouraging local war-born industries and providing jobs for returned soldiers. Lord Beaverbrook's abortive *Daily Mail* campaign for "Empire Free Trade" had few Australian converts but prepared the way for the Ottawa Agreement, which established preferences for British Trade. The Ottawa Agreement strengthened Australasia's and Canada's competitive position in the United Kingdom and extended preference to British over American goods throughout the British Commonwealth.

The Ottawa Agreement, while it served to alleviate an immediate crisis, was never wholly acceptable to Australia. Beaverbrook's Empire Free Trade idealism was rejected because it ignored the rapid growth of Australia's secondary industry and Australian determination to capture growing markets in Asia and Europe. In Australian eyes, the Ottawa Agreement was essentially an emergency measure preparatory to a complete reappraisal of Australia's position in a changing world. Consequently, the post-World War II position, in which British-Australian trade links ceased to be an overriding consideration in the formulation of Australian economic policies, had its roots in the past. The growth of Australian secondary industry made it inevitable that Australia should become more than a source of food and raw materials for Britain and the need to discover new sources of capital for the development of vast newly-discovered deposits of iron ore and other minerals revealed the Ottawa Agreement as inadequate for the postwar world. The United States of America, which had replaced Britain as Australia's most valued friend and neighbor in the war against Japan, gradually and inevitably grew more and more important to Australia as a trading partner and a source of capital.

Even before the war, Australia had begun to look to the United States for capital. In 1921, a Labor Government in Queensland, finding it increasingly difficult to raise money in London, took the unprecedented step of floating two loans in New York. According to one commentator, this proved a bombshell for the City of London which had hitherto assumed that the Commonwealth and States of Australia were entirely dependent upon the City of

London, which could call the tune. However, the Queensland gesture was a gesture only, rather than a radical change of policy. Edward Granville Theodore, Queensland's Premier, had no wish to change British financial dictatorship for American. He feared that in a non-competitive market interest rates might rise and he faced the prospect of having to rewrite £24 million in Queensland loans due to mature in London in 1924-25. Having made his point, Theodore, an astute financier who later became Treasurer in a Commonwealth Labor Government, went to London and arranged a compromise under which London's virtual black ban on Queensland was dropped.

In 1925, the conservative pro-protectionist Bruce-Page Federal Government roused "surprise and disappointment" in London by deciding to raise a loan of $100 million in New York. "The most influential authorities state that the London market is distinctly hostile to Dominion borrowing outside Britain," reported the Australian Press Association on 9 July, "which would be bad for the prestige of London as a financial centre and bad for British trade as America is sure to see that trade follows the loan." The financial editor of the *Morning Post*, however, was not unduly perturbed. "The City is keenly discussing the possible details of the Issue," he reported. "In some respects the arrangement has been well received because the change is regarded as calculated to help the general exchange position, and to throw some of the burden of financing Australia upon New York. At the same time, there are regrets that even for a brief time America rather than the home country, should be meeting the necessities of Australia." On 20 July, when the books were opened in New York, the Australian loan was oversubscribed within an hour. However, London had no immediate cause for concern. By the end of the decade, American loans to Australasia had reached only two per cent of the American grand total of foreign investments, lowest on the list with the exception of Africa.

Three days after the Australian loan was oversubscribed in New York, the American Fleet paid its second full-dress visit to Australia under the command of Admiral Robert E. Coontz, who had been executive officer aboard the *Nebraska* in the Great White Fleet seventeen years before. "The arrival today of the United States Fleet marks one of the outstanding events in the history of the Pacific," declared the *Sydney Morning Herald* on 23 July. Admiral Coontz, forgetting his dismissal of Admiral Sperry's oratory as "an awful fizzle", was equally effusive. "As I stand on the quarter-deck of the flagship *Seattle*," he said in a message to the people of Australia, "and see the hospitable shores of your fair land through the morning mist, my heart beats faster as memories are revived of our visit to your country, whose whole-hearted hospitality is so deep and so lasting." The Australian Prime Minister, Mr. Stanley Bruce, for all his morning clothes, spats and British accent, declared: "The future prosperity and peace of all countries bordering the great Pacific

Washington, an inspiration to the young
Commonwealth

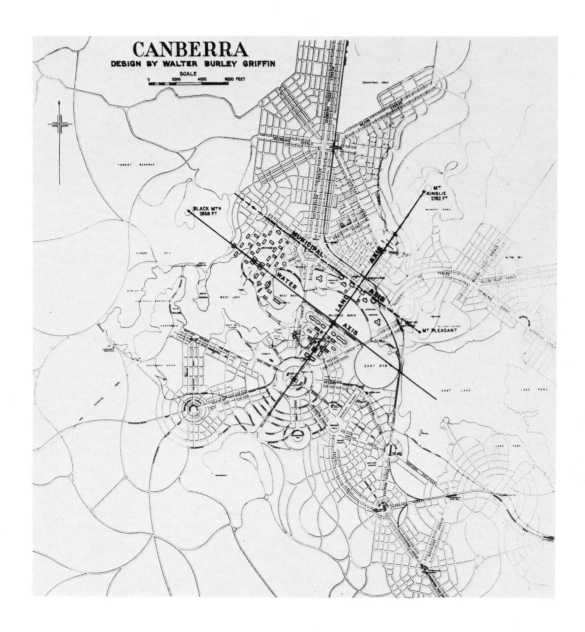

Plan of Canberra. American architect Walter
Burley Griffin planned the Australian capital

Ocean can best be assured by mutual intercourse, mutual understanding, and mutual sympathy."

The technological and military changes that had taken place between the two visits were emphasized by the fact that before Admiral Coontz saw Australia's hospitable shores through the morning mist, a seaplane from the Royal Australian Navy flew out to greet the American Fleet. The Australian Associated Press correspondent aboard *Mississippi* reported by wireless: "At 8.25 this morning (21 July) an Australian seaplane came out of the rain and mist and circled above the fleet. Owing to the unfavourable weather no airman was expected. Commander Newton White, Staff Aviation Officer, commenting upon the feat, said, 'It was a very gallant effort. I am sorry we were unable to send up a 'plane to meet him but we did not expect him in the rain'." At this time, ships of the Royal Australian Navy totaled twenty-five, including the three criusers, *Adelaide*, *Brisbane* and *Melbourne* and the fast "Flotilla leader" *Anzac*. In accordance with the provisions of the Washington Conference, H.M.A.S. *Australia* had been sunk but two 10,000 ton cruisers, two ocean-going submarines and a seaplane carrier were under construction.

Recalling the 1908 visit, the *Sydney Morning Herald* emphasized that it had coincided with "the idea of a fleet of Australia's own." The present cruise, the newspaper added, "should help to drive home the significance of seapower [and], above all, to emphasise once again Australia's peculiar interest to the Pacific, and the necessity, if we are to be properly safeguarded, for all those facilities of naval defence which ought to be the natural adjunct of a fleet in these waters." Consequently, "With fitting enthusiasm, and with that hospitality which is not merely an obligation of kinship, but which is a tradition of our people, the glad hand of welcome will be extended to a friendly Power, the despatch of whose majestic fleet to these shores, after engaging in one of the most impressive manoeuvres ever staged in times of peace, has been inspired by a desire to knit more closely together two great English speaking democracies in the common bond of brotherhood. Constituting as it does an interchange of courtesies, the visit is invested with special interest and significance because of Australia's vital share, along with the United States, in the welfare and fortunes of that vast and rich domain whose waters wash their long coastlines."

The late twenties and early thirties of the twentieth century was the Jazz Age in Australia as well as in America. While Australian governments tried to recapture the booming pioneering spirit of the nineteenth century, by financing back-to-the-land experiments to stem the flow of people to growing cities, the young kicked up their heels in the Charleston and looked about for records to be broken and for older people, whom they held responsible for the war, to be shocked with louder, more raucous music, new sexual mores, light and skimpy clothing, faster cars and increasing consumption of tobacco and alcohol. Faced with persistent and irritating trouble on the waterfront, the Bruce-Page Government tried to turn back the clock by coercive legislation that would have restricted the traditional privileges and powers of trade union leaders and trade unionists. The 1929 election produced the greatest electoral landslide in Australian history until the 1975 victory of the Liberal Party under Malcolm Fraser. With the Great Depression just around the corner, Labor was swept into office with the gentle, indecisive son of a Catholic railway worker. James Henry Scullin, as Prime Minister, and Edward Granville Theodore, Federal Treasurer.

Using a cricket bat like a flail, instead of with orthodox Gentlemen versus Players stance, a young Australian cricketer named Donald Bradman began, in the same period, a career which broke every existing batting record. He led the Australian team in an unbroken series of Test victories against England and brought himself a popular esteem in Australia rivaling that of Babe Ruth in the United States. Although tennis was still "lawn tennis", a name redolent of lazy summer afternoons of leisurely play in white flannels, hard-hitting Jack Crawford and other young hopefuls pointed the way to the high-powered international competition to come. In those days Australia's first Davis Cup champion, Norman Brookes, found himself sufficiently rewarded with a knighthood from the Queen. Forty years later, Davis Cup champions looked forward to nothing less than a million-dollar professional career. Meanwhile horseracing, which Mark Twain had found to be the universal Australian sport, had by the 1930s reached the stage when devotees were prepared to embalm the heart of a great horse, Phar Lap, as Americans had embalmed the jersey of footballer Red Grange.

The twenties were not all sport and jazz and political shenanigans. The young record-breakers included Charles Lindbergh, who, at the age of twenty-five, flew the Atlantic solo in 1927 in the *Spirit of St. Louis*, a $6,000 plane he had practically built himself. Charles Kingsford-Smith, an Australian bank manager's son, with Charles Phillipe Ulm, an Australian of French descent, Harold W. Lyon, of Maine, and James Warner, of Kansas, flew the Pacific for the first time in *Southern Cross*, a secondhand three-engined Fokker bought on borrowed money from Hubert Wilkins, the Australian-American explorer, himself an aerial record-breaker. With Kingsford-Smith and Ulm as pilots, Lyon as navigator and Warner as wireless operator, *Southern Cross* made the 7,389 miles crossing from San Francisco to Brisbane in three hops, in a little more than eighty-six flying hours. The hop from Honolulu to Fiji was the longest nonstop flight then made, Lindbergh's epic loner notwithstanding.

Southern Cross would not have flown the Pacific if it had not been for the generosity of Captain G. Allen Hancock, of Los Angeles, a wealthy American

Charles Lindbergh was admired in Australia too

Charles Kingsford Smith's flight from San Francisco to Brisbane was backed by American cash

master mariner interested in aviation. Neither the Australian nor the United States Government made any contribution to the flight. When they conceived the idea in Sydney, following news of Lindbergh's Atlantic crossing, Smithy and Ulm were too poor and unknown to raise sufficient money to buy a plane. As both had excellent war records, the Returned Soldiers League prompted Mr. J. T. (Jack) Lang, then Labor Premier of New South Wales, to grant them £3,500. With this money they went to the United States and put down a deposit on Wilkins's old Fokker, which had seen sterling service in the Arctic. Locke Harper, Californian representatives of the Vacuum Oil Company, advanced them sufficient to finish paying $6,000 for the Fokker, minus engines or instruments. The aviators then had to take out a mortgage on their machine to pay back Harper. Mr. Sidney Myer, a Melbourne businessman visiting San Francisco, handed them a cheque for £1,500 to help buy the three Wright whirlwind engines needed for the plane, which they had christened *Southern Cross*.

They still needed money to repay their loan and equip *Southern Cross* for the flight which Australian "experts" and Press were already condemning as foolishly impractical. When, as Smithy said later, the seats of their pants were hanging out, Mr. Andrew Chaffey, President of the Bank of California, introduced them to Captain G. Allen Hancock. Hancock invited them for a twelve day cruise on his 1,400-ton yacht *Oaxaca*. Two days before they arrived back at Los Angeles, Hancock called them into *Oaxaca*'s chart room. "I'll buy the machine for you, boys." he said and their financial troubles were over.* In 1930, Smithy flew *Southern Cross*, with a Dutch co-pilot, on the first around-the-world flight and was accorded a tumultuous welcome in New York.

Sir George Hubert Wilkins, the Australian explorer from whom Kingsford-Smith and Ulm bought *Southern Cross*, was an inveterate traveler and amateur scientist. Born on a farming property at Mount Bryan, South Australia, on 31 October 1888, he stowed away on a ship at Adelaide before he was twenty-one and arrived in England in 1909 after an adventurous voyage through the Middle East. In England he made a living as a freelance photographer-journalist and at the same time learned to fly. In 1912, he was a war correspondent in the Balkans and in 1913 accompanied Vihjalmur Stefansson's expedition to the Arctic.

Wilkins was already an experienced Arctic explorer when World War I broke out. He won a Flying Corps reputation as pilot and aerial photographer and after the war competed for the £10,000 prize offered by the London *Daily Mail* for the first England-Australia flight. Wilkins's plane crashed in

*I am grateful to Beau Sheil's and Colin Simpson's *Caesar of the Skies* (Melbourne, 1937) for the financial details of above. By the mid-thirties, both Kingsford-Smith and Ulm had perished while flying. Kingsford-Smith was knighted in 1932.

Crete and two other Australians, Ross and Keith Smith, both with distinguished records in the Royal Flying Corps, won the prize. In 1921, Wilkins was a member of Shackleton's last expedition to the Antarctic. Over the next ten years, the Australian explorer, backed by the American Geographical Society, made many pioneer flights in the Arctic, earning amongst other honors, a knighthood from King George V. During this period he spent five summers and parts of twenty-six winters in the Arctic regions and eight summers in Antarctica.

Based in the United States, Wilkins turned to submarine exploration under the Arctic ice cap, a project outlined in his book *Under the North Pole.* His experiments in the submarine *Nautilus* brought him further world-wide attention and preceded the atomic-powered *Nautilus* by twenty-seven years. While a resident of the United States he was frequently consulted by the American, British, Australian and Canadian governments as an Arctic expert and scientific specialist in meteorology, geology and botany. He was also a musician and an expert photographer. His Arctic and Antarctic travels continued until his death, at the age of seventy, in Framingham, Massachusetts, on 3 November 1958.

In 1929, the new Labor Government gave notice that the world was changing when Prime Minister Scullin put forward the name of Sir Isaac Isaacs, a liberal-minded, cultivated Australian-Jew and a judge of the High Court, for successor to Lord Stonehaven as Governor-General of Australia. This was the first time any Dominion had proposed a non-British Governor-General and King George V firmly rejected the notion. Lord Passfield, the British Labor Government's Dominions Secretary, referred the matter to the British Law Officers who made the extraordinary ruling that while British ministers no longer had the right to advise the King directly on Australian matters, Australian ministers had no legal right to advise His Majesty on anything at all. The only obvious conclusion, that the King should act in his own right, did not appeal either to His Majesty or anyone else, as it was clean against the British convention of a constitutional monarchy with a non-political head of state.

A way out of the dilemma was sought by referring the matter to the next Imperial Conference. The Conference decided that the King "should act on the advice of His Majesty's Ministers in the Dominion concerned." In effect, this meant that the King was now supposed to follow the advice of seven different sets of Ministers, most of whom he could not meet, on matters about which he could not be supposed to have the slightest real knowledge. George V tried to persuade Scullin to withdraw Isaac Isaacs's nomination. When he refused the King gave way and announced, with the best grace he could summon, the appointment of the first native-born Australian as Governor-

General of the Commonwealth. The decision opened the way for the extraordinary anomaly, seventeen years later, that when the Dominion of India fought the Dominion of Pakistan, the King of the British Commonwealth was at war with himself. In short, from 1929 on, the Dominions, in fact if not in theory, were self-governing republics with no more than the trappings of monarchy and, by the second half of the century, even the trappings were ceasing to have the popular appeal they once had.

On 29 October 1929, a day still retained in the memories of an older generation as Black Tuesday, the post-World War I euphoria ended and a grim new age began. Herbert Hoover (who had once managed a gold mine in Western Australia and been offered a tip by a British Lieutenant-Governor shown over the workings) had just been elected President of the United States on a ticket which promised a "final triumph over poverty." American technology, American free enterprise, American salesmanship, American democracy, seemed to promise that the century of the common man was something more than a political cliché. The Stock Market was a casino, with jazz orchestras blaring in all the big buildings round, burlesque shows part of the reward due to successful "homo boobiens", as H. L. Mencken called the new genus Americana, pioneering adventure open to all who frequented speakeasies and defied "the noble experiment" of prohibition, a world which procreated Al Capones as well as business tycoons, two-bit gamblers and idealistic presidents.

Within two years of Hoover's election there were thirteen million unemployed in the United States, and respectable ex-managers, ex-clerks, ex-investors, who hung about street corners in their best clothes, would not have smilingly waved aside a tip from a Lieutenant-Governor or anyone else. From the Western Australian goldfields, Herbert Hoover had gone on to apply to world problems precepts of common humanity learned among gold diggers in Australia. After World War I, he organized American help for war-wracked starving Europe. Maynard Keynes, the English economist and publicist who preached the end of *laissez faire* and inaugurated the "new economics", said the President-to-be was the only man at Versailles with commonsense and practical magnanimity sufficient to make the postwar world fit for heroes to live in. Instead, because of the cussedness of things as they were in a world where man's goodness did not match his cleverness, his political memorial was not "the good society", but a proliferation of shantytowns satirically labeled "Hoovervilles".

Depression spread throughout the world, not excepting Australia. The prices of wool and wheat, sustainers of the between-wars Australian economy, fell sharply, British investors called home their capital, and export prices generally slumped by fifty percent. Long-term London and New York lending for Australian Commonwealth and State projects virtually ceased until after

World War II. The newly formed Loan Council, supposed to rationalize government spending, had no money to distribute. Between 1929 and 1930, the national income dropped from £640 million to £560 million. By 1933, nearly one-third of Australia's workforce was unemployed. In October 1929, States met Commonwealth at a Premiers' Conference which recommended retrenchment all round. Prime Minister Scullin called in Sir Otto Niemeyer of the Bank of England for advice. Sir Otto recommended further retrenchment. The economy went from bad to worse.

Conservatives tightened their belts and advised others to do the same. Radicals rebelled. In the Federal Government, Theodore, reinstated Treasurer despite charges that he had been involved in questionable operations in connection with Mungana mines in Queensland, advocated policies which seemed to many very like repudiation of overseas debts. Such suggestions shocked orthodox Labor men like Joseph Aloysious Lyons, who had acted as Treasurer during Theodore's temporary disgrace, and James Edward Fenton, Acting Prime Minister while Scullin was in London to attend the Imperial Conference.

The reinstatement of Theodore, and Scullin's ineffectual politics drove Lyons out of the Labor Government and party. Others followed him into the new party he formed in collaboration with the conservatives, the United Australia Party, pledged to decency, honesty and nonrepudiation under the slogan "All for Australia and the Empire." In December 1931, a landslide election swept Labor from office and Lyons became Prime Minister. Meanwhile, in New South Wales, the Lieutenant-Governor, Sir Phillip Game, dismissed the Premier, Jack Lang. Lang had defaulted in his payments to London bondholders in defiance of the Premiers' Plan to reduce expenditure by twenty percent, to lower interest rates and increase taxation. In subsequent State elections the United Australia Party won power in New South Wales and Victoria.

In America, Franklin Delano Roosevelt, descendant of that intrepid whaling skipper Delano Roosevelt who had defied Governor King and colonial sealers early in the nineteenth century, became President of the United States, a few months after Joseph Lyons was elected Prime Minister of Australia. Less hidebound than Lyons, Roosevelt immediately asked Congress for powers beyond the Constitution and obtained them without much difficulty. He formed a National Recovery Administration (NRA) and launched the New Deal which skirted nearer democratic socialism on the Australian model than anything that had hitherto been attempted in the United States. A Supreme Court decision, which upheld the rights of two brothers to raise chickens in New Jersey and sell them in New York, destroyed the legal basis of the NRA and restored the Constitution.

Described by columnist Westbrook Pegler as "tricky, stubborn and strong as a bull", President Roosevelt persisted with what he believed to be the

General Thomas Blamey knew American troops
as well as his own Australians in New Guinea

Right: *General Douglas MacArthur got to know*
Australians in the war in the Pacific against
Japan

people's will. He created a state apparatus which had many of the advantages and some of the disadvantages of social democracy as understood in Australia. He borrowed hugely for public works, encouraged trade unionism, subsidized actors, writers and artists, played havoc with the laws of supply and demand in the production and disposal of farm produce, and created the sort of money Australian Premier Jack Lang had in mind, according to a *Bulletin* cartoon, which showed Financier Lang handing Alice in Wonderland wads of bank notes. "Will they buy anything?" asks Alice. "Oh! no," replies Lang, "but think of the fun if they were real."

One thing President Roosevelt, Prime Minister Lyons and Premier Lang had in common: they could not produce full employment in peacetime. It took World War II to do that and by 1939 World War II was just around the corner. Joseph Lyons died in April 1939, and Robert Gordon Menzies became Prime Minister of Australia. Franklin Delano Roosevelt was re-elected in 1940 and again in 1944, the only man till then to break the record of two terms in the White House.

War orders from Britain and France had by then made the wheels of United States industry speed up again. In Australia, also, the war ended depression. Prime Minister Menzies took it for granted, as perhaps a majority of Australians did, that once Britain was at war it was Australia's duty to fight beside her in defense of the British Commonwealth. Like President Wilson, the new Leader of the Labor Party, John Joseph Curtin, had repudiated the Kaiser's War as an evil outcome of Great Power politics. He now saw Hitler's War, as President Roosevelt saw it, a threat to small nations, human dignity and the rights of the common man.

World War II and its sequences in Korea and Vietnam brought to a head tendencies implicit in the way the world was going between the wars and indeed as far back as the 1890s. On 29 June 1950, four days after a North Korean Army crossed the 38th parallel, thus violating the United Nations' recognition of South Korea, the Australian Prime Minister (Mr. Menzies) placed Australian forces "at the disposal of the United Nations through the United States authorities in support of the Republic of Korea." This was the first time Australia had gone to war without waiting for Great Britain, in support of a cause that was primarily American, although the United States acted as the spearhead of an international force pledged to uphold the prestige and authority of the United Nations.

On 12 July 1951, long before the Korean War ended, Prime Minister Menzies, who retained all his sentiments of loyalty towards Queen and Empire, nevertheless signed the Pacific Security Agreement between Australia, New Zealand and the United States (ANZUS), a pact in which Britain had no part, despite the known wish of the British Government to be included. By the 1960s, Australian troops were heavily engaged alongside Americans in the tragically ill-judged Vietnam War of which Britain tacitly disapproved though conservative, traditionally pro-British Australian Ministers, unhesitatingly accepted America's version of the fighting as an act of aggression by North Vietnam against South.

To extreme right and extreme left opinion, ANZUS, the American-inspired South East Asia Treaty Organization (SEATO) that followed, and the Vietnam War, were all no more than virulent anti-Communist gestures, dictated by contemporary ideological reasons; part of the Cold War in which two superpowers, the United States and the Soviet Union, faced each other belligerently from behind mounting piles of atomic weapons. More accurately, both pacts and the superpowers themselves could be seen as logical outcomes of processes that had begun when the United States discovered that manifest destiny did not stop at the Pacific coast; when Russia under the failing Czars began an industrial expansion which war and revolution slowed but did not stop; when Edmund Barton accepted leadership of the Australian Commonwealth which, in 1905, returned the first national Labor Government in world history; and when a resurgence of nationalism in Asia and Africa began to break down the old dominance of Europe.

When Mr. Menzies declared in 1950, through his Minister for Foreign Affairs, that Australia's destiny was linked "for all time" with the destiny of the United States, he was admitting the logic of events as well as echoing sentiments expressed by a liberal, Alfred Deakin in 1908 and a radical, John Curtin in 1941. The world had changed and the destiny of nations with it. Despite the British genius for compromise there was no way in which Australia's desire for economic and political autonomy could be reconciled with an imperial unity which the British themselves, despite Joseph Chamberlain and Lord Beaverbrook, had never taken seriously. World War I and the Great Depression had brought the old Victorian England of *laissez faire* and free trade crashing to the ground. The new England flirted with socialism or based its hopes on trade associations, oligopolies and giant American-style multinational corporations rather than on a revival of Empire.

Between the wars, an isolationist America and a parochial Australia had averted their gaze from Hitler's ambitions in Europe and Japan's aggressiveness in Asia. Now that the war was over, and the sun had set on the British Empire, Australia realized that autonomy involved also the axiom that politics, external as well as internal, are about power. In short, Australia needed powerful friends. If Britain was no longer automatically available, the obvious alternative was to turn towards the United States. Reasons more tangible than the bonds of kinship, about which Admiral Sperry and Admiral Coontz had waxed so eloquent, prompted the United States to respond to Mr. Curtin's appeal and to accept Mr. Menzies' complaisance: the availability of Australia as an assembly and supply base had been an important factor in the island-hopping victory against Japan. The southern continent did not lose its strategic importance once peace had come again to the Pacific.

Australian-American rapprochement did not mean, as leftist critics asserted, the subservience of Australia to the United States, nor, as rightists hoped, that the United States was committed to intervene on Australia's behalf in any crisis that appeared to threaten Australia's security. To begin with, the two countries differed radically in their early assessment of Japan's role in the postwar world. Australia feared that a revived Japan might attempt to emulate the revived Germany after World War I, and embark on a new career of aggression. America, on the other hand, soon began to regard an economically-strengthened Japan as a necessary counterbalance to Communist China. The contretemps was resolved by ANZUS which was, in effect, an American assurance to Australia that the United States would not stand aside if such a contingency occurred.

Other conflicts of opinion were not smoothed over so easily. It was soon apparent that ANZUS was not an automatic guarantee of the kind Australia believed she possessed when the Pax Britannica extended east of Suez. America not only did not support Australia's intervention in the Suez crisis but was actively opposed to it and, to many Australians brought up on the theory that Suez was vital to Australia, appeared the chief reason why the ill-judged Franco-British-Israeli action failed so ignominiously. Nor did Australia show any enthusiasm for America's support of Quemoy, Matsu and Taiwan against Communist China's attempts to blast out potential stepping-stones for Chiang Kai-shek's return to the mainland. During the Indonesian-Malaysian confrontation in 1963, the United States maintained a stony silence when the Australian Foreign Minister, Sir Garfield Barwick, asserted that for the purpose of ANZUS Borneo was in the Pacific area.

Nevertheless, ANZUS remains the keystone in Australia's security structure. This is as true of the Labor Party as of the Liberal-Country Party. Although Mr. Gough Whitlam, when he became Labor Prime Minister in 1972, asserted the right of the middle and small powers to contract out of Great Power conflict, he did not repudiate ANZUS or allow his appeal for "zones of peace" excluding Great Power rivalries to blind him to the fact that, in the ultimate test, power is important and Australia lacks the power to stand alone in a potentially hostile world.

Australia's politicians are aware that Asia has replaced Europe as the locale of conflicts potentially dangerous to international order. ANZUS gives Australia the right to be consulted in the event of any such conflict leading "to an armed attack in the Pacific Area on any of the parties" to the treaty or "the island territories under its jurisdiction, or on its armed forces, public vessels or aircraft. . . ." On the other hand, no party to ANZUS is committed to do more than "act to meet the common danger in accordance with its constitutional processes. . . ." The leaders of the three main political parties in Australia would have agreed with the late Mr. Arthur Calwell, when, as Leader of the Labor Party he declared, "We want the American presence, strong and powerful, in Asia and the Pacific. We want it because Australia needs it until all nations are prepared to disarm."

11 *Partners in in the Future*

On 20 February 1962, as the sun dropped below the horizon of the Indian Ocean and darkness moved over the face of the earth, the lights of Perth, State capital of Western Australia, blazed as brightly as a star in the black immensity of space. One hundred and fifty miles above the earth John Herschel Glenn, Jr, a forty-year-old Colonel of the U.S. Marines, strapped on a foam contour couch in a Mercury space capsule, *Friendship 7*, surveyed the spectacle as he sped overhead at a speed of five miles per second. Fifty-four minutes and thirty-one seconds earlier he had hurtled into space from Cape Canaveral, Florida, to become the first American to orbit the earth.

"Just to my right I see a big pattern of lights apparently right on the coast," Glen reported to Astronaut Leroy Gordon Cooper, U.S. Airforce major and capsule communicator at Muchea, on the hills northeast of Perth. "I can see the outline of a town and a very bright light just to the south of it."

"Perth and Rockingham you're seeing there," Cooper told him. "They've turned on the lights for you."

"The lights show up very well," Glenn replied in the few seconds left before the silver-black darkness closed him in again. "Thank everybody for turning them on."

There was no time for more but the gesture pleased Glenn beyond measure. In the bright light of a shortened day he had seen the green-gold earth in all its beauty. The sun on white clouds over the Americas, vivid patches of emerald green water about the West Indian islands, dense banks of cloud above the Atlantic, the coast of Africa with the Atlas Mountains clearly visible, dust storms chasing across the Sahara, a brilliant rainbow-hued sunset over the Indian Ocean. Then a moment or two of inky blackness before white moonlight silvered the sky and down below, poignant reminder that he carried with him the thoughts and prayers of millions, lights in house windows and on open porches as well as in streets and parks and on public buildings.

John Glenn hurtled over Perth and across the Australian continent three times on that historic orbit. When in contact with Muchea, Glenn reported

228

readings on the instrument panel and the positions of all the switches. The temperature inside his space suit was seventy degrees Fahrenheit. The oxygen main tank held sixty per cent, ninety per cent in the secondary tank, which meant it was leaking. The relative humidity was thirty-six per cent. All the warning lights were out except the fuel quantity light. Soon he was over the Hawaii tracking station ready for the reentry phase, culmination of three years' intensive preparation. Later, Glenn described his experience:

> We were in the re-entry phase of the flight now. We had trained for this and knew most of the things that would happen. There was the bright orange glow around the capsule which we had expected. There was the dead silence over the radio as the communications were blacked out as a result of ionization caused by the heat. There was the build-up of G forces again as I was pressed back into the couch. There were also some events that were not normal. . . . I could see flaming chunks go flying by the window. Some of them were as big as six to eight inches across. I could hear them bump against the capsule behind me before they took off, and I thought the heat-shield might be tearing apart. . . . This was a bad moment. But I knew that if the worst was really happening it would all be over shortly and there was nothing I could do about it. So I kept on with what I was doing— trying to keep the capsule under control—and sweated it out.*

Millions of people around the earth were concerned, too. The tension lasted thirty seconds. Then *Friendship 7* splashed down and navy frogmen swarmed round to release her from the giant parachutes that had checked the last minutes of flight. Twenty thousand technicians and naval personnel around the world had made the orbit possible. They included seven astronauts associated with Project Mercury—each man picked as mentally and physically suited for training in the most hazardous of all professions—exploration of space. Among the seven were Gordon Cooper at Muchea and Malcolm Scott Carpenter, a U.S. naval commander, who three months later, 24 May 1962, saw the lights of Perth from *Aurora 7* on another three-orbital flight, followed by Walter Marty Schirra, who made a flight of six orbital passes in October the same year. The last Mercury flight, before the Apollo moon mission began, was the twenty-two orbit mission of Astronaut Gordon Cooper, Jr., who saw Western Australia from the same angle as John Glenn only many more times.

Man's conquest of space began on 4 October 1957, when the Soviet Union sent up *Sputnik*, the first man-made moon, or artificial satellite, into orbit around the earth. Three months later, the United States sent its first satellite,

Into Orbit, by the Seven Astronauts of Project Mercury (Cassell, London, 1962), for which I am indebted for most of the information above.

Explorer, into orbit. The Russians launched a rocket to the moon in 1959. On 12 April 1961, the first man in space, Russian Cosmonaut Yuri Gagarin, orbited the earth in one hour and forty-eight minutes, compared with Magellan's thirty-six months, George Francis Train's eighty days and George Schuster's 169 days in the 1908 New York to Paris around the world car race. Later in 1961, American astronauts made their first short journeys into space before John Glenn's complete orbit on 20 February 1962. An eight-day orbit by America's *Gemini 5* in late 1965 proved that man can live and work in space for the time it would take to journey to the moon and back. Early in 1966, the Russians achieved a soft-landing of an unmanned spacecraft on the moon and, the culminating triumph, when *Apollo 11* reached the moon on 20 July 1969 and Neil Armstrong, Michael Collins and Edwin E. Aldrin, Jr., extended America's manifest destiny from earth to the stars.

Australia, because of its favorable geographical position and close political and economic ties with the United States, has been intimately involved in the international space adventure from the first. The United States spent more than $U.S.40 million creating tracking and other space-watching stations in Australia, plus about $U.S.4 million a year on maintenance. Australian scientific and other personnel man these stations. Consequently, Australia now has a large number of scientists and technicians trained in the many aspects of space technology, radio communication and electronics. More than a thousand Australians, including the staff of the CSIRO's* radio telescope at Parkes, New South Wales, played a vital part in the *Apollo 11* moon mission, especially in making sure that clear, good-quality television pictures crossed the quarter of a million miles of space when the astronauts touched down. NASA's switching station at Deakin, in the Australian Capital Territory, was the only major switching station in the southern hemisphere. Had it suffered a breakdown the whole moon mission would have had to have been abandoned.

The partnership began in 1957 when a cooperative program was initiated in connection with the International Geophysical Year, a thirty-month period of intense international research activity. During this period joint facilities for scientific observation and space communication were jointly established. In February 1960, following the organization of NASA (the National Aeronautics and Space Agency), the U.S. Government proposed that the Geophysical Year program should be continued and extended with the object of facilitating space flight operations and "contributing to our mutual scientific knowledge for the benefit of man; and the development of space vehicles of advanced capabilities including manned space vehicles." The Australian Government agreed and, in addition to Muchea (later moved to Carnarvon), space tracking and communication facilities were established at Woomera, in South

*Commonwealth Scientific and Industrial Research Organization.

Australia, Tidbinbilla, A.C.T., Honeysuckle Creek, A.C.T., Orroral Valley, A.C.T., and Cooby Creek, Queensland. At Woomera, in addition to the U.S. Deep Space Station, the Smithsonian Institution set up an Astrophysical Observation Station.

In 1969, Australia's giant radio telescope at Parkes was used in conjunction with another 210-foot antenna in the United States to carry the historic television pictures of the first manned landing on the moon. The picture everybody remembers—Neil Armstrong's leg searching for the surface of the moon—was first seen in the briefing room at Honeysuckle Creek tracking station near Canberra, A.C.T. "Who said we'd miss it?" exclaimed somebody at the back of the room when the picture began to glow on the screen. "We've got it, all right," exulted someone else. Ed Renouard, the scan converter technician at Honeysuckle Creek, heaved a sigh of relief. "Today we really fired 'The Beast' in earnest," he said afterwards. "Suddenly all those hours of training seemed worth it. I heard Buzz Aldrin say 'TV circuit breaker in', and suddenly on the screen I saw the sloping strut of the lunar module's leg against the moon's surface."*

At Houston, Texas, they heard Aldrin say, "Oh, you got a good picture, huh?" Houston greeted the event with characteristic matter-of-factness: "Okay, Neil, we can see you coming down the ladder now." A white padded leg with a heavy boot searched gingerly downwards. "It takes a pretty good jump," said Armstrong. Then the marvel became historic fact: man stepped from planet earth to satellite moon. "That's one small step for a man, one giant leap for mankind," said Armstrong with one of what Norman Mailer called the astronauts' rare "swoops of hyperbole". "That first hour on the moon was hardly the time for long thoughts," said Armstrong afterwards. "We had specific jobs to do." At Honeysuckle Creek it was 12.56 P.M. Monday, 21 July. Someone had stuck the title of a popular song, "Fly me to the Moon", on the operations room notice board. Someone else had scribbled: "and back."

Four scientists from the Australian National University at Canberra were among the privileged scientists in about 150 laboratories around the world to investigate the moon rocks the three astronauts brought back from space. Neil Armstrong's first act when he stepped onto the moon, while still holding onto the module ladder to keep his balance, was to scoop up a handful of moon surface and put it in his trouser pocket. The astronauts later used long-handled implements to collect more rocks. The samples collected were brought back to earth in a sealed container and subjected to a quarantine period before being examined by biologists, chemists and geologists at Houston. Dr. S. R.

*First On The Moon, A Voyage With Neil Armstrong, Michael Collins, Edwin E. Aldrin, Jr., Epilogue by Arthur C. Clarke (London, 1970).

Taylor, an Australian working as the first visiting scientist with the Lunar Science Institute at Houston, was among the small preliminary band of scientists who examined the rocks. The lunar samples brought to Australia were tested at the Lucas Heights atomic reactor near Sydney.

As a compliment to Australia, NASA in 1971 named Apollo 15 *Endeavour* after Captain James Cook's *Endeavour*, from which Midshipman James Matra was the first American to see Australia on 20 April 1770. Apollo's *Endeavour* sprang a leak when its drinking water was being chlorinated on 30 September, while the command ship was circling the moon, and mission commander David Scott asked whether Cook's *Endeavour* had ever experienced a similar mishap. Mission control at Houston told Scott, fellow moon-walker James Irwin and command ship pilot Alfred Worden that it had. On 11 June the ground staff at Honeysuckle Creek transmitted the full story, read by Scientist-Astronaut Joe Allen on the day the spacemen had spent photographing and observing the moonscape:

It was 11.00 P.M. on 11 June 1770, a clear moonlit night, when Her Majesty's ship *Endeavour* under command of Captain James Cook, sailed serenely under fully-furled sail within the waters of the Great Barrier Reef off Australia's northeast coast. Then disaster struck. The ship hit a reef. With a grind and a roar, the *Endeavour* rose from the bow and came down hard, empty water casks broke their lashings and lay in a tangle with the rigging on the deck. Captain Cook dashed to the deck in his drawers, which must have compared with the astronaut's constant wear garment, a kind of long underwear. Captain Cook directed repairs to the ship. The leak was fixed, and *Endeavour* sailed safely to port, then to England. And that's the end of your history lesson for the day.

"That's quite an analogy," commented Scott, glancing out at the moonscape which, compared with Joseph Banks's first impression of Australia, "the back of a lean cow . . . her scraggy hip bones . . . stuck out", had "a stark beauty all of its own . . . like much of the high desert in the United States." In the two hundred years that separated the two events the world of men had changed beyond comparing.

Although Australia's independent space program has been necessarily limited the Commonwealth joined the space club in its own right in November 1967, when it launched a satellite, WRESAT, off the launch pad at Woomera, the South Australian rocket range. WRESAT went into orbit at a height of 200 miles and 100 minutes later passed over Carnarvon, in Western Australia, to complete its first orbit of the earth and to earn official classification as a successful satellite. Australia thus became the fourth nation, after Russia, the United States and France, to have put a satellite into orbit from its own territory. The Australian Weapons Research Establishment at Woomera built

WRESAT in collaboration with the University of Adelaide. A U.S. Redstone rocket, touched off by an American engineer, launched WRESAT into space. The satellite burnt itself out reentering earth's atmosphere after an orbital life of more than forty days. However, Australia as yet lacks the technical maturity and financial resources essential to any country which wishes to play an independent role in man's conquest of space. Consequently, she remains at present in a state of what Lord Casey, as Minister in Charge of CSIRO, called "scientific colonialism."

Nevertheless, Australia's CSIRO has developed a world reputation in several scientific fields, notably radio astronomy and agricultural research. The CSIRO's Division of Radiophysics began operation during World War II in the field of radar. After the war, the Division became a world leader in the new science of radio astronomy, which it largely pioneered. Recognition of this came quickly from the United States, where the Carnegie Corporation and the Rockefeller Corporation contributed more than $U.S.2 million towards the cost of the giant radio telescope at Parkes, New South Wales. Since 1961, the Parkes Catalogue of Radio Sources has grown to be the most complete in the world. In 1962, the discovery of mysterious objects called "quasars" followed precise determinations made at Parkes. Quasars, according to one theory, are enormously luminous stars. According to another, they are the debris of a "local" explosion in space and owe their luminosity to their relative closeness to the earth.

In addition to collaboration in the exploration of space, the United States and Australia have developed a partnership in defense which has survived several changes of government and seems likely to continue for a long time to come. During World War II, although there was no formal alliance, the Australian people became aware that their survival as a free people depended upon Washington not London. The millions of American servicemen who passed through Australia or were stationed here were a tangible demonstration of America's direct involvement in the defense of Australia. Australian and American troops fought the Japanese in New Guinea and shared in the occupation of Japan. Although Australian armed forces were small by American standards they nevertheless comprised ten per cent of the population and earned a high reputation for efficiency and initiative.

In the postwar years the threat of Communism, rather than unrealistic fears that a resurgent Japan might threaten the peace of the Pacific, prompted a continuing alliance, formalized in the ANZUS Pact and SEATO. Australia, besides backing United States efforts with sea, land and air forces in Korea and Vietnam, has provided locations for a $U.S.80 million U.S. Naval Communications Station on Northwest Cape, Exmouth Gulf, Western Australia; a $U.S.225 million Joint Defense Space Research Facility at Pine Gap near Alice Springs, in the Northern Territory; and a smaller defense project at Nurrungar, near Woomera, in South Australia. Despite recurrent political criticism a wide range of Australian opinion accepts these bases as part of the "mutual deterrents" which, as seems likely to many in Australia as well as in the United States and elsewhere, are the best guarantee of peace in our time. Majority opinion in Australia has eagerly embraced the current policy of détente but has no desire to see the United States let down its guard.

Since 1958, when President Eisenhower successfully proposed the demilitarization of the Antarctic, Australian and American scientists have collaborated in a continuing study of Antarctic meteorology, geology, biology and other sciences from the U.S. base at McMurdo Sound and the Australian base at Mawson. Soviet scientists have accepted invitations to share in these studies. Earlier this century British, Australian and American explorers outlined the geography of this vast forbidding region. British scientific bodies, with help from the Royal Navy, organized three large expeditions between 1901 and 1912. The first and third were under Captain R. F. Scott, R.N., the second under his lieutenant (later Sir) Ernest H. Shackleton. In a secret, record-breaking dash unhampered by scientific research, the Norwegian Raol Amundsen reached the Pole on 14 October 1911, a few weeks before Scott. The Australian poet Douglas Stewart has celebrated the heroism of Scott's last journey, in which he and four companions lost their lives, in a poetic drama *The Fire on the Snow* (1944) which has been widely broadcast.

Australian explorer, Sir Douglas Mawson, who accompanied the Shackleton Expedition of 1908-9, carried out valuable Antarctic exploration on behalf of the Australian Government between 1911 and 1931. In 1928, the United States took up where Commander Wilkes had left off in the mid-nineteenth century, and dispatched a series of expeditions under Admiral Richard Byrd, who was the first to use aircraft for Antarctic exploration, worked from a permanent base which he called Little America. In 1947, the Australian Government authorized expenditure of £200,000 on preliminary planning for a new and continuing Australian National Antarctic Research Expedition concerned with scientific investigation rather than geographical exploration. The first wintering party organized by Group-Captain Stuart Campbell of the R.A.A.F. sailed in *Wyatt Earp*, originally a Norwegian 400-tonner bought by Australian-born Sir Hubert Wilkins for the American explorer, Lincoln Ellsworth, who made several notable flights over Antarctica, two of them with Hubert Wilkins.

In 1952, Langley George Hancock, a sheep-farmer at Mulga Downs, near Wittenoom, Western Australia, decided to fly down to Perth before the summer "wet" made private flying impossible. Storm clouds were black above him when he set out and soon forced him to seek shelter by flying low along the gorges between the flat-topped mesa-like hills of the Pilbara, which resemble America's Badlands. At close range the dark red walls of the narrow gorges looked to Lang Hancock like iron. They mostly were. During the next "dry" he took another look from the air and traced the iron walls for seventy miles without a break. He landed his plane in the spinifex and took samples. He believed he had found a bonanza. Although a sheep-farmer he knew enough about mining to appreciate his find. Back in the thirties he had discovered seams of blue asbestos in Wittenoom Gorge, pegged the area and opened a mine which he sold to the Colonial Sugar Refining Company. CSR formed Australian Blue Asbestos Ltd., built a township and continued mining there until high costs forced a closure in the mid-1960s.*

In the early 1950s, Lang Hancock could not exploit his new discoveries. Since 1938, the Australian Government had banned the export of iron ore, following the refusal of watersiders to load pig iron at Kembla for export to Japan. Consequently, Japan wished to import iron ore direct from known deposits at Yampi Sound, off the coast of Western Australia, later mined for home consumption by Broken Hill Pty. Ltd. In 1960, the Government lifted the export ban. By then, Lang Hancock had been all over the Pilbara looking for iron ore. He found mountains of it. The ban lifted, he wrote to mining companies all over the world inviting participation. The only reply came from Rio Tinto of Britain, which merged two years later with Consolidated Zinc and became a British-owned international metals group.

Rio Tinto geologists were not at first unduly impressed with the deposits of limonite iron ore Lang Hancock showed them. Nevertheless, they stayed in the area for more than a year, mapping and sampling Hancock's discoveries, which were shown to contain 1,000 million tons of between fifty and sixty per cent iron. Then, on 11 September 1962, two geologists landed from a helicopter on a mountain Lang Hancock had spotted from the air in 1958. They found it to be an almost solid lump of high-grade hematite. Subsequent drilling showed an ore-body of about 500 million tons averaging more than sixty per cent iron. The mountain now bears the name Mt. Tom Price after an American engineer. How this came about is a classic story of postwar Australia, and explains how she has become one of the major areas of American investment.

Lang Hancock, soon to become the richest man in Australia, flew to London to see Rio Tinto's chairman, Sir Val Duncan. This is how he tells the story of what happened. "I think I'll ring Edgar Kaiser," said Sir Val. Hancock, like most other Australians, knew the name. Henry Kaiser was the American construction man who, during World War II, had turned from building dams to building ships. In next to no time, he was mass-producing them at the rate of one every four days. Besides providing a continuous

*The New Australia, by Colin Simpson (London, 1971).

supply of food, arms and ammunition across the Atlantic to submarine-beleaguered Britain, Kaiser's Liberty ships became the main Pacific supply line to Australia and the islands. Henry's son Edgar Kaiser, who started as a shovel foreman on his father's Boulder Dam project and became construction manager for Grand Coulee, the world's biggest dam, was by 1962 chairman and chief executive of Kaiser's Industries Corporation, the parent firm of more than one hundred companies. "Of course," continues Lang Hancock, "Billy Muggins from the bush didn't think Sir Val could ring up a bloke on the other side of the world and say, 'Look, Edgar, I want to dob you in for forty million', but that's what he did."

Mr. Tom Price, a vice-president of the Kaiser Steel Corporation, flew out to inspect Lang Hancock's leases. "There are mountains of iron ore here," he reported. "It is just staggering." So Hamersley Holdings was born in 1962 with Conzinc Rio Tinto holding 54 per cent interest, Kaiser Steel, 34.5 per cent and public shareholders, 11.5 per cent. In 1964 Hamersley Holdings obtained letters of intent from Japanese steel mills to take 65.5 million tons of ore and 17.9 million tons of iron pellets. This was the "go" signal for what is expected to continue to be the biggest iron mine in the world. In an incredibly short time, the company built the town of Tom Price, 182 miles of railroad to Dampier on the coast, and the port of Dampier itself. In 1966, the first iron ore was shipped to Japan.

Lang Hancock and his partner, Ernest Archibald (Peter) Wright, of Perth, receive royalties amounting to $2\frac{1}{2}$ per cent of whatever Hamersley receives for its ore. In 1974, royalties to Hancock and Wright amounted to $5.43 million, or just over $15,000 per day. Nor does there seem any chance of the bonanza petering out. South Australian Russel T. Madigan, Hamersley Iron's managing director, considers that the Pilbara region contains an ore body something like one hundred million million tons of thirty per cent iron and more as against two hundred thousand million tons in North America. Pilbara iron is mostly high grade. "What you use for road metal here," one Kaiser Steel expert told Colin Simpson, "we in the States call high-grade hematite." Current estimates suggest that at the present rate of usage, the Pilbara has iron enough to supply the world's needs for the next 100,000 years and more.

Lang Hancock's success story is an extravagant rather than an exceptional product of Australia's postwar mineral boom, which inflation has pricked but by no means deflated. Australia had long been known to possess raw material sufficient for an industrial structure yet in the 1950s the continent appeared to have serious deficiencies in its mineral resources. Until the Pilbara discoveries, it had been thought that iron-ore reserves were sufficient only for domestic needs. There appeared to be no oil deposits of commercial interest, no natural gas, no bauxite or nickel in significant quantities. There had been a brief uranium boom in 1953-4, when prospectors scoured the land with geiger counters instead of pickaxe, pan and dry-blower, adding the Northern Territory's Rum Jungle to South Australia's Radium Hill as a source of supply for a diminishing demand. By the 1960s, everything had changed. Australia was found to be rich in iron, bauxite, oil, uranium and natural gas, and had huge deposits of open-cut coal. International consortia, with the United States prominent in most of them, soon overshadowed but did not eliminate efforts by local groups to exploit these new riches.

Tom Price, the steelman who pioneered Hamersley Iron, was not the only American to introduce American money, methods and machinery into Australia's mineral upsurge. Two Californian companies, Utah Construction and Mining Company and the Cyprus Mines Corporation, each own a third of Goldsworthy Mining Company, first to begin iron production in the Pilbara. Mt. Goldsworthy, as it is known, holds reserves of about 50 million tons of high-grade ore and has similar deposits at Shay Gap, fifty miles inland and Kennedy Gap, further east. Japanese steelmakers have contracted to take more than 88 million tons of Mt. Goldsworthy ore and although inflation brought about a reduction in Japanese economic activity and a consequent readjustment of delivery for Mt. Goldsworthy and other companies concerned, the basic position remains.

The Mt. Newman Mining Company, third of Pilbara's "Big Three", mines deposits at Mt. Whaleback, in the Ophthalmia Range. Stan Hilditch, an Australian prospector who discovered more iron with less publicity than Lang Hancock, located Mt. Whaleback in 1957. Samples sent to his partner, C. H. Warman, a Sydney engineer, assayed 68.8 per cent iron. Waiting for the export ban to be lifted Hilditch prospected a number of other promising areas. American Metal Climax (Amax) optioned the Mt. Whaleback lease and made a geological survey which confirmed the existence of huge reserves. Amax invited Australian, Japanese and British participation. The upshot was that Mt. Newman is a sixty per cent Australian proposition, with the prestigious Broken Hill Proprietory Ltd. holding thirty per cent, Pilbara Iron (largely the Australian Colonial Sugar Refining Company) holding another thirty per cent, and a British mining house, Selection Trust, five per cent. B.H.P. manages the operation which sells ore to B.H.P. as well as to Japan. With the completion in 1976 of its expansion program which will increase annual production and shipping capacity to 40.6 million tons, capital investment by the Mt. Newman consortium will have reached almost $700 million. An American contractor, using international migrant labor, built 265 miles of railway from Newman to Port Hedland, the nearest port, in fourteen months. Using American-designed line-and-sleeper-laying machinery, engineers and workers created a world record by laying 4.35 miles of line in one day. A town had already been established at Mt.Newman, but Port Hedland, already used by the Mt. Goldsworthy Company, needed further dredging and land reclamation, work done by American and Japanese contractors, besides new harbor installation. Within two years of Mt. Newman's operational beginning in 1968, a Japanese ore carrier lifted the first load of iron for Japan. By 1975, Mt. Newman was producing iron ore at a rate exceeding 30 million tons a year.

Australia's iron-ore El Dorados went into production just before world inflation called a halt to a spectacular minerals boom of which the Pilbara discoveries were only a part. By then, Australia had become the world's third largest producer of iron ore, next to the Soviet Union and the United States; the world's biggest exporter of bauxite, the ore of aluminium, from huge deposits in Cape York Peninsula, in Arnhem Land, Admiralty Gulf and the Darling Ranges in Western Australia; had signed contracts to supply Japan with nickel concentrates worth $U.S.64 million from the Western Mining Corporation's Kambalda Mines in Western Australia; seen Poseidon nickel company shares leap from a few cents to $190 following announcement of fabulous proven ore reserves; heard the overexcited announcement that the "world's richest" uranium reserves existed at Narbarlek in the Northern Territory; begun mining manganese, essential to United States and Japanese steel production, at Groote Eylandt in the Gulf of Carpentaria. . . .

The amazing story of Australia's mineral explosion does not end there. Until recently, Australia had to import gasoline and oil from the United States and the Middle East. Following the discovery of commercial oil fields in Queensland (Moonie), at Barrow Island (off the northwest coast) and in Bass Strait, Australia now produces more than half its oil and gasoline requirements and promises to produce sixty per cent of requirements for the next twenty-five years. In addition, natural gas has been found in such vast quantities that it has replaced coal gas in domestic use in Brisbane, Melbourne, Adelaide and Perth and, in due course, Sydney. Australia is the chief producer of rutile, abundant in beach sands, a product essential to the manufacture of titanium, the light but strong metal used for the construction of spacecraft and rockets. New South Wales, hitherto Australia's chief source of coal, has been outstripped by Queensland, where Australian-American-Japanese interests are mining huge open cuts. There have also been fresh discoveries of copper, scheelite, antimony, molybdenum, vanadium, phosphates and salt. Salt by the 1970s promised to be more valuable on the export table than gold.

In short, during the 1960s Australia became one of the world's major quarries while remaining the biggest sheep run and one of the biggest wheat farms. The boom, inevitably attended by dubious company promotions and hysterical stock market gambles, laid down positive assets through government and private investments that will continue to pay dividends long after fly-by-night, get-rich-quick efforts have been forgotten. New towns have appeared in desert places, new railways opened up new territories for human occupation, new or refurbished ports provide modern outlets for vast hinterlands which offer more than rich quarries to exploit. Port Hedland, in northwest Australia, is a case in point. Twenty years ago it was a Graham Greene limbo of lost hopes sweltering above mangrove mud flats in one of the world's worst climates, relic of a romantic past based on pearls, bêche-de-mer and gold. Now, Port Hedland is one of the fastest growing towns in Australia, provided with all modern conveniences and with a population of about five thousand which should have tripled itself by the end of the present decade.

The mineral explosion is not the only reason why Australia has become one of the major areas of United States private investment. Stable government and steady development in a restless postwar world has made the southern continent seem a haven of affluence untouched by major political scandals or upheavals and free from race riots or party violence. Until the postwar period, Britain was the main source of overseas capital in Australia. After the war, the rate of American investment increased and reached a crescendo in the mining boom during the 1960s, moving ahead of total British investment, which nevertheless is still considerable. While American investment in Australia is comparatively small in the general pattern it has increased at more than twice the rate of American overseas investment in general. This investment is partly represented by the formation of subsidiary companies able to market goods competitively behind Australia's tariff wall. The main areas of investment have been oil refining, motor vehicles and non-ferrous metals. Large investments have also been made in other industries, notably agricultural and construct: on equipment, domestic appliances, fertilizers, pharmaceutical products and rubber—plastics.

American interests have also been prominent in the postwar development of Australia's remaining frontier—the Northern Territory. In February 1970, the *Wall Street Journal* drew attention to the rate at which rich Americans and American companies were "gobbling up" what Australians call the "Top End". The *Journal* reported that between sixty and seventy per cent of the upper half of the Northern Territory was held by Americans under long-term leases. "There are spots in the Northern Territory where the Stars and Stripes flies boldly from a station's flagpole—alongside (or instead of) the Australian flag," reported Bryan Boswell in the Sydney *Sunday Telegraph* on 15 February 1970. "And the accents of the drovers are strictly Texan drawl; as Stateside as the Jeeps they drive and the Camel cigarettes they smoke. If it weren't for the gum trees and the Brahman bulls the endless plains could be the Panhandle— the signposts pointing to Laredo instead of Katherine." According to the American Embassy in Canberra there are more than 3,000 Americans with land in Australia because, as the *Wall Street Journal* put it, Australia has "the cheapest developable land in the world." Much of this land now provides work and a future for hundreds of Australians, even if some of them develop a Texan drawl and smoke Camels.

Investing big money and using modern methods, American managers have turned huge areas fit only for a few wild cattle into viable Texan-style ranches. According to the *Wall Street Journal* some promoters are "experienced ranchers come to settle a new frontier", others are "multi-millionaires seeking novel and exciting outlets for excess funds." Two of the best known are companies, the Dillingham Corporation, whose Australian operations were established by Ben Dillingham II, and King Ranch (Aust.) Ltd. Dillingham leased 750,000 acres of territory bordering Arnhem Land and in the first two years spent more than $U.S.2 million in development, including a mini-town of modern houses for the seventy Australian stockmen and their families employed on the ranch. There is a school, attended by Aboriginal and white children, wells, roads, fences and 10,000 head of cattle. By 1980 the company will have spent up to $U.S.10 million on development. Other investors attracted by the Top End include banker Robert Rockefeller, rancher Robert Kleberg, oilman Nelson Bunker Hunt and the entertainer Art Linkletter.

Using trace elements over huge areas, American enterprise is also developing large areas of southwestern Australian sandplain. "On country that was supposed to be worthless you're seeing cattle and sheep on clover crops," Pioneer coachman Laurie Campbell told Australian author Colin Simpson in 1971.* "The Americans went for this land because there was a lot of it, and no big timber, so it was easily cleared. Of course, they used a lot of trace elements and fertilizer. The best fertilizer they used was the one Australians wouldn't have put into it. Money." Actually, the idea of making this area fertile with trace elements did not originate in the United States but with Australian agronomists at the Esperance Downs Research Station of the Western Australian Department of Agriculture. After several setbacks (some caused by ignoring local advice, others due to inadequate plowing and sowing by Australian contractors) the area began to show promise. Americans involved in development include Allen Chase, Art Linkletter, David Rockefeller, Benno C. Schmidt and the film actors Robert Cummings and Rhonda Fleming. Britain is represented by the family of Lord Mountbatten of Burma, former Viceroy of India, who own a 10,000-acre property east of Esperance, a southern port for a district which in 1954 supported 36 farmers working 20,000 acres and now provides for more than 600 farmers on a million acres.

Not unnaturally, with a large proportion of the motor industry controlled by General Motors, Chrysler and Ford, three of the four largest advertising agencies financed from America, and with an increasing number of multinational corporations centrally directed from overseas, many Australians ask themselves: Who owns Australia? In the *Anatomy of Australian Manufacturing Industry* (Sydney, 1967), E. L. Wheelwright and J. Miskelly indicate that

*Colin Simpson, *The New Australia* (London, 1972), pp.547-8.

240

of the 340 biggest companies operating in Australia, more than one-third are foreign owned and these account for two-fifths of the total assets. In manufacturing and mining, two-fifths of the corporations investing in Australia are foreign controlled and account for half the total assets. Most American capital is the form of "direct" investment in subsidiary companies controlled by multinational corporations. The Labor Party has shown greater concern about these developments than the more pragmatically minded Liberal-Country Party coalition. The Australian public shows little apparent anti-Americanism. American brand names appear to be a marketing advantage rather than otherwise.

The use of foreign capital and expertise to develop Australian resources is not new. In his Presidential Address to the Australian Institute of Mining and Metallurgy in June 1967, Sir George Fisher, chairman of the Mt. Isa lead mine in Queensland (the American Smelting and Refining Company owned half the shares), strongly supported the use of overseas capital. He pointed out that from the beginning, Australian mining had depended upon overseas money and technical assistance for initial "take-off" although at a later stage Australian investors usually bought out foreign interests. Sir George instanced Mt. Isa, Mount Morgan and Broken Hill Proprietory Company in its mining days as concerns made possible by foreign investors. He contended that Australia lacked capital resources and technical knowledge sufficient to benefit from the minerals explosion without American and other overseas help. He agreed with the current insistence that where possible provision should be made for an Australian equity in all mining operations but added that Australian investors should be prepared to share the period of high risk as well as reap the benefit of accomplishment.

Similar arguments were used in 1969 by Sir Ian McLennan, chairman of Australia's largest company, Broken Hill Proprietory Ltd., when he said: "Australian industry has developed to its present extent, and this particularly applies to recent mineral developments, only with the help of substantial financial assistance from overseas. . . . Currently this figure runs at about twenty-seven per cent. It is certainly not overwhelming." The history of B.H.P., almost as remarkable as the Lang Hancock saga, is a case in point.

On 5 September 1883, Charles Rasp, a German boundary rider on Mount Gipps sheep station in the far west of New South Wales, chipped off some heavy black rock he thought might be tin at a place called Broken Hill in the Barrier Range, not far from the South Australian border. Trained at Hamburg as a chemist in edible oils, Rasp had come to an open-air life in Australia to repair his lungs. Riding the vast lonely paddocks he kept his eyes open for minerals, which he identified from books kept in his hut. Rasp showed the specimens to David James and Jim Poole, two bullock drivers, and together they pegged out forty acres of the great iron-stone outcrop as a tin mine.

Sending samples to an assayer in Adelaide, they discovered Rasp's specimens to be carbonate of lead with silver.

Rasp, Poole and James decided to broaden their partnership into a syndicate of seven. Each member contributed £70 towards the expense of sinking a shaft. The syndicate pegged out six more blocks of forty acres and employed a miner to dig. Although they did not know it, they had leased about two miles along the line of a lode that was to prove richer, for each foot of lode, than any metal discovered in Australia. "For twelve months," Rasp said afterwards, "it was really doubtful whether we would make anything out of it."

In August 1885, the four leaders of the syndicate floated Broken Hill Proprietary Company, destined to be Australia's largest mining and industrial corporation. The new company's first smelting, carried out by a company in Melbourne, returned 35,600 ounces of silver from forty-eight tons of ore, for a return of nearly £7,500 in cash. Before long the mine was paying its own way and the company was doing its own smelting with two Nevada furnaces bought in New South Wales. Soon it was apparent that Broken Hill was Australia's Comstock lode, although Ballarat's goldfields had attracted more people than either Comstock or Broken Hill. The men who migrated to Broken Hill were looking for work, not a fortune, but the area soon had all the symptoms of a boom town: streets, sidewalks, hotels, gambling dens, a railway and hordes of parasites. By the end of the 1880s Broken Hill had a population of 20,000 and the mine had a market value of more than £6 million, with shares selling at more than £400 each. By then all Australia was caught up in a silver boom that equalled the earlier Comstock excitement in the United States.

In 1886, B.H.P. directors decided to look in the United States for a man with sufficient experience to manage the fabulous monster they had conjured up. William H. Patton, superintendent of the world's most productive mine, Consolidated Virginia, was persuaded to come to Australia as general manager at Broken Hill at what was for those days the fabulous salary of £4,000 a year. Herman Schlapp, an Iowan metallurgist trained at the Royal School of Mines at Freiburg in Germany, was also engaged as the first of a long line of American metallurgists and technicians who served Broken Hill. Patton brought in experienced miners from Nevada and introduced modern methods of extraction which enabled the men to work ground hitherto too dangerous to touch. He soon discovered that Broken Hill ground was different from Comstock and new methods had to be devised to cope with creeping ground and other problems.

Meanwhile, Herman Schlapp had supervised construction of fifteen furnaces employing more than a thousand men. Other companies were now in operation, either building smelters or sending ore away to be treated at Port Pirie and elsewhere. A fall in the price of lead and silver, Broken Hill's chief ores, steadied the boom but by the first decade of the twentieth century Broken Hill had a population of 35,000 and was still Australia's most productive area, producing valuable zinc from tons of silver-lead tailings. By then B.H.P. had transferred its smelting operations to Port Pirie and was also mining at Iron Knob, across Spencer Gulf from Port Pirie, although pig iron was a secondary consideration to the production of the silver-lead furnaces. By this time, Guillaume Delprat, a Dutchman who had managed large mines in Spain and Canada, was B.H.P.'s general manager. In 1911, Delprat advised the company to guard against Broken Hill giving out by extending its operations into steel. The directors agreed and B.H.P. began a new phase in its development.

Again the company turned to the United States for its initial expertise. Guillaume Delprat brought in David Baker, a young Philadelphian consulting engineer, who endorsed the economics of a steel-making project and designed a comparatively large steelworks for the operation at Newcastle, New South Wales, conveniently situated between coalfields and water transport. The Governor-General opened the new works on 2 June 1915, when the first red-hot ingot rolled from the mill. Delprat and Baker read the signs of the times aright. B.H.P.'s original mine has long been worked out and all the company owns at Broken Hill nowadays is a gigantic slag heap that may one day be worth processing for zinc. B.H.P. remains, however, Australia's biggest and only steel company with huge and growing plant at Newcastle and Port Kembla, south of Sydney, where it began operations in the 1930s when it absorbed its only rival, Australian Iron and Steel Ltd. When B.H.P. began steelmaking, more than seventy per cent of its shares were owned overseas. Now only about sixteen per cent are held abroad.

Americans contributed substantially to the development of Western Australia's famous Golden Mile, at Kalgoorlie, which was discovered during the 1890s and turned out to be the world's richest single golden lode. In 1899, Lake View Consols, with Henry Clay Callahan from Colorado as manager, produced £80,000 worth of gold, to become the world's richest single producer. Ralph Nichols, a New York mining engineer, managed the nearby Great Boulder mine, Perseverance. His acuteness uncovered a share-dealing fraud perpetrated by an assayer and an underground-manager who "salted" a new lode, after buying low-priced shares, and then leaked rumors of a rich find. Nichols promptly sacked the culprits, who had made several thousand before the fraud was discovered. As a result of this and similar frauds the West Australian State Government appointed a Royal Commission which ended West Australia's first but by no means last get-rich-quick mining boom.

London mining consultants Berwick Moreing & Co. were chiefly responsible for increased efficiency in Western Australian mining. They sent out a team of mining engineers, including twenty-two-year-old Herbert C. Hoover, who had not long left Stanford University, to inspect or manage English mining companies. These experts introduced American mining methods and proper production costing. On Hoover's advice, Berwick Moreing bought the Sons of Gwalia mine 100 miles north of Kalgoorlie and installed Hoover as manager. The mine continued production until comparatively recently. It was here that a State Governor offered the President-to-be a tip when the young man had finished showing him over the mine. Like everyone else in Gwalia, the manager lived in a corrugated-iron hut in desert heat under conditions which no present-day miner would contemplate. In 1905, still employed by Berwick Moreing, Hoover visited Broken Hill, New South Wales, where he floated the Zinc Corporation to treat tailings from the dumps. The Corporation went through many vicissitudes before good management produced the first dividends.

Patton, Schlapp, Baker, Callahan, Nichols and Hoover were first on a long honor roll of Americans who have contributed to the development of modern Australian mining and industry. Dr. Edward Dyer Peters, American copper expert, pioneered Tasmania's Mt. Lyell lodes which Robert Carl Sticht, from New Jersey, later managed with remarkable success. T. A. Rickard, journalist historian of American mining development, visited Australia many times and wrote a series of notable articles for the American Institute of Mining Engineers. Julius Kruttschmitt, American manager for Mt. Isa during the 1930s, was partly instrumental in securing more money from American Smelting and Refining Company to save Mt. Isa from collapse. Although an Australian company, Ampol Petroleum, pioneered the search for oil in Western Australia, it had to bring in America's Caltex and Britain's Shell to find the kind of money for exploration that Australian investors did not have. Esso-B.H.P. drilled Australia's most prolific wells in Bass Strait. American technicians and managers have been equally prominent in the recent minerals boom.

Australia, like America, enters the last quarter of the twentieth century in a mood of intense spiritual unrest. This may not have yet penetrated to the breezy, informal, sporting and beer-drinking masses, which form the mis-leading American stereotype of the typical Australian, yet it shows itself in Australia's traditional art, literature and music as well as in a widespread youthful counterculture, environmental protest, economic unease, political unrest and the women's liberation movement. All these are transferred to ordinary Australians (from Britain as well as America) through the mass media and represent a universal malaise rather than a local phenomenon. Nevertheless, the last quarter of the twentieth century represents to many Australians not only the swan song of British Liberalism but the deathbed repentance of sensitive Americans appalled at some of the consequences of

Americanization. Technological progress and widely-spread affluence no longer add up to the good life.

This mood of rejection, common among educated Australians as well as an intellectual elite, fails to give due credit to the obvious social advantages that technological expertise has brought to Australia and Australians. British concepts of the welfare state and the place of trade unions in economic life, heavily Australian accented though they are, brought social dignity and freedom from the threat of devastating poverty to the average Australian but Americanization, in the sense of technological expertise applied to economic production and human problems, has made the good life possible over enormously wide fields.

Labor-saving machinery has lifted the burden of sweated labor from the backs of men in the frontline of national development, as anyone knows who has seen the huge earth-moving machines working the iron-ore deposits at Mt. Tom Price, or Mt. Newman. Nor, as critics assert, are men merely ciphers in complex economic calculations, as workers who live in airconditioned houses of Pilbara company towns and ports soon learn. Trade unions, which once had to fight to obtain a living wage and minimal working conditions, are now entrenched institutions, geared to obtain increasing shares of a common affluence threatened by more complex conditions than employers' greed or the conventional wisdom of *laissez faire* economic theory. Women, in particular, have been beneficiaries of the labor-saving devices that are a part of Americanization, in a manner that perhaps compensates for the increasing substitution of processed for natural foods, air pollution, and computerized thinking.

Against the advantages brought by labor-saving machinery and domestic appliances, which are the basis rather than the apex of the good society, we have to set the fact that modern mechanical and social forces threaten to destroy the cohesive moralities that hold societies together. There are no longer common standards automatically acclaimed by established churches, established political parties, established social conventions. Although governments and institutions still operate as if the people they represent or seek to serve accept an evolving conventional wisdom, rapidly evolving concepts of morality, human relationships and artistic expression increasingly attract the young and bewilder the old. Political and religious leaders nowadays lack the confidence that once enabled them to say *this* is right and *that* is wrong.

The vague concept of "democratic standards", which provided the social dynamic of new societies like the United States and Australia, now faces unprecedented challenges from those who insist on carrying democratic processes to what they consider their logical conclusions in intellectual, social and political promiscuity—doing one's own thing in one's own way. In literature, music and art, experiment and innovation are valued above traditional standards or professional competence. In education, egalitarianism rates higher marks than excellence and teachers are more and more expected to teach what students want to know rather than what society thinks they should know. Authority, in any shape or form, has become a dirty word.

The process has not as yet gone so far in Australia as in the United States but Australian culture and educational practice have always been largely derivative and ideas and climates of opinion travel quickly. Until the mid-twentieth century Australian sources, except for a deeply-rooted local democratic tradition, were mostly British. Now they are increasingly American, so far as a younger generation is concerned. In earlier days, those who liked to keep up with the intellectually chic seized on the latest English vogue. Now just as eagerly they embrace American vogues. More serious social debate also tends to follow American rather than British trends. "Campaigns on pollution, students' rights, Women's Lib., Aboriginal land rights, nuclear disarmament," comments Australian business leader Norman B. Rydge, "follow prior overseas campaigns in predictable pattern after predictable pattern, with the participants borrowing the trappings of their intellectual godfathers. Even the Aboriginals, who of all people have a good enough cause in their own right, are aping the protest style of the American Black Power movement."

The immense ticker-tape shower which greeted President Johnson during his triumphant Australian tour in 1966 expressed Australian feelings in an American manner. So did the students who lay down in the street in front of his car with its bullet-proof plastic bubble. Ironically, following the President's visit, the Victorian Chamber of Manufactures was inundated with letters from Americans who wanted to migrate to Australia to enjoy a slower, easier pace of life. True, many of the thousands of Americans who migrated to Australia during the 1960s have found Australia more British than American, especially if they sought a new life beyond the cities. On the other hand, many of them have contributed to the Americanization they were trying to escape, or have left Australia for the same reason they left America—because it wasn't Utopia. Names like Ford, Kellog, Heinz and General Motors, and phenomena like supermarkets, regional shopping complexes and lubritoriums, have become as much part of the Australian scene as the American.

On the other hand, there is an increasing sense of Australian identity which positively rejects Americanization. The late Mr. Harold Holt, Prime Minister when President Johnson visited Australia in 1966, discovered this. The millions of Australians who greeted the President so effusively in Sydney and Melbourne reacted against the Prime Minister's enthusiastic reiteration of the slogan used in the Presidential election campaign, "all the way with LBJ." This was going much further than most Australians wanted to go although many of them also rejected the antiVietnam War campaign Mr. Holt was endeavoring to denigrate. While most Australians reject the politically-motivated antiAmericanism of the extreme left they have no desire to become an American satellite, however much they look to the United States as a Big Brother who will stand by them if they get into trouble.

Michael Kahan, an American Research Fellow in the Department of Political Science at the Institute of Advanced Studies, Australian National University, Canberra, found that one of the more frequent questions he was asked during his four years' stay in Australia was: Is Australia becoming like America? "The answer is a sharp and cynical 'no' " he wrote in the *Australian*, 18 January 1971. "Take-home fried chicken and late-night films are not America. Nor is pollution, big cars and expressways. These are the surface things that can be touched by Australia. Beneath them is the pain of wondering who one is and where one is going, the recognition of cupidity and, however hypocritical at times, the longing to ask questions and to hear answers. America, beneath its fear and disgusting facade, is vital. It is brutal in its tolerance, grudgingly admiring of the eccentric expression. To become like America, Australia would have to give up too much: It would have to give up anonymity and learn to hate and love; it would have to think and take notice of the next person. It would have to recognize its problems."

This is the answer to those who reject the obverse side of the advantages Americanization has brought to Australia: an obverse reflected in student unrest, moral uncertainty, the racist slur, political disquiet, spiritual misgiving. These things are already apparent in contemporary Australian literature, art and music, among students and intellectuals, and widely disseminated through the mass media. They represent a challenge as well as the predictable patterns of behavior about which Norman B. Rydge complains. Although Australians have long been more adult, more sophisticated, more widely aware of other people and other countries, than Michael Kahan credits, the average Australian, in so far as there is such a creature, has tended towards the kind of innocence once habitual to Americans: an innocence which assumes that they live in God's own country and represent a spearhead of human progress.

All such comparisons and parallels between Australia and America can be misleading as well as illuminating. The parallels are no more than girders from which bridges of sympathetic understanding can be built provided there remains a mutual realization that different environments have produced different peoples. As that observant pro-American Englishman John Buchan once remarked, half the misunderstandings between Britain and America arise from the fact that neither will regard the other for what it is—a foreign country. The parallels between Australia and America are closer than the parallels between Britain and America. Nevertheless, Australia remains basically British whereas America is a vast cosmopolis in which millions have no sentimental or institutional ties with Britain. An Australian feels at home in Britain whereas in America, divergencies in speech, food, fashions, social habit and political behavior are more irritating than they would be if possession of a common language did not lead to expectations of greater kinship than actually exists.

The discovery, during World War II, that Australia was peripheral to British military and strategic thinking came as a great shock to many Australians. They now have to accommodate themselves to the idea that America, too, has global responsibilities and political strategies in which Australian interests are not necessarily paramount. Certainly, Australians do not feel, as the extreme left asserts, that they have transferred from British tutelage to American tutelage, exchanged an Imperial Mother for a democratic Big Brother. Rather, as best they can, Australians are groping to establish an international identity for themselves and if in the process they sometimes speak or act brashly it is the brashness of eager youth rather than the snarling impotence of disillusioned old age. Meanwhile, mutual comprehension is best attained through a realization that an appreciation of differences is as essential to understanding as a comparison of similarities.

Appendix

The degree and complexity of Australian-American diplomatic, trade, defense, financial and sporting relationships since World War II, and the parallels between cultural and social developments, are too extensive for adequate treatment in a book of this sort. The most obvious, if not always the most important, of these relationships and parallels have been dealt with in the main text of this volume. Other and by no means less intimate or far-reaching developments are summarized in this appendix. When he visited Australia in 1971, Professor Hartley Grattan, of the University of Texas, the man largely responsible for making Australia known to Americans, pointed out that the problems of industrialization and urbanization have caught up with Australia and made the American experience more relevant, both as a warning and an example. Professor Grattan believes that Australians should build a country that is meaningful to them and valued by them. They can do this, he says, by using their critical judgment, accepting those influences useful in building the kind of society Australians want and rejecting those without relevance to Australian history or conditions.

In education, as Professor Grattan observed, Australia has a reasonably respectable tradition of providing basic education for all children in every corner of a vast continent, however remote the pupil's home or impoverished the family or the district. This has been achieved by central direction and uniform standards. Both cut across American concepts of what education should be. Consequently, most American educationists who have visited Australia have found more to deplore than to praise. There has been insufficient realization, on both sides, that different countries have different problems and that development is historically and environmentally as well as ideologically conditioned. Since the Fulbright Scheme provided for academic cross-fertilization in the 1950s, and the introduction of Dr. H. S. Wyndham's comprehensive scheme in New South Wales during the same decade, there has been greater mutual understanding of local problems and accomplishments.

The Fulbright Scholarships Exchange Scheme provided for the exchange of scholars and students between the United States and certain other countries established under an act of Congress sponsored by Senator J. W. Fulbright in 1946. The section of the agreement relating to Australia was signed at Canberra on 26 November 1949. It involved the exchange of students on the financial basis of a debt of $5 million owed to the United States by Australia as a result of wartime lend-lease and surplus property settlements. The first Australians to be awarded scholarships under the scheme went to the United States in 1950 and the first Americans came to Australia in 1951. In 1953/4, 115 exchanges took place, divided almost equally in number between the two countries. The United States Education Foundation in Australia with a board of seven members representing both countries advised on the selection of participants. In the fifteen years of its existence the scheme brought 684 American scholars, students and teachers to Australia to study and work and sent 866 Australians to the United States. In 1965 it was replaced by a truly reciprocal program financed by $A180,000 each from the United States and Australian Governments and administered by the Australian American Education Foundation, with its headquarters in Canberra.

An American Chamber of Commerce was established in Sydney in 1961 with sixty members. The Chamber aims to represent the American business community in Australia on questions of trade, commerce, finance, industry and taxation; to interpret the Australian business point of view to American businessmen; to seek to protect America's high commercial reputation in Australia and to promote or oppose legislation and other measures affecting the commerce and financial interests of members. The Chamber receives enquiries from potential migrants from the United States and has assisted Australian companies in obtaining franchises, for licencing manufacturers and also in obtaining a toehold in the United States for Australian products.

The sporting links between Australia and the United States are too well known to need elaboration. Less known is the contribution such famous Australian sportsmen as Reginald Leslie (Snowy) Baker and Henry Christian (Harry) Hopman have made to American sporting successes. Snowy Baker was probably the greatest all-round athlete Australia ever produced. He excelled in twenty-nine different sports. He was in the championship class as a footballer, rower, wrestler, track athlete, swimmer, diver, horseman, gymnast, fencer and boxer. He was a top-notcher in almost every other type of athletic activity. Snowy Baker went to the United States in the early twenties at the age of nearly forty, to make films in Hollywood and stayed on to work as sporting coach at a Los Angeles Country Club.

Harry Hopman, captain of the Australian tennis teams which won the Davis Cup for Australia in 1939, 1950-53, 1955-57, 1959-62, 1964 and 1967, went to the United States in his mid-sixties and now conducts the West

Side Tennis Coaching School, Forest Hills, New York, where he hopes to train American Davis Cup champions. In addition to Hopman a succession of Australian tennis personalities now live in the United States, mostly as professional players. A number of Australia's champion swimmers and other athletes have also migrated to the United States for business or professional reasons. Meanwhile, baseball has a big following in Australia although it has not taken the place of cricket or Australian Rules football in the public imagination. Nevertheless, baseball registers more in Australia than cricket in the United States despite the fact that cricket once tetered on the edge of becoming America's most popular summer sport.

"There is a parallel but not a close similarity between Australia and America," says the late P. R. Stephensen in *The Foundations of Culture in Australia* (Sydney, 1936). Provided we keep this warning in mind the similarities and differences between Australian and American literature and art make fascinating study. The parallels are tempting but dangerous if carried too far. In simplified terms: first a genteel period, then a period of national assertion, now a period of spiritual unrest. In each phase, Australian writers have owed something to American as well as to British influences. Rolf Boldrewood (T. A. Browne), leading novelist of the genteel period, derives from James Fenimore Cooper as well as from Sir Walter Scott. Henry Lawson, the quintessence of Australian nationalism at its best, was deeply read in Bret Harte. Steele Rudd, Australia's Mark Twain if we think of Mark Twain as the frontier humorist rather than the disillusioned democrat, created a Dad and Dave stereotype later generations of country folk have had difficulty in shaking off. Henry Handel Richardson's *Fortunes of Richard Mahony*, apex of Australian realism, rose from the same deep wells of European realism as Theodore Dreiser's *An American Tragedy*. Martin Boyd's Anglo-Australian dilemmas have something of the same motivation as Henry James's masterpieces. Anyone who reads contemporary Australian prose must detect the influence of John Steinbeck, Ernest Hemingway and Norman Mailer.

In prose, spiritual concern is not so apparent as post-Hemingway realism. The oustanding example is Patrick White, who won the Nobel Prize in 1974. His first major success, *The Tree of Man* (1955), appeared in New York before it was published in London. White repudiated what he called "the dreary, dun-coloured offspring of journalistic realism" together with racially exclusive egalitarianism, the "Digger spirit" and other clichés.

Randolph Stow, whose first novel appeared in 1956 when he was twenty-one, also represents the new wave in Australian fiction. His novels impress American and English critics as major contributions to contemporary Australian letters, especially *To The Islands* (1958), an Australian *Heart of Darkness* in which a disillusioned missionary journeys through the bush "to the islands", an Aboriginal phrase for death, in search of some spiritual nucleus which would make his life again meaningful. Early in the 1970s Randolph Stow went to the United States as a creative writer under a Harkness Award. He is one of a number of Australian writers who have lived and worked in the United States, including Christina Stead, whose Australian novels *Seven Poor Men of Sydney* (London, 1934) and *For Love Alone* (New York, 1944), won her a high place in Australian literary estimation. Most of her later novels have American or European backgrounds.

Until the 1960s, the best-known Australian author in the United States was Arthur Upfield, whose rough-edged detective stories about the outback adventures of his Aboriginal sleuth "Boney" helped form the American image of Australia as a vast arid land of wide open spaces and small dilapidated towns. Jon Cleary's *The Sundowners* (1952) and D'Arcy Niland's *The Shiralee* (1955), both made into successful American films, helped perpetuate the image. Morris West, Australia's latest international best-seller, has broken away from the Australian and New Guinea locales of his early work and fictionalizes world problems in his highly professional novels, *The Devil's Advocate* (1959), *The Shoes of the Fisherman* (1963), *The Ambassador* (1965) and *The Tower of Babel* (1968).

Meanwhile, Thomas Keneally, George Johnston, Peter Mathers, David Ireland, Thea Astley and Elizabeth Harrower, among others, have brought a new sophistication to the Australian novel. Earlier urban novelists, like Ruth Park and Kylie Tennant, dealt sympathetically with slum dwellers and the working class from the older realistic tradition of the "bush" novelists and short-story writers. Now, like many contemporary Americans, Australian novelists are more concerned with the tragic plight of man in an increasingly menacing world and are grappling with the complexities of sex and marriage. They endeavor to present and elucidate problems without attempting to provide neatly packaged answers. In Australia, as in America, mind-probing has replaced muck-raking as the contemporary mode.

Ronald McKie, first Australian journalist to receive a Smith-Mundt Fellowship from the U.S. State Department, is well-known in America for his best-selling war documentaries *Proud Echo* and *The Heroes* and for analytical social studies of Southeast Asia, an area in which he has specialized. His first novel *The Mango Tree* won the 1974 Miles Franklin Award for Literature (which Randolph Stow had won in 1958). Although not experimental in form or content *The Mango Tree* breaks as completely as Patrick White's novels with the dun-colored realism of an earlier Australian tradition and has none of what one critic has called the "rough-edged and radically nationalist" ethos that marks so much early twentieth-century writing in Australia. "This is a novel beautifully written, sensitively evocative of the joy and pain of growing up," the Miles Franklin judges commented.

Ivan Francis Southall, who has won American, European and Australian awards with his books for children, is another Australian author well-known in the United States. In 1973 he lectured in America on children's literature at the invitation of the Library of Congress, and again in 1974 as the American Library Association Arbuthnot Honor Lecturer. *Hills End* (1963) was chosen as a notable book by the American Library Association. Ivan Southall's books have been translated into ten different languages and in 1969, the Japanese Government honored him with the Children's Welfare & Culture Encouragement Award. Originally, Ivan Southall made his name with the Simon Black books of physical and aeronautical adventure (Southall won a DFC as a pilot in the R.A.A.F.). Of recent years, however, his books are sensitive studies of teenage youth "searching for answers to questions that have often been avoided or forgotten by an older generation."

In poetry, American influences are not so apparent as in prose. During the nineteenth century Australian poets were mostly thin musical echoes of the Great Romantics. During the nineties, their work either reflected the Celtic Twilight or echoed the galloping rhymes of Kipling. Christopher Brennan, the major poet of the early twentieth century, was nurtured on French symbolism which owed its theory, if not a great deal of its practice, to Edgar Allen Poe. During the 1930s, Frank Wilmot ("Furnley Maurice") experimented with the techniques of the American realists Edgar Lee Masters, Carl Sandburg and Vachel Lindsay. T. S. Eliot was a major influence on Kenneth Slessor, whose work has been hailed by American critics. Among modern poets Judith Wright won the *Britannica* award for literature in 1964, while A. D. Hope, James McAuley, Evan Jones and Chris Wallace-Crabbe, though not conspicuously influenced by American example, have visited or studied in the United States.

The beatniks and the poets of America's underground have had a major influence on Australia's new crop of younger poets. The Commonwealth Literary Fund has been responsible for subsidizing more volumes of poetry than ever before and magazines such as *Poetry Australia* (1964-) and *New Poetry* (1965-) provide outlets for emerging poets. The work of Allen Ginsberg, William Carlos Williams and Charles Olson are major influences on much of the new poetry appearing in these publications. "With each visit I make to this country," said Professor Grattan in 1971, "I am more disturbed by the intensity of American influence—not all of which I can accept as good for Australia. . . . Australia needs to improve her capacity for critical judgment of the influences flowing from the United States. Australians should not reject all these influences but, with wit and judgment, accept those that are useful in building the kind of society they want."

A new school of Australian playwrights, also influenced by the American underground, is at the same time trying to do so with the wit and judgment Professor Grattan recommends. Australian theatrical entrepreneurs bring Broadway and off-Broadway successes to Sydney and Melbourne stages, often before they appear in London, and the repertoire of Australian "little theatres" usually includes more American plays than British. Consequently Australian audiences are familiar not only with *Damn Yankees, Fiddler on the Roof, Hello Dolly! The Pajama Game, The Music Man*, to name but a few of the hit musicals of recent years, they are also familiar with Eugene O'Neill, Tennessee Williams, Arthur Miller and Edward Albee among others, on stage as well as on film. Australian international theatrical successes like Ray Lawler's *Summer of the Seventeenth Doll*, derived from Tennesee Williams's romantic-realism rather than from contemporary British drama.

The new playwrights not only reject what they consider the debased standards of commercial theatre and the "powdered clutch of the theatre-going middle class", but what David Williamson, one of the most successful of the new dramatists, calls the dictation of "a cultured élite who preferred overseas theatre and films because they are convinced that there is nothing here worth writing about or investigating." The new writers, almost all deriving from student protest, write what Geoffrey Serle describes as "comic colloquial, anti-authoritarian, satirical and sometimes savage plays" on subjects dredged from Australian history and contemporary life. They produce them for eager young audiences in makeshift improvised theatres in the backstreets of Sydney, Melbourne and Adelaide and occasionally in Canberra's more formal Theatre Centre.

American influences on contemporary art have been much more direct and disturbing than American influences on literature. Australian art, as an independent cultural activity, originated with the Impressionists and neo-Impressionists at the end of the nineteenth century and the beginning of the twentieth. These artists saw Australian landscape through Australian eyes and made full use of the tonal values of Australian light. The tradition continued but soon breakaway schools showed the influence of more recent European developments. Until the 1960s the most influential of the new tendencies coalesced about left-wing social-realists and a heterogeneous group influenced "by abstract art, expressionism, surrealism, cubism and dada."*

Meanwhile, the work of William Dobell, Russell Drysdale, Sidney Nolan, Arthur Boyd and Albert Tucker gave Australian art an international status never enjoyed by Australian literature or drama. While symbolism and naturalism have continued to be major influences, what Geoffrey Serle describes as a "total break with the local past" occurred between 1965 and 1966 when "young artists returning from overseas introduced the urban international New York-derived style of colour painting—hard-edge, optical or colour-field." This was followed in 1967 with a visiting exhibition of contemporary

*This necessarily simplified account of a complex and confused period, and what followed, is indebted to Bernard Smith's *Place, Taste and Tradition* (Sydney, 1945) and Geoffrey Serle's *From Deserts The Prophets Come* (Melbourne, 1973).

American painting which had a major influence on younger Australian artists. Meanwhile, the Australian public has become so bemused by contemporary art that the Federal Government felt justified in paying more than a million dollars for Jackson Pollock's *Blue Poles.*

American architect and townplanner, Walter Burley Griffin, who had been with Frank Lloyd Wright for some time when he designed Canberra, met with what Australian architectural historian Robin Boyd describes as "maddening frustrations" when he struggled to put his plan on the ground. "Griffin saw it as a Capital Splendid, imposing and splendid from the start with grand perspectives and great flights of steps reflected in placid lakes, all set on axial lines between the natural features of the site," says Boyd. "The suburban areas were not strong elements of Griffin's plan but these, characteristically of Australia, grew most rapidly." In 1955, a new central authority took control and Canberra returned to the principle of planning although, according to Robin Boyd, it was too late to return to the principle of wholeness which Griffin had learned from the Chicago School and Frank Lloyd Wright.

Nevertheless, Lake Burley Griffin now anchors the two parts of Canberra into an imposing whole and serves as a perpetual reminder that the American architect who spent the best years of his professional life in Australia did not dream in vain. At the foot of Russell Hill, where Walter Burley Griffin sited an imposing Market Place, the simply-conceived Australian-American Memorial for World War II now stands. On either side spreads a complex of defense buildings, commonly referred to as the Australian Pentagon, on a site planned by American architects Skidmore, Owings and Merrill, with buildings designed by Australian architects Buchan, Laird and Buchan. Skidmore, Owings and Merrill also designed the giant Shell House on the corner of Bourke Street and William Street, Melbourne, a building supervised by Buchan, Laird and Buchan.

Sydney and Melbourne, long architectural outposts of Victorian England, have increasingly given way to Americanism for, as Robin Boyd commented in the *Sunday Australian*, 12 September 1971, so far as Australia is concerned "the only modern architecture in the world is modern American architecture." This generalization applies more to the city centers than to the suburbs where a growing number of houses, set in gardens grown with gum trees and native shrubs, have an Australian quality lacking in the pseudo-Spanish and pseudo-colonial bungalows popular earlier in the century. The suburb is the essential Australia and here more Australians are endeavoring to be Australian rather than pseudo-British, pseudo-Spanish or pseudo-American. Meanwhile, American design has influenced suburban shopping centers and American-style motels have changed the accommodation pattern throughout Australia.

Intellectually, Australia has contributed to American science and thought more than most Americans are aware. Australian neurologist Sir John Eccles, who won the Nobel Prize for Medicine (jointly) in 1963, has been Distinguished Professor, State University of New York since 1968. Melbourne immunologist Sir Frank Macfarlane Burnet, who won the Nobel Prize for Medicine (jointly) in 1960, has remained in Australia but his work is well-known and influential in the United States and the Harvard University Press has published some of his books. Both these men are major figures in modern medical science but at lower heights there is a constant exchange of scientific ideas and practice between Australia and the United States. The CSIRO has an international reputation and produces a wide range of journals which make its work widely known overseas. The growth of research in Australian university departments has been accompanied by a proliferation of specialist scientific journals well known in the United States.

During the 1960s, the intellectual level and technical sophistication of Australia's capital city daily and weekly press made considerable progress. Nevertheless, *Time, Newsweek* and *Reader's Digest*, all now with Australian offices and a higher proportion of Australian content, continue to be widely read in Australia. American comic strips are ubiquitous in the Australian press and American TV programs jostle British TV programs at Australia's peak viewing times. Latterly, however, with Federal Government direction and support a greater proportion of locally-made TV features are being prepared for American and British showing, in addition to nature and travel pieces which have always had something of an international audience.

The Australian-American Association, which was established in 1936, is the longest-lived of the various organizations that have through the years helped cement mutual understanding between the two countries. It began at a time when America was little understood in Australia, when there were difficulties about war debts, import quotas and protective tariffs. Founded in Sydney, the Association spread to Melbourne, Adelaide, Brisbane and Perth where AAA Hospitality Centers flourished during World War II. Annual Coral Sea celebrations are an important part of its wide range of postwar activities which include publication of a magazine *Pacific Neighbours*, sponsorship of international scholarships, and Community Cooperation projects which link towns in Australia with towns in the United States. American-Australian Associations, with similar aims and activities, operate in New York, San Francisco, Los Angeles and Honolulu.

ACKNOWLEDGMENTS
SOURCES AND ARTISTS

COLOUR PLATES

1. *Major Johnson with Quarter Master Laycock, one sergeant and twenty five privates of ye New South Wales Corps, defeats two hundred and sixty six armed rebels* [Castle Hill] *5th March 1804*. Watercolor, artist unknown. Rex Nan Kivell Collection, National Library of Australia.
2. *The Battle of Bunker Hill*. National Army Museum, from *Australia's Heritage*, Paul Hamlyn.
3. *King's Table Land, Blue Mountains, New South Wales, the appearance of a new road*. Watercolor, Augustus Earle, 1793-1838, Rex Nan Kivell Collection, National Library of Australia.
4. *The Oregon Trail*. Oil painting by Albert Bierstadt. Butler Art Institute, Youngstown, Ohio.
5. *Post Office San Francisco, California*. Stokes Collection, New York Public Library.
6. *Hindley Street*, [Adelaide, South Australia] *from King William Street* [1851]. Lithograph, Samuel Thomas Gill, 1818-1880. Rex Nan Kivell Collection, National Library of Australia.
7. *Australian gold diggings*. Oil painting, artist unknown. Rex Nan Kivell Collection, National Library of Australia.
8. *The Mines of Placerville, California, 1885*. By A. O. D. Browere. National Cowboy Hall of Fame and Western Heritage Center, Oklahoma City, Oklahoma.

BLACK AND WHITE ILLUSTRATIONS

Christopher Columbus, p.4, line engraving. *William Dampier*, p.5, line engraving. *Sir Joseph Banks*, p.10, mezzotint. *Bay whaling off the Boyd Town Light House, Twofold Bay, N.S.W.*, p.29, etched by J. Carmichael, engraving from William Henry Wells' *A geographical dictionary or gazetteer of the Australian Colonies*, Sydney 1848. *Rival whaling crews*, p.38, from *Making New Zealand*, Vol. 1 No. 4, New Zealand Department of Internal Affairs. *Bungaree, a native of New South Wales. Fort Denison, Sydney Harbour in the background*, p.41, oil painting, Augustus Earle. *The Omeo Track, Bullock Team*, p.54, *Australasian Sketcher*, July 5, 1880. *Overlanders fight off Aboriginals*, p.68, Hamilton.

John Batman's famous treaty with the blacks, Merri Creek, Northcote, June 6, 1835, p.77, painting, George Rossi Ashton, Petherick Collection. *Hon. William Charles Wentworth*, p.82, photograph. *Henry Parkes*, p.92, photograph from Ravenscroft Album. *Rev. John Dunmore Lang*, p.95. *Charles Wilkes*, p.100, line engraving. *Escape of Fenian convicts from Fremantle, West Australia*, p.106, *Australasian Sketcher*, July 8, 1876. *Yankee Digger* [c.1858], p.126, watercolor, Edward Charles Moore. *Australia—News from home*, p.127, oil print, George Baxter, Rex Nan Kivell Collection, National Library of Australia. *Off for the holidays? outside Cobb's Office, Bourke Street*, p.131, *Australasian Sketcher*, December 24, 1881.

Eureka Stockade, p.143, Henderson, Mitchell Library, The Library of New South Wales. *On the Murray River at Echuca, 1876*, p.154, oil, P. J. Lysaght. *Ned Kelly, the day before his execution*, p.160, photograph. *New South Wales Court at Philadelphia*, p.165, *Illustrated Sydney News*, October 12, 1876. *The Exhibition Building, Melbourne*, p.166, from *Illustrated Handbook of Victoria*. *The Tarrant Car*, p.190, *from R.A.C. Golden Jubilee 1903-53*, R.A.C.V., 1953. *T-Model Ford*, p.191, from George Gilltrap's Auto Museum. *The first Australian-built aeroplane made by J. R. Duigan and flown by him in 1910*, p.195, from *The Australian Encyclopaedia*.

Canberra design by Walter Burley Griffin for the Federal Capital Design Competition 1911, p.213, National Library of Australia. *Kingsford Smith with the 'Southern Cross' c.1930*, p.217, National Library of Australia. *General Blamey at the front*, p.222, The Australian War Memorial. *General MacArthur at the front*, p.223, The Australian War Memorial.

Benjamin Franklin, p.11, Historical Society of Pennsylvania, from *The American Heritage Book of the Revolution*, 1958. *The Boston Massacre*, p.15, Metropolitan Museum of New York, gift of Mrs. Russell Sage, 1910. *Illinois Chief, Black Hawk*, p.40, property of the Illinois State Historical Library. *Lewis and Clark parley with Indians*, p.48, *The Westerners Brand Book*, Los Angeles Corral, 1947. *Crossing the Ute Pass, Colorado*, p.55, State Historical Society of Wisconsin. *Weapons of the frontier*, p.65, *The Westerners Brand Book*, Los Angeles Corral, 1947. *Indian attack on an emigrant train*, p.69, *The Westerners Brand Book*, Los Angeles Corral, 1947.

William Penn's Treaty, p.76, courtesy of the Pennsylvania Academy of Fine Art, from *The American Heritage Book of Great Historical Places*, 1957.

Thomas Jefferson, p.81, Peale, New York Historical Society. *Gen. Andrew Jackson Jan. 1815*, p.85, steel engraving, from K. B. Dawson's *Battles of the U.S.*, Vol. 11, New York, 1858. *Escaping slave*, p.105, from *Lincoln and His America*, David Plowden, Viking Press, New York, 1970. *James Stuart Hanged in San Francisco*, p.112, California Historical Society. *Wells Fargo Gold Shipment, Deadwood*, p.117, Library of Congress, from *The American Heritage History of the Great West*, 1965. *Mississippi Paddle-wheeler 'Gipsy'*, p.155, Tulane University of Louisiana, from *The American Heritage Picture History of the Civil War*, 1960. *Billy the Kid*, p.161, *The Westerners Brand Book*, Los Angeles Corral, 1947.

Washington, p.212, Library of Congress, Washington, D.C. *Charles Lindbergh*, p.216, Library of Congress, Washington, D.C.

Every effort has been made to locate original copyright holders of illustrative material, and any omissions are regretted.

258